W9-CIH-851

Forever Lucy

By Joe Morella and Edward Z. Epstein

Judy: The Films and Career of Judy Garland
Rebels: The Rebel Hero in Films
Lana: The Public and Private Lives of Miss Turner
Paulette: The Adventurous Life of Paulette Goddard
Jane Wyman: A Biography
Loretta Young: An Extraordinary Life
Rita: The Life of Rita Hayworth
The "It" Girl: A Biography of Clara Bow

FOREVER LUCY

The Life of Lucille Ball

by Joe Morella
and Edward Z. Epstein

Lyle Stuart Inc.   Secaucus, New Jersey

Published by Lyle Stuart Inc.
120 Enterprise Ave., Secaucus, N.J. 07094
In Canada: Musson Book Company
A division of General Publishing Co. Limited.
Don Mills, Ontario

Queries regarding rights and permissions should be addressed to: Lyle Stuart, 120 Enterprise Avenue, Secaucus, N.J. 07094

Manufactured in the United States of America

9 8 7 6 5 4 3 2

Library of Congress Cataloging-in-Publication Data

Morella, Joe.
   Forever Lucy.

   1. Ball, Lucille, 1911-   . 2. Entertainers—
United States—Biography.   I. Epstein, Edward Z.
II. Title.
PN2287.B16M6 1986   791.45′028′0924 [B]   86-14409
ISBN 0-8184-0414-0

To our families.

*Our sincere gratitude to the many
individuals who granted interviews
in connection with this book.*

*Special thanks to:
Patrick B. Clark, Steve Eberly,
Chris Kachulis, John Madden,
Bill Edwards and Buddy.*

Forever Lucy

PROLOGUE

The Split 1959

There was no script. No director to yell "Cut!" No characters to hide behind. The harsh confrontation was all too real. This was not "Lucy and Ricky." This was Lucille Ball and Desi Arnaz at the very peak of their TV success.

They were both desperately unhappy. Arnaz wanted out of the "ideal" marriage. He had told Lucy earlier in the day, after yet another heated argument at the studio, that they should divorce. The subject of divorce had come up often over the years—it had usually been Lucy who brought it up. (Once, she *had* divorced him. But a passionate reconciliation the night before made the divorce null and void.)

On this occasion, fifteen years later, when Desi mentioned divorce, Lucy stared at him coldly and walked away. Later that evening, at home, she asked him if he had meant what he said. He told her he had.

"Why don't you die then?" she retorted. Her piercing blue eyes left no doubt about the intensity or sincerity of her feelings.

Desi informed her he had no intention of dying. She cursed him and insulted him and spewed out all the things she would do to him. Her threats about breaking him financially meant little to him; when she called him a two-timer, a drunk, a bum, he had heard it all before.

Lucy's anger was justified. Desi's drinking, gambling and womanizing were well-known to Hollywood insiders. Both he and Lucy were fiercely jealous and mistrustful of the other's affections, and this had caused years of friction. But the two had always reconciled. In the past there had been lots of "ecstasy and sex." Not this time. Lovemaking was not on the agenda. In fact, they hadn't slept together in over a year.

The argument raged. The children's names were brought into it—the only reason Lucy and Desi were still together was for the children. The kids' welfare was all that either at this point really cared about.

The threats continued. Both husband and wife had gathered information on each other's outside activities. "I've got enough on you to hang you," Lucy declared.

The "battling Arnazes" owned an antique pistol converted into a cigarette lighter that through the years had been used as a joke by one or the other to diffuse an argument. But this night, when she pointed the pistol at him and pulled the trigger, shrieking: "I could kill you!", he, as always, lit his cigarette. But then he changed the ritual. Instead of storming out, he calmly countered her threats by simply showing her a slip of paper which had a man's name, address and telephone number. She reddened. It was the name of a man she was having an affair with. Arnaz said, "Don't ever threaten me again."

Soon the most adored couple in America would no longer be man and wife. An image would be shattered—yet the public still refused to believe it.

The Woman, 1986

Careful public relations over the years has downplayed the turmoil in her life. Softened the edges. But behind the grinning mask of America's favorite female clown there are many faces, many roles.

Determined actress. Passionate lover. Failed wife. Successful wife. Loving mother. Tortured mother. Loyal friend and relative. Business tycoon. Enduring star. Devoted grandmother. Showbusiness Legend.

Lucille Ball is ever-mindful and concerned about the image she projects to her legion of admirers. "They don't want me to grow up," she recently observed accurately.

Today she often speaks nostalgically of Desi Arnaz. He is the man with whom she made showbusiness history. They were married for nineteen years (after the first eight years they had even retaken their vows in a Catholic ceremony). Late in the marriage they had had two eagerly awaited and adored children, one of whom was thought of as "America's most famous baby." They had parlayed the top-rated television series into a showbusiness empire. The lives of "Lucy and Ricky Ricardo" seemed intertwined with the lives of Lucille Ball and Desi Arnaz until their explosive parting.

Lucy proved that she could not only survive but triumph in the aftermath. She entered a second, enduring, and this time happy, marriage. She continued with her first love—work. But today, after more than a half-century in the topsy-turvy all-consuming world of show business, the scars are visible. Lucy looks, sounds and acts like a weary veteran. The long voyage has taken a heavy toll.

She's been described as "a two-fisted drinker." There is no doubt that she has long been a tough character on the set, someone who knows what she wants and always gets it, no matter what. She is wary, watchful and difficult to get close to.

Even her detractors, however, cannot dispute her talent or her appeal.

Amazingly, through the decades, millions of people have meshed the zany "Lucy" character, as portrayed on TV, with the real-life Lucille Ball, even though her private life has been the antithesis of "Lucy's." To countless millions, "Lucy" is real yet somehow separate and apart from reality.

In reality Lucille Ball had the same problems that many parents had. Desi, Jr. began drinking at thirteen. He has fought a long battle with alcohol and drugs. For years this information was suppressed, but other aspects of the boy's private life could not be hidden from the public.

After all, to the public and the press, Desi, Jr. (although he *never* portrayed the character on television) was thought of as "Little Ricky." His private life became fodder for sensational coverage: "Desi, Jr. to Wed Patty Duke." The marriage didn't happen, although the relationship reportedly produced a son (Lucille Ball's comment on that allegation: "She never proved a thing").

"Desi, Jr. to Wed Liza Minnelli." That marriage never took place either.

Lucie Arnaz gathered her share of headlines. An early marriage ended in divorce. An affair with Burt Reynolds wound up as "a good friendship." Lucie's second marriage, to actor-writer Laurence Luckinbill, took place when Miss Arnaz was many months pregnant.

To their mother's chagrin, the private lives of the children were far more controversial than her or Desi's lives had ever been. Later headlines blared: " 'Little Ricky's' Climb From Hell...'" " 'Little Ricky' Joins Stars That Battle Booze, Drugs..."

When people learned of Lucille Ball's and her family's problems, they commiserated but did not judge as they do with so many other superstars. After all, "Lucy" was family. And what family, even a royal family, doesn't have problems?

16

Even when the press portrayed Lucy's role as mother in a negative light, mothers sympathized with *her* when the Arnaz offspring led convention-defying lifestyles.

Lucille Ball's own youth had hardly been conventional. By fifteen she was living on her own in New York. She became a model, a showgirl. By twenty-two she was in the fast-paced world of Hollywood. When she met Desi, she was living with another man. When Arnaz wanted to get married, she just wanted to live together. As her first husband has noted, Lucy was a lady ahead of her time.

And Lucille Ball was also a lady determined to succeed. As far as most people are concerned, her life began in October, 1951, when the first "I Love Lucy" episode was broadcast. Within six weeks, the names Lucille Ball and Desi Arnaz were household words.

But it had taken eighteen years to achieve "overnight" superstardom. Lucy now looks down on life from the lofty heights of money, influence and position. But it was not, of course, always that way.

BOOK I

1

Celoron, such an obscure little town in upstate New York that it is not even on most maps, is a suburb of Jamestown and was Lucille Ball's birthplace on August 6, 1911. Shortly after her birth, her mother, Desiree Hunt, and father, Henry Ball, moved from the Jamestown area and settled in Butte, Montana.

Desiree, nicknamed DeDe, was a pretty, vivacious young woman. "She had a lot of spunk and personality," recalls a Jamestown friend. "It sure as hell took a spirit of adventure to pick up and move to the wilds of Montana, but DeDe came from a long line of American pioneers."

In Montana, DeDe became pregnant with her second child. Then tragedy struck—a typhoid epidemic took the life of Henry Ball. Lucille remembers everything that happened that terrible day: hanging out the window, begging to play with the kids next door...the doctor coming...her mother weeping...a bird that flew in the window...a picture that fell off the wall.

Lucille was almost four.

Pregnant and alone, Desiree took Lucille and moved back with her father, "Grandpa" Fred Hunt. It was 1915.

Lucy's grandfather resumed the position of family patriarch. He was a character, a jack-of-all-trades, a one-time woodcutter, mailman, bon vivant, hotel owner and a Jamestown furniture factory worker. He was interested in politics, social reform and would later campaign for labor leader and Socialist candidate Eugene V. Debs and read the *Daily Worker.*

His attitudes about life, especially about family closeness and survival, determined the manner of Lucille's upbringing and her outlook on life.

He was, in the words of his other granddaughter, Cleo, "An enormously earthy, humorous man with a great sense of roots and heritage." A neighbor remembers him differently. "He was a bit of a nut, always pushing some kind of cause to better people's lives. Lots of energy and drive. I liked him."

What kind of child was Lucille? "A very original, dynamic, unusual child," remembered cousin Cleo. "She saw things in a way nobody else did."

Lucille's flair for acting emerged at a very early age. On one occasion a few months after her father's death, Lucille insisted on running next door to visit some kids who had the measles. DeDe looped a rope around Lucy's waist and hooked it by a trolley to the clothesline so that "Miss Busybody" could run freely back and forth, still harnessed. Suddenly, DeDe realized the trolly had stopped jingling. She looked out the window and overheard her daughter charming the milkman: "Oh, mister, *somehow* I happened to get caught in this silly old clothesline. Do you think you could get me loose?"

The charming little Lucille was soon no longer queen of the mountain. Desiree had a son. She named him Fred, after her father. "Even to this day," according to Cleo, "Lucy suspects Fred was her mother's favorite, although DeDe devoted her entire life to Lucille."

"My brother Fred was always very, very good," remembered Lucille. "He never did anything wrong—he was too much to bear. I was always in trouble, a real pain in the ass. I suppose I wasn't much fun to be around."

DeDe and her younger sister Lola (whose daughter Cleo would be Lucille's lifelong friend and business associate) were the only children of Fred C. Hunt and Flora Belle Orchutt.

Lucille's memories of Grandma Flora Belle are vivid, "A real pioneer woman and pillar of the family. She was a nurse and a midwife, an orphan who brought up four pairs of twin sisters and brothers all by herself." Grandpa first met Grandma when he owned a hotel and Flora Belle worked there as a maid.

The Hunts were a close-knit family. It was a blow to all when Grandma died. Lucy has recalled, "When she died at fifty-one, it was almost too much to bear. All I remember is holding onto my brother Freddie's hand, walking to the funeral."

Grandpa Hunt had an insatiable love of life which found its greatest expression through his grandchildren:

"He got us up early, otherwise we might miss something. Sunsets. He loved them and made us love them. He wore an old cardigan sweater and a wide-brimmed hat always on the tilt. Played rickey-tick piano and sang naughty ditties.

"He always made things—playhouses in trees, teeter-totters, doll houses, tents, bobsleds, stilts. In the winter it was skating and sledding and fishing through the ice for muskie. In the summer, boat rides and groaning picnic baskets."

Her early years had their share of happy memories. "Suppose I give you a few quick items from my childhood," Lucille mused to an interviewer. "There was, for example, the time when a skunk got into the tent in our back yard where my brother and I were sleeping. On another occasion we had a tragedy. The chicken coop back of our house caught fire, and I've never gotten over the fact that the hens roasted rather than leave their chicks. Then pretty soon I was twelve years old and playing basketball and softball and doing an Apache dance in a Masonic revue. I hurled myself into the dance so enthusiastically I threw one arm out of joint, but I finished the performance. . . .

"Yeah, I guess I am real mid-America, growing up as a mix of French-Scotch-Irish-English, living on credit like everyone else, paying $1.25 a week to the insurance man, buying furniture on time. But it was a good full life. Grandpa took us camping, fishing, picking mushrooms, made us bobsleds. We always had goodies. I had the first boyish bob in town and the first open galoshes."

Her childhood had its unhappy memories as well. Lucy's mother had married a sheet metal worker, Ed Peterson, described by Lucy as "a handsome-ugly man, very well read. He was good to me and Freddie, but he drank too much."

For a while, Ed, DeDe and the children lived in Jamestown, but when times got rough they returned to Grandpa's house in Celoron. Lucy recalls, "When I was about seven, Ed and mother moved to Detroit, leaving me with his old-fashioned Swedish parents, who were very strict. I had to be in bed at 6:30, hearing all the other kids playing outside in the summer daylight. Maybe it wasn't that traumatic, but I realize now it was a bad time for me. I felt as if I'd been deserted."

Although this period might have seemed forever to Lucy, DeDe said it lasted "more like three weeks than three years."

Lucy's happiest memories have been of her childhood with Grandpa. Life at Grandpa Hunt's was hectic, not unlike the zany family of *You Can't Take It With You.*

The most important part of her childhood, at least from Lucy's point of view, was Grandpa's love of vaudeville. "There were those five-cent streetcar rides into Jamestown to 'do things.' See the vaudeville show, which he loved. Every week something new. It gave us a closeness, let us know someone cared."

At the vaudeville shows with Grandpa, Lucy saw Tom Mix movies and Pearl White serials. "Wow! I knew I had to be a part of it," Lucy remembered. "I tried out every year for the Scottish Rite revue. I got with the Jamestown Players."

Young Lucy did a play entitled *Within the Law,* which had a *Sadie Thompson*-like plot. The local reviews compared the youngster with Jeanne Eagles—"someone I had never heard of."

Desiree's marriage to Ed Peterson didn't endure, but the man had an important effect on young Lucy's life. "It was my stepfather who introduced me to the Chautauqua circuit, then at its height as a platform for lecturers, musicians, actors," Lucy later recalled. Her mother and stepfather drove her miles through the snow to the theater. "One night a monologist named Julian Eltinge was appearing. A female impersonator yet. Ed insisted I go. There sat this man with one light bulb, a little table and a glass of water, creating a whole world out of nothing, making people laugh and cry. It was magic. I can still see him, lank and tall. He looked like Lincoln."

Like many youngsters, Lucy had feelings of frustration and of reaching-out-and-trying-to-please. "I found the quickest and easiest way to do that was to make people laugh."

She discovered at the age of twelve that she could make people laugh. "Bernard Drake, the principal of my school recognized my urge for approval," remembered Lucy. "I'd do anything for a smile—sell tickets, fix the stage, clean the office—and, recognizing my need, he saw to it that I had a part in school plays and operettas. My mother and stepfather also encouraged me to act, dance and sing."

Wanting to be an actress was considered a rather dubious goal in Celoron, New York, especially in the 1920s. The word actress still had a "wicked" connotation.

A young man who later became an M.D. and practiced in nearby Olean, New York, "used to walk Lucy home from school" when they were classmates at Jamestown High. His mother, however, made him stop seeing Lucille because she had become known as "the Jamestown hussy."

Cleo remembers, "Lucille was always a wild, tempestuous, exciting child... with enormous energy, flair, style. She took us all over, particularly me, who was eight years younger.... She was a reactor—she reacted to everything. Always conning us to be in her plays and was always in hot water with somebody. Running away was reacting. She'd inveigle me into going with her—I had a piggy bank. It was always very dramatic when we were caught. And that was the point. What she really wanted was to play a scene."

23

For example, "One summer, she conned me into running away. It was only to nearby Fredonia, but in her sneaky way she really wanted to catch up to a groovy high school principal who was teaching there. He played it very cool, calling Mom and telling her we were staying overnight in a boarding house. On his advice, when we got home DeDe acted as if we hadn't been away. That devastated Lucille, no reaction, nothing."

DeDe Ball was obviously a remarkably understanding and modern woman for the 1920s. If Lucille wanted to be an actress, then that's what she could be. In Cleo's words, "DeDe was never bound by the social conventions of the day. She didn't mind the ridicule of the neighbors. Lucy said she wanted to play the saxophone? She got a saxophone. Freddie a cello? He got a cello. She never cried poor." (Lucy had taken up the saxophone in high school not because of an interest in music but simply because she had a crush on a football player and wanted to get into the school band so she could go on the team's out-of-town trips.)

Continuing her recollections of DeDe, Cleo also stated, "She allowed us to express ourselves. She taught us character, values, involvement. She operated on the theory that none of us would ever disgrace Grandpa. It was a relationship based on trust."

DeDe even allowed Lucille to drop out of high school at fifteen and enroll at the John Murray Anderson—Robert Milton Dramatic School in New York City, though she wasn't overjoyed about it. But go to New York Lucy did. Not once, but many times, between 1926 and 1933.

Before tackling Broadway, Lucy had had some minor stage experience in Jamestown. In addition to attending the Chautauqua Institute of Music, she had appeared in local Masonic revues and played a lead in the Jamestown High School production of *Charley's Aunt*.

"I played the lead, directed it, cast it, sold the tickets, printed the posters and hauled furniture to the school for scenery and props." A portent of things to come.

Her enrollment at the Anderson-Milton Dramatic School wasn't a momentous event. Shortly after Lucille began, DeDe was notified that she was "wasting her money." A school official recommended that Lucille withdraw, since it was obviously futile to attempt to make "this gawky girl" into an actress.

"This dope—that's how I thought of him then—couldn't see what I had to offer," Lucy remembered. "I wasn't discouraged—delayed, yes, but not discouraged. I was struck by the lightning of show business."

Discussing the school, Lucy subsequently said, "I was shy, terrified. I was terribly frightened. I never put forth my personality. I just stood there rigid. Bette Davis was the star pupil. There was nothing shy about her. I can see her now, starring in plays while I hid behind the scenery. And I took elocution, and Robert Milton made me repeat 'water' and 'horses' because I pronounced them 'worter' and 'hasses.' I was so miserable mother brought me home, and I spent the next few months writing. Poetry."

During her stays in New York City, Lucille often got homesick. "I grew physically ill," she remembered. "I'd run home for a while, then gather up my courage and go back. For years, I never even got inside a theater. But I sure managed to burn up a lot in train fare."

Years later, giving insight to her character, she confided: "Ever since I was fifteen years old and the director of the school told me to forget about acting and apply my energies to some other field, I've been determined to make him eat his words. I told myself, 'Someday, I'll have writers turning out material just for me.'"

Tragedy struck Grandpa Hunt's household in 1927. Freddie had received a .22 rifle as a Christmas gift. "You can shoot it on your twelfth birthday," he was promised. On the birthday, Grandpa set up a target in the back yard. Naturally, all the neighbor kids were there to watch. Suddenly, a six-year-old child ran across the line of fire and was accidentally hit by a bullet.

The child was crippled for life. The embittered parents took Grandpa Hunt to court and charged that he had "made a target" of the boy.

The court ruled that Fred Hunt had to await trial in Mayville, the county seat. Grandpa was forbidden to leave the city limits while the trial was pending. The house in Celoron had to be sold to pay for legal fees. This tragic incident changed all their lives, but most affected was Grandpa, and Lucy noted, "It broke his heart and spirit."

This shooting incident in Celoron provided the basis for countless rumors which plagued Lucy for years. One farfetched story widely circulated is that Lucille, as "a wild young girl," had been hanging around with a group of "rowdies" and for fun they shot a boy from a moving car.

Ed and DeDe, along with DeDe's sister Lola, now separated from her husband, moved Grandpa and the children into a rented house in Jamestown. Ed still had his job at the factory. DeDe went to work in a department store and Lola took up nursing. To help out, Lucy, now a gawky teen-ager, got a job as a soda jerker in Jamestown. She was fired because she always forgot to put the bananas in the banana splits.

"This is no kidding," she recalled years later. "I've told this story hundreds of times but nobody's ever used it—maybe because it sounds so phony. But it's true. It's just that so much junk went into the split that by the time the bananas came due I'd forget them every time."

Times were rough for the family in the late 1920s and in 1929, after Lola died, Cleo went to live with her father in Buffalo. Lucille continued her treks to New York City, where DeDe arranged for her to stay with some friends.

Lucy's version of these early years of struggle was, "I never even finished night school. I couldn't wait to get into show business, and at that time show business meant vaudeville to me." But getting her break presented a problem. "I never met anybody who knew how to get into vaudeville, so I decided to be a show girl and I answered a call for an Earl Carroll tryout. I was tall and thin, but measurements weren't the whole bit then. Other things counted too, although I can't remember what. I rehearsed for two weeks, then a man said to me, 'Miss Belmont! (that's who I decided to be) You're through.'

"He didn't say why, but I found out later that I was so young and so dumb I wasn't contributing anything.... I don't know why they picked me in the first place. Earl Carroll's show girls had great bodies, which looked fine in abbreviated costumes. I didn't. I went home and cried. I asked some of the girls I'd met, 'What'll I do now?' and they said, 'There'll be other calls. Maybe there'll be a Shubert call, but, of course, you won't make that.' I was a teen-ager and Shubert girls were *femmes fatales,* dripping diamonds and minks, but I was picked for a Shubert show anyhow. We rehearsed for two weeks, and I was fired again. That time I really suffered."

Life as a show girl in New York in the 1920s was rough. Lucy recalled, "Shubert girls were the living, bitchy end. They didn't want any fresh competition. They'd say, 'Think you're pretty cute, don't you?' 'Call that a figure?' 'Go home!' Horrible things to say to a kid self-conscious about being skinny anyhow. I planned ways to kill myself so I wouldn't have to go home and tell everybody I'd lost another job. I thought, 'I'll get killed faster in Central Park because cars go faster there. But I want to get hit by a big car—with a handsome man in it.' Then I had a flash of sanity. I said to myself, 'If I'm thinking this way, maybe I don't want to die.' So I regrouped my forces."

Discussing struggling kids of later generations: "I don't understand kids today who get easily discouraged and yap about 'doing their own thing.' Don't they know what hard work is? Where are their morals? I always knew when I did wrong and paid penance." Comments like these reflect Lucy's somewhat rigid philosophy of life.

Recalling her show-girl days, "I also had a grab on respectability. My grandparents raised me to have a conscience. I was very observant. I watched the other girls make their mistakes. I turned down a lot of so-called 'opportunities' because they were only 'maneuvers.' My ambition wasn't high. I just wanted to work."

While trying out for chorus girl jobs, Lucy invented a glamorous autobiography. She said that she had been born in Butte, Montana, which to her seemed a cut above Jamestown. To gather information for her Montana background, she wrote to any town in Montana big enough to have a Chamber of Commerce and memorized all their handouts. "I think I knew more about Montana than lots of the natives."

The Montana birthplace also provided her with nicknames easy for casting directors to remember—they labeled her "Montana" or "the Buttean."

Lucy managed to wangle a chorus job in the third road company of Ziegfeld's *Rio Rita*. However, during rehearsals the stage manager told her, "It's no use, Montana. Go home. You ain't meant for show business."

Although she did go home a number of times, she wouldn't give up. She kept returning to New York, supporting herself with odd jobs: soda jerking, clerking, anything to keep going. At one point she was so broke that she only had four cents to her name, a penny short of the then five-cent subway fare. "So I panhandled for a penny," she has related. "A man offered me ten dollars, but I said firmly, '*Mister, I only need one cent!*'"

She landed a job in the chorus of the Broadway musical *Stepping Stones*, but the job lasted only a few weeks. Then came a chorus job in *Step Lively*, but she was fired two weeks later when the choreographer decided he only wanted girls who could do toe work. ("Toe work? I couldn't even do heel work!")

At first Lucille hated the casting directors and choreographers who couldn't see through the facade to the talent she knew was inside her. But she learned that burning up energy by hating was hurting no one but herself... especially since the people she hated weren't even aware of how she felt, nor could they have cared. Lucy later philosophized, "I loathe bitterness. It shows in everything you do and eats the liver right out of you."

This was a time when Lucille literally didn't have a nickel for a cup of coffee. She was eating only when she could find a "one-doughnut man." "This," she has explained, "is a guy who sits at a counter and orders doughnuts and coffee. He drinks his coffee, eats one doughnut and puts down a nickel tip. I'd do a fast slide onto his stool, yell for a cup of coffee, pay for it with his nickel, and eat the other doughnut.

"I was still trying to get into show business, but in the meantime I had taken a cheap, dark, dismal room of my own and I was starving to death," she said of this period. "Then one morning I picked up a paper and saw the word 'model.' I said 'Okay, I'll model.' I looked up a place that needed models for size ten to fourteen coats. 'Coats will cover my missing figure,' I thought, and I got the job."

She alternated between modeling and chorus girl jobs. "I tried starvation in all its forms," Lucy subsequently said, "and none of them was satisfactory. In a show, five weeks rehearsal without pay was the rule, and that's too long for a girl to fast.

"I had a hall room, fifth floor back and would sometimes try to prepare food over the gas jet. I would save up a little money from modeling and get a show job. For a week or two I'd live on hope and ambition and hoard my money. Then hunger would prove too much for me. I'd eat hearty, run out of funds and leave the show before the money started coming in. It never occurred to me to ask for an advance, so I don't know whether I could have gotten one or not.

"After repeating that experience two or three times, I made up my mind there was nothing to the hunger theory, so I decided to stick to modeling and really learn the business."

Finally working steadily, Lucy met another model who told her, "My husband's a commercial photographer and you're the type he needs for an assignment." So in addition to earning twenty-five dollars a week as a model in the garment district, Lucy picked up extra money by modeling in fashionable department stores and becoming a commercial photographer's model. She also posed for artists. Then she got a job modeling at Hattie Carnegie's chic salon. Hattie suggested she become a blonde and she did.

While modeling at Carnegie's was a step up in prestige, it

only increased her salary to thirty-five dollars a week, so she continued her other assignments with illustrators such as McClelland Barclay and John Lagata, while still trying to break into show business.

The strain was too much but she wouldn't slacken her pace. "Slow down, honey," advised a fellow model, "you look kinda pale." But Lucille had no time to waste. She was working. Then one afternoon at Carnegie's she was stricken with pains "which pierced my insides." The diagnosis was malnutrition and fatigue. Once again Lucy had to return to Jamestown.

Lucy learned from the experience. "I worked hard and was ill for two years from the work and missed out on everything," she later said. "I was only eighteen, but I even learned from that. It taught me that without your health, you ain't got nothin'. Remember that, kiddo. I had no survival technique, so I didn't survive. But where I was different from the other dumb show girls is that I learned from every experience, and some of them don't."

Lucy recovered her health in Jamestown and became friendly with a girl named Gert Kratzert, a hairdresser. The two girls talked of "the big city," Lucille longing to return to New York, and Gert dreaming of the city's excitement. One afternoon, they stopped talking and boarded a bus for New York City.

They took a room at the Hotel Kimberly at 74th Street and Broadway. Gert found work in the beauty parlor of the Amsterdam Hotel and Lucy got her old job back at Hattie Carnegie's. The charm of New York eventually wore off for Gert and, homesick, she returned to Jamestown. Lucy stayed on determined as ever to have a successful career.

Finally a break came when Liggett and Myers chose her as the Chesterfield poster girl, and Lucy was on twenty-four-sheet billboard posters for the cigarette company.

Concerning her love life during these days: "Love? I was always falling in love." Her small-town upbringing and feelings of responsibility to her family's "good name" determined Lucy's attitudes. Unlike many New York models, Lucy was discreet about her romances.

There is a story about a bullet that richocheted into the bathtub in her hotel room, which over the years has given rise to the rumor that Lucy was "a gangland moll." Lucy's explanation: "A gang war was going on around the corner. I didn't hear the bullet whang into the tub, but the water suddenly began to disappear. I got out and tried to mop the floor. That's all there is to the story."

Although she was relatively successful at Carnegie's, she still dreamed about a show business career. It was the summer of 1933 when she wandered over to Broadway one sweltering day and stood in front of the Palace Theater, hoping to see some actors. Then, "Sylvia Hollow, a New York woman agent I knew, said 'How'd you like to leave this heat?' I said, 'I'd love to' and she asked, "How about California? I've just come from Jim Mulvey's office upstairs. He had twelve girls leaving to be poster girls in the next Goldwyn movie and one of them can't. You're a poster girl, aren't you?'"

Her Chesterfield poster qualified her.

She met Mulvey and he said, "All right." Lucy made a long-distance call to her mother and went back to say goodbye to Hattie Carnegie. "She gave me a coat, a hat and a dress," Lucy remembered, "and said, 'God bless you. It'll be good experience, and, if you don't like it, you can come back to work.'"

Even though these seven years had been rough, two decades later, at the peak of her TV fame, Lucille Ball obviously decided that the "tough struggle" image need not be continued. "People keep saying that success came to me the hard way, after a long struggle. This myth is ridiculous. The truth is just the opposite: I have *never* been out of a job. In my early days in New York, I was hardly starving, I was making good money as a model. Then I went to Hollywood and Sam Goldwyn immediately placed me under contract. Some struggle!"

2

Desi Arnaz, a sixteen-year-old boy who up until then had lived in the pampered world of Cuban aristocrats, was, that summer of 1933, also embarking on a new life—one which was forced on him. A revolution was raging in Cuba.

Desiderio Alberto Arnaz y de Acha III had been born on March 2, 1917, in Santiago, Cuba. His father, Desiderio Arnaz II, was a Cuban senator and mayor of Santiago. A wealthy landowner, his property included three ranches, a townhouse, an island in Santiago Bay, a racing stable and several cars and speedboats.

Dolores, Desi's mother, was considered one of the ten loveliest women in Latin America. Desi was their only child.

Desi's memories of his youth are vivid: "The world was my oyster. What I wanted I only needed to take. Ambition, incentive, opportunity, self-reliance, appreciation of what I had meant little to me. At sixteen I had my own speedboat, motor car, ringside tables at cafés and a fast-swelling case of what, in a language I couldn't speak at all then, is called a fathead."

Desi has said that from his birth to his teens he couldn't recall ever having faced a worry or a strain. His future was blueprinted and assured: he would be sent to the United States to attend the University of Notre Dame, he would study law, and then, as the offspring of one of Cuba's number one politicians, he would return to a ready-made practice.

But in August, 1933, the hopes and aspirations of the aristocratic Arnaz family were shattered.

Desi explained, "One morning, I heard gunfire in the distance. Down the road I saw a mob of several hundred advancing on our house. Rumbles of revolution against the Machado government had gripped Cuba for some time. But this was it! My father was miles away in Havana. I was sixteen and alone in the house with my mother. Outside, screaming junta forces were slaughtering our cattle, burning our buildings."

Desi dashed for the garage. Luckily, they had $500 in cash in the house. His mother took that and their Chihuahua and met Desi at the rear of the house. They hopped into a car and drove out the back road across the fields. When they stopped to look back, their glorious ranch house, containing all their cherished possessions, was ablaze. They watched as it disintegrated and crashed to the ground.

"God help us!" His mother moaned. "We'll never reach Havana."

"In Havana we had relatives," Desi remembered, "but the trip was a nightmare. I fixed a junta flag to the radiator of our car. Whenever we encountered troops out to kill every patrician they could find, I turned the wheel over to my mother and, standing on the running board, I yelled 'Viva la revolucion!' at the top of my lungs. In this way we reached the capital, where an aunt living on the outskirts took us into hiding. What had happened to father in Havana we could not find out at first—he had disappeared.

"In one stroke, all of the life we had known was shot out from under us. All Cuba was in chaos. In Havana, two hundred to three hundred bombs were exploding every day. I saw men dragged to their death behind horses, machine-gunned for simply daring to walk past terrorist police."

At his aunt's house, Desi and his mother finally learned that his father, a supporter of deposed President Machado, had been arrested and thrown into Morro Castle with the rest of the Cuban Senate. He remained there for six months and, according to Desi, he was released only because he had remained neutral and the United States was demanding an end to the bloodshed.

The Arnazes had spent the $500 and when Señor Arnaz was released from prison, haggard and worn, he told his wife and son that all their property had been confiscated.

They had no choice—they had to leave the country. But there wasn't enough money for all of them to go. Señor Arnaz, as a political undesirable, was in the greatest danger, therefore he left first for Florida. Desi was to join him as soon as possible and Señora Arnaz would stay hidden in Cuba.

Señor Arnaz was able to send for Desi within a few months. But the outlook for life in Miami was dismal. At first, they lived in a dingy rooming house on the outskirts of town. Arnaz had no job and he and his son ate canned beans warmed on a hotplate in an attic cubicle.

"We are refugees," Arnaz told his son, "worse off than the poorest peon at home. There are no jobs for refugees here."

Desi remembered, "To save the five dollars rent, we moved into an unheated warehouse filled with rats. We found sticks and rushed around, trying to kill the rats. The spectacle of my father, a highly-educated and honored man, doing this was such a shock that I wept. I couldn't see how we could survive in America— seemingly so big, so cold and cruelly competitive."

America was a far cry from the Cuba Arnaz had known. Years later, Desi recalled that he was surprised most of all by the absence of dividing lines between the upper and lower classes. "Here there were millions of average people who owned nice homes, cars, expensive appliances. Each man was equal to his neighbor."

Desperately looking for work, one morning Desi noticed a

man building something in his back yard. It was a birdcage. Young Arnaz was hungry, but he couldn't speak English, so he tried to explain, in Spanish and with gestures, that he needed a job.

"Can't savvy you, kid," the man said. "Now run along."

Desi was about to leave when the man's wife came out of the house. She was Cuban. Through this couple Desi got a job cleaning canary cages. "I went around with my little whisk broom and droppings can, earning twenty-five cents per cage cleaned and off this the Arnazes II and III lived for some weeks."

Like most immigrants to the United States, Desi learned the language and customs of America the hard way—embarrassing experiences, being "taken," often misunderstood.

Potential disaster raised its head when the Immigration Service hauled in the Arnazes. Since they had entered the country illegally and were not permanent residents, they could not work in the United States. They were told to leave the country for six weeks and return with proper entry papers.

They were stunned. They had no money to leave and had to continue working in order to eat. But the law was clear. Young Desi offered the following solution: "It struck me that if America was as open hearted to the weak and distressed as advertised, maybe the rule could be given a small bend. I told my father, who spoke English, to suggest that I be allowed to stay on and clean cages, which would finance his leaving. When he returned, I would go away for the prescribed time while he took over my job."

Luckily for the Arnazes, the Immigration official decided to look the other way. And Desi has noted, "That, I know now, was the turning point of my life. A refusal by the official—which he had every right to make—would have sent me shuffling off into the shadows.

"We skipped out of there, two glad and grateful señores. Father left for Puerto Rico, where he had friends, with the few dollars we had, to stay for six weeks and get his entry papers. I went back to the canaries. When his time was up he returned, and I worked my way to Cuba by boat, assured my mother we were well, stayed out my time and returned with my papers."

Nineteen thirty-four and nineteen thirty-five were rough years for the Arnaz men, living hand to mouth. Señor Arnaz had pooled some funds of other Cuban refugees and formed the Pan-American Export-Import Company, Inc. The firm had one truck, which Desi drove, and one product, bananas. They sold one load to pay for the next and operated the entire company on a shoestring. When one shipment of fruit was completely spoiled, the company went broke.

Desperate for work, Desi decided to get a job in a band. "I walked into a jai-alai fronton in Miami and boldly asked for a job with the band. In Cuba, where everybody is musical, I had amateurishly sung a bit and played the guitar.

" 'Can you handle the drums?' the manager asked.

"I lied that I could.

"That night, I whacked vigorously away as the fronton band played the march that brought the players onto the court. Musically, it was low as you could get, but I was delighted. From there, I talked myself into a singing job in a tough waterfront café. I got one dollar a night, plus tips, but not for long. When I did a soprano version of 'Moon Over Miami' once too often in fractured English, the customers began throwing salt shakers."

"Kid, you're dead until you learn the lingo," Desi's boss told him. "Why don't you go to school?" he suggested.

Desi hadn't realized that higher public education in the United States was free. He had been thinking of the expensive private schools in Cuba, which only the upper classes could afford to attend. Realizing the need for some sort of education, and especially the need to speak English well, the young Cuban enrolled in a Miami high school. The best-liked boy in the school was Sonny Capone, whose father was Al Capone, the notorious racketeer. Sonny and Desi had an immediate rapport. Desi has recalled, "Nobody judged Sonny for what he couldn't help, only for himself. For school graduation, the custom was to

37

pick your closest buddy to accompany you to the stage when you received your diploma. When I was graduated, I picked Sonny Capone, my best pal."

Desi was voted "most courteous" in his class, but the greatest reward from his education was that, after a fashion, he could pronounce words in English up to five syllables.

Before his twentieth birthday in 1937, he wangled a job in a big-time rhumba band at the swank Roney Plaza Hotel in Miami Beach. They needed a singing guitarist, so he borrowed a tux and went for a one-night tryout. He sang what has become his most famous number, "Babalu."

"Before I even finished, the crowd was cheering, beating hands as if Bing Crosby had suddenly materialized. I stood stupefied until, looking into the audience, I spotted all my classmates. They'd all turned out, bringing their parents, to raise the roof in support of me."

The management, thinking that Desi was a hit, kept him on. Soon he was making fifty dollars a week, a huge sum for 1937. Mrs. Arnaz was sent for, and when she arrived from Havana the family rented a pretty cottage near the hotel.

3

When Lucille Ball arrived in Hollywood in 1933, the top box-office stars in the country were Greta Garbo, Norma Shearer, Wallace Beery, Marie Dressler, Joan Crawford, Gary Cooper, Clark Gable and Mae West.

The Depression was at its peak, but Lucille was, for the time being at least, riding high with a contract—with options—for $150 a week as a Goldwyn Girl.

She almost hadn't gotten the job. At that time director Busby Berkeley was instrumental in selecting the Goldwyn Girls. Later Berkeley would move to Warner Bros. and cinema immortality via *42nd Street* and other film musicals.

Berkeley recalled: "Goldwyn called me in one day and said, 'I want you to come up to the projection room. I've made some tests of girls from New York and I want you to see whether you like them.' We ran them and there were two girls that I liked very much. But Goldwyn didn't like them. The next morning I went by his office and asked his secretary, 'Mary, did he send for the two girls that he didn't like but I did?' She smiled and said, 'Yes, he did, Mr. Berkeley.' The two girls I had picked were Barbara Pepper and Lucille Ball."

"Lucy never was the Hollywood type," remembered Berkeley. "She worked very hard to get her breaks.... She was very much a positive thinker. I used to tell her, 'Why don't you get an agent? You can go far in this business.'"

Twenty-two-year-old Lucille appreciated such words of encouragement, which were few. "She sweated out every goddamn break she got," recalls an ex-Goldwyn executive. "Opportunities never 'fell into her lap.' She was one of dozens of girls at the studio watching and waiting for *the* opportunity. The difference between Lucy and the others was that she was a *worker*. That, and Jesus, what energy! If I had to use one word to describe Lucille Ball then it would be *energy*."

She was, as always, eager to learn and her industriousness didn't go unnoticed. She accepted any kind of role available: extra, walk-on, bits. She never lost hope that her attitude, hard work and learning from mistakes would pay off. "Meanwhile, she was earning a living in the business she wanted to be in," observes an ex-Goldwyn Girl. "Things could have been a lot worse for her."

Lucy appeared in ten films while under contract to Goldwyn in 1933 and 1934. They can mostly be characterized as junk, albeit commercial junk of the day. Four were Goldwyn films— *Roman Scandals,* with Eddie Cantor; *Nana* (Goldwyn's ultra-expensive Anna Sten vehicle which bombed); *Kid Millions*— another Eddie Cantor vehicle in which Lucille, as a blonde, was an unsmiling Goldwyn Girl; and *Bulldog Drummond Strikes Back,* starring Ronald Colman and Loretta Young. She was unbilled in all these productions and unbilled in parts she had in *Broadway Through a Keyhole, Blood Money, Moulin Rouge* and *The Affairs of Cellini*. These were 20th Century pictures released through United Artists. She also did extra work in *Bottoms Up* and *Hold That Girl* for Fox.

40

One of the people who befriended Lucy in her early days was George Raft. "He loaned me money for my rent once, and it took me years before I could pay it back," Lucy remembered. "I've never forgotten him for it. He gave away a fortune in the early days in Hollywood."

Although Lucille was never out of work, she wasn't progressing very far. "It galled her that schleps with no talent were getting billing while she wasn't," recalls a friend. "But she didn't let it get her down. She didn't scatter her energies by hating this one and that. She knew she wouldn't benefit by doing that."

The time had come to make a decision. "I was with Mr. Goldwyn a year and a half. Then I asked him if I could go, for by that time I was a last-year's Goldwyn girl and I'd been relegated to the back row. Mr. Goldwyn was very nice. 'You can do better,' he said, 'and I'm sorry we don't have more for you to do here.' So I moved over to Columbia, where my principal work was being chased before a camera by Ted Healey and his Stooges."

Lucy signed with Columbia Pictures in the fall of 1934 and became a seventy-five-dollar-a-week contract player, a substantial salary drop from Goldwyn. But it was, she hoped, an opportunity to become something more than a permanent show girl.

In those days Columbia was strictly a B-picture studio. There, in addition to being cast without billing in comedy shorts starring The Three Stooges, Lucille was given extra and bit work in Frank Capra's *Broadway Bill, Jealousy, Men of the Night, The Fugitive Lady* and *Carnival*. The last film, in which Lucy had a small role as a nurse, was the fifteenth in which she appeared, but it was the first picture in which she received screen billing. It was released in 1935.

On the strength of her Columbia contract, Lucille sent for her mother (who had divorced Ed Peterson), brother and grandfather. She rented a small, white-frame bungalow for the family to live in, in a modest neighborhood on a tree-lined street. Thirteen forty-four North Ogden Drive.

In the 1930s this little house would provide Lucille and her family with a secure, happy home base. But in the 1950s that address would plague Lucille Ball because of certain political activities supposedly carried on there.

Lucy was intent on making it in the movies. But the family had no sooner settled into their new home when Columbia dropped Lucy's option. The studio had decided to disband its stock company, which also included Gene Raymond and a pretty young blond actress, Harriet Lake, whom Columbia boss Harry Cohn had renamed Ann Sothern. Lucy and Ann became friends and have remained so to the present.

Not one to waste time brooding, Lucy hustled over to the RKO studios and was lucky enough to land a job there, although she took another salary cut to fifty dollars a week. Lucy recalled, "I had a call from a friend, Dick Green. He said, 'RKO is looking for ex-Bergdorf girls.'" That was supposed to be a slightly higher caste of model. "Anyhow," Lucy went on, "I had worked a fashion show at Bergdorf's, so RKO tagged me."

Lucille's first film there was *Roberta*. She was typecast as a clotheshorse, complete with ostrich feathers, and she descended a staircase in a fashion show sequence. She herself has called the part "halfway between an extra and a bit." As usual, no billing.

After *Roberta*, RKO put Lucy under contract and into their talent school. She studied under studio drama coach Lela Rogers, mother of Ginger Rogers, who was coming into her own as one of RKO's top stars. Lucy later recalled, "When I was a beginner at RKO it was wonderful having Lela Rogers give us a stage, scripts to get our teeth into and an audience. That constitutes acting experience..."

She worked with Lela a couple of years and did several plays. "Lucy was a shrewd politician," noted a studio executive from that era. "Lela never at any time had any fears that Lucille would try to take over Ginger's top spot at the studio. Lela guarded Ginger like a drone watching over the queen bee. Of course, you couldn't blame her. She *was* Ginger's mother."

Lucy "ground 'em out." She was unbilled in *Old Man Rhythm*, played a florist's clerk (she had one line of dialogue) in the Ginger Rogers-Fred Astaire classic *Top Hat* and bits in *The Three Musketeers* and *Winterset*.

About these RKO days, Fred Astaire remembers, "Everyone liked Lucille very much. She was a lady very determined to make good, I could see that. And she had talent. She was just doing small bits in my pictures, but you knew somehow or other there was a lot of something going on there."

Lucy began speaking up. She marched into her studio bosses and complained about being an extra. Her determination must have been evident, since they began giving her small speaking roles. Her first RKO screen billing came with a small role in *I Dream Too Much*, a film starring opera singer Lily Pons and upcoming actor Henry Fonda. Lucy and Fonda later became friends and sometimes double-dated with Fonda's roommate, James Stewart.

"Lucy usually didn't date guys her own age, though," recalls a friend. "She preferred older men. Men who knew their way around."

One actual incident that could have been straight out of "I Love Lucy" occurred during these early RKO contract years. One day Lucy was supposed to have publicity portraits taken. It was to be the most important photo-sitting she had had up to that time, the kind of expensive session that wasn't scheduled very often.

Excitedly, she went to make-up. The make-up man was brusque and told her he couldn't work on her because Katharine Hepburn (RKO's top star) was due any minute. Lucy implored him to help, explaining how important the photo session was. Reluctantly he agreed.

Lucy had with her a box containing some caps for her teeth. (Her smile was marred by a couple of chipped teeth and one missing tooth on the side, and she had had expensive caps made.) As she got into the make-up chair, she placed the box containing her caps on the counter. Barely ten minutes later, an assistant came dashing in: "Hepburn's coming! She's on her way!"

Lucy was practically thrown out of her chair. A few moments later Hepburn breezed in, businesslike as always. "Hallo," she said to Lucy as she went over to the make-up chair, concentrating on her script. The make-up man hustled Lucy out, and, in the anteroom, Lucy realized she had left her "teeth" on the table. And she couldn't have portraits taken without those caps!

She went next door and explained her predicament to a friendly wardrobe lady, who told her to go to a small window connecting wardrobe and make-up, through which she could talk to the make-up man. Lucy opened up the window and tried to catch the man's attention, but he pretended not to see her. She became angrier by the minute as he continued to ignore her.

A tray of coffee was resting on the window ledge. Absolutely frantic and totally frustrated, Lucille picked up a container of coffee and hurled it at him. It missed him but splattered all over Katharine Hepburn, drenching her.

Hepburn didn't utter a word. She sat motionless for a moment, then got up and went home, leaving word that she would be unable to work that day. She was filming an expensive costume picture, *Mary of Scotland,* and the day's production loss cost the studio thousands. Lucy was careful to avoid her for the next few weeks, but Hepburn didn't hold a grudge.

RKO cast Lucy in another small role, this time as a member of a summer stock company, in a turkey called *Chatterbox.* She made four other films in 1936: *Follow the Fleet,* another Astaire-Rogers blockbuster, in which Lucy played one of Ginger's sailor-minded girl friends; she played a script girl in *Farmer in the Dell,* a B-movie with Jean Parker and Esther Dale; and had a bit in the less-than-memorable *Bunker Bean.*

Finally she was assigned a good second lead, playing the blond dancer-fiancée of Gene Raymond in another Lily Pons picture, *That Girl From Paris.* But the film was only a routine programmer and didn't get any major attention.

Lucille was still frustrated. Her progress was painfully slow, but at least her salary provided her family with a stability they hadn't enjoyed in years.

At home, Grandpa was active in socialist causes and was regarded by neighbors here, as he had been in Jamestown—"a real character."

Cleo, now seventeen, came to live with the family. Lucy had gotten Grandpa a job in the RKO woodworking department, but it was short lived. So Grandpa Hunt, or "Daddy," as Lucy, Cleo and Freddie called him, took to fooling around in the garden and making objects of wood in the garage. He also "took to nipping."

"He was forever fighting the establishment," recalls a neighbor. Once when the city of Los Angeles refused to allow him to cut down a tree in front of their North Ogden Drive house ("it blocked his view of the world going by") Grandpa Hunt secretly hacked away at the tree's roots, carefully replacing the sod after each session. One day during a rainstorm, as he planned, the tree fell over—unfortunately, right onto Lucille's new yellow convertible.

In his later years, Grandpa retired to his "corner." It was a place behind the front door where he read the *People's World* editorials and copies of *National Geographic*. And like many old people he tried to get any one he could to listen to his views on life and politics.

Lucy had taken over as the family organizer by now. It was she who got the family together for picnics in Griffith Park and led all the parades Grandpa used to lead. She has admitted that these early years in Hollywood were her "hey-hey" period socially. She had a new beau every night, went to all the clubs, loved to dance and have a good time.

Though RKO had graduated her to speaking parts, Lucy was still dissatisfied. She decided to try the stage again and it looked as if her "big break" had finally arrived when she landed the lead in a musical comedy headed for Broadway called *Hey Diddle Diddle*, starring former silent screen star Conway Tearle. But the play opened at the McCarter Theatre in Princeton, New Jersey, on January 21, 1937, and closed in Philadelphia the following month.

Lucy later said, "If Conway Tearle hadn't died during the tour, *Hey Diddle Diddle* would have made Broadway."

She went back to Hollywood and RKO where they didn't exactly pull out all the stops in honor of her return. She was assigned a small supporting role in the Guy Kibbee comedy, *Don't Tell the Wife*.

While in San Francisco publicizing the picture, she saw a young dancer, Ann Miller, in a night club. Lucy was responsible for helping Ann secure a contract at RKO.

Ann remembers it vividly. "They had sent Lucy up to appear at the premiere. After the film opened, she and Benny Rubin, who had been a comedian and was at this point a talent scout, did a couple of the nightspots together. I was appearing at the Beau Tamerin and they saw me. Lucy told Rubin, 'Better call up Sam Briskin [he was head of RKO] and tell him we've seen this girl and she's great and they ought to give her a test.'

"Lucy Ball is, to me, of all the people I've met in this town, the most down-to-earth person. She has a great sense of humor and a good heart which a lot of these people don't have."

Ann says she was only thirteen when she was signed by RKO. There was some problem about her working in films because of her youth and she had to secure a fake birth certificate. "Lucille and Ginger Rogers stuck by me and upheld my fake age and fake birth certificate so the studio would keep me under contract."

Miss Miller says she herself mentioned to a wardrobe lady that she was only thirteen. "That's how it got around, and somebody threatened to turn my mother, and producer Pandro Berman, into the child labor union because I wasn't being schooled on the set. Lucy came forward and said, 'Look, I was there when she signed and her mother said she was eighteen years old. Why don't you just drop it and let it go at that?'"

Lucille Ball finally got *her* "big break" when director Gregory La Cava cast her as a wise-cracking would-be actress in RKO's prestige picture for 1937, *Stage Door*, which starred the studio's two biggest female stars: Katharine Hepburn and Ginger Rogers. Ann Miller and Eve Arden were also in the cast.

Discussing *Stage Door,* Ann Miller remembers, "It was like dog eat dog on that picture—even though everyone was very friendly. They were writing the script on the set and I remember there was quite a lot of tension between Ginger Rogers and Katharine Hepburn. Lucy helped relieve a lot of the strain because she would always laugh and joke and kid. Eve Arden was the same way, and thank God for them."

Ann also recalls that Ginger and Lucy were very close friends, really chums.

About Eve Arden, Lucy later noted: "She and I competed for years—one of us would be the lady executive and the other would be 'the other woman.' They were the same roles, for we'd walk through a room, drop a smart remark and exit. I called us 'the drop-gag girls.' I didn't dig it at all, for in such parts you lose your femininity."

Though they may have competed for parts, off-stage the actresses became and remained close friends.

Lucille scored a hit in *Stage Door* and RKO renegotiated her contract. She got a substantial raise and was cast as Irene Dunne's sister in *The Joy of Living.* She also got a role in *Having a Wonderful Time* as one of Ginger Rogers' roommates at a recreational camp. Lucy wangled a small role for her cousin Cleo in that film. And off set, she played camp counselor, organizing "fun and games" for the cast and crew.

At last Ball's career was gaining momentum. She got another break when radio star Phil Baker, broadcasting from Hollywood early in 1938, signed her as featured comedienne with his show. She was an instant hit. Then CBS radio comedian Joe Penner requested Lucy as his leading lady in his RKO film, *Go Chase Yourself.* Though *Having a Wonderful Time* was produced first, it was released after the Penner picture.

The public was starting to appreciate Lucille Ball. As was typical of Hollywood, the studio began glamorizing Lucille's past with official and almost totally fabricated biographies that read like this: "She's flown over South American jungles to shoot crocodiles from the sky; once she took an open-cockpit plane up in weather twenty degrees below freezing to effect the rescue of a schoolboy; she plays a fast game of polo; has a hobby of woodcarving; owns a profitable flower shop; and is one of Hollywood's best-dressed actresses. Such is a portrait of Lucille Ball, RKO Radio contract player who is fast climbing the ladder of cinema success."

They identified her birthplace as Butte, Montana, and her father was incorrectly labeled an electrical engineer with the Anaconda copper company. Her mother was described as a concert pianist. To account for the seven years Lucy struggled in New York, RKO summed it up as follows: "After a year and a half in New York, Miss Ball joined a stock company and traveled with them throughout the east."

Studio biographies such as these were not unusual and the misinformation they contained would be repeated and believed through the years.

In 1938, since she had been such a hit on Phil Baker's show, Lucy was signed for weekly appearances on Jack Haley's CBS radio program, "Wonder Show."

Lucy had gotten her wish. She was working as hard as any woman could. In 1938 she appeared in seven films. One of them—*The Affairs of Annabel*—was important for her.

In *Annabel* she played a fading actress with an over-enthusiastic press agent, Jack Oakie, who gets her involved in publicity capers that land her in jail. The film did so well that RKO quickly threw together a sequel, *Annabel Takes a Tour,* released the same year.

Then came a featured part in *Room Service,* but even Lucy couldn't overshadow Harpo, Chico and Groucho Marx as they romped through the film version of the successful play. Lucy's other film released in 1938 was a "B" production, *The Next Time I Marry,* a comedy with James Ellison and Lee Bowman.

It had been a busy five years. Lucy herself has candidly summed it up: "I came out to Hollywood to do an Eddie Cantor picture with twelve to fourteen show girls, right? They had more experience, more money, knew their way around. Yet I made it and they didn't. Why? Maybe because they turned down more working jobs for social opportunities and I did just the opposite. As a result, I've never been out of work in this town except for two hours once between contracts."

Lucy did have time for some social life, however. In 1938 she was dating Broderick Crawford and they became engaged for a brief period. One of her other beaux was a sexy Cuban named Mario who had quite a reputation as an uninhibited lover. She also dated Brian Donlevy and, a bit later, "wonder boy" Orson Welles.

At this time, David O. Selznick was screen-testing every actress in Hollywood under forty for the most coveted role of them all: Scarlett O'Hara in *Gone With the Wind*. Lucille realized she wasn't exactly perfect for the part, but Selznick had asked studios to submit their contract actresses for auditions.

RKO casting chief Ben Piazza summoned several of his studio's actresses, including, of course, Lucille. Piazza explained that the studio wanted the girls to try out for the role of Scarlett and gave them script pages with three scenes from the film. He told them to study the pages and be ready to audition in three weeks.

Filing out of the casting office, Lucille was bewildered. "This is ridiculous!" she exclaimed. "Me play Scarlett O'Hara? Impossible!"

However, Lucille had no choice but to comply with her studio's wishes. She worked on the early scene in which Scarlett tries to charm Ashley, "I do declare, Ashley Wilkes, I don't for the life of me understand what you see in that skinny little Melanie..."

Lucy practiced in front of a mirror, but felt she couldn't make herself sound like Scarlett. The accent was giving her trouble.

She made an appointment with Will Price, the southern scholar who had been hired by Selznick as an adviser on the film. As always she was an eager pupil and Price helped Lucy to approximate a Georgia accent. She returned for more lessons and became friendly with Marcella Rabwin, Selznick's executive secretary. Miss Rabwin was sympathetic to Lucy, who appeared scared.

One story of Lucille's encounter with Selznick: It rained in Los Angeles on the day of her audition, and her drenched Studebaker just about made it to the Culver City studio.

She was dripping wet when she arrived at Marcella Rabwin's office, and out of breath, she panted: "I just dropped by to say I can't make the audition today."

"But you're here, aren't you?" queried Marcella. "You might as well stay. Mr. Selznick is looking forward to meeting you."

Lucile was petrified. "Mr. Selznick! You mean I'm supposed to see *him* today? But I can't!"

Marcella assured her she could. "You'll feel better after I get you an aspirin."

"But I don't need an aspirin."

"Then I'll pour you some brandy."

"I don't drink brandy."

"Then I'll make you some nice hot tea."

Marcella took Lucy into Selznick's office and helped her out of her wet boots. She brought the tea and suggested that Lucille practice her lines before Selznick returned from lunch. Lucy dropped down on a couch and spread the script pages in front of her. She drank the tea and went over the lines. She fell to her knees.

"Ah do declah, Ashley Wilkes, ah don' foh the lahf of me understand what yo see in that skinny little Melanie," she read.

"That was a very good reading, Miss Ball."

Lucille jumped at the sound of the voice behind her. She turned and saw Selznick's burly form. Her blue eyes widened.

"I . . . I was just practicing," she said.

"Yes, and it was very good indeed. Please go on." He went to his seat behind his desk.

"Go on?"

"Yes, I'd like to hear you do all three scenes."

Lucille attacked the scenes with all the energy she could muster.

The last was the film's final scene where Scarlett utters the famous lines: "I'll think about it tomorrow, at Tara. Tomorrow, I'll think of some way to get him back. After all, tomorrow is another day."

As she finished, tears rolled down Lucille's cheeks. Selznick seemed genuinely moved. "Very good, Miss Ball."

"Did you really think so?" She was hopeful.

"Yes. We'll let you know our decision. Thank you for coming."

"Then I can go now?"

"Yes. Here, let me help you."

As he came from around his desk to assist her, Lucy suddenly realized—or so the story goes—that she had played all three scenes on her knees!

Perhaps for an afternoon, Lucille Ball, like dozens of other hopefuls, fantasized about playing the most important role of the decade. But soon it was back to reality and, for Lucy, back to RKO.

Nineteen thirty-nine was another hectic year of work. And Lucy was steady-dating Columbia director Alexander Hall, ex-husband of actress Lola Lane. Columnists hinted that Lucille would be the next Mrs. Hall. What columnists didn't tell readers back in these days was that while Lucy maintained her own apartment she was living with Hall.

Lloyd Nolan remembered: "I first met Lucy on location of a movie I was doing with Fred MacMurray, *Exclusive*. The film was being directed by Al Hall. It was almost childlike, Lucy's interest and enthusiasm in everything and everybody. Everything was an adventure. Everything was a great burst of joy to her and it was infectious."

As a result of her *Annabel* films Lucille was being touted as one of the "luminaries in the 1939 Galaxy of New Stars." But instead of building her into an "A" picture star, RKO cast her in five potboilers: *Beauty for the Asking; Twelve Crowded Hours; Panama Lady; That's Right You're Wrong*, a film version of Kay Kyser's radio show; and *Five Came Back*, which presented Lucy in her first "heavy" dramatic role. She believably played a hardboiled tramp stranded with eleven other passengers in a South American jungle after an airline crash. (The film was remade seventeen years later as *Back From Eternity* with Anita Ekberg playing Lucy's role.)

By now, Lucille Ball was established as "Queen of the B-movies" at RKO. She was making big money—about $1,500 a week—and had certainly succeeded in making a name for herself. However, she had no illusions about her status in films and no intention of letting up on the hard work.

In 1940, RKO starred Lucy in four more forgettable films (including *The Marines Fly High*, with Richard Dix and Chester Morris; *You Can't Fool Your Wife*, with James Ellison; *Dance, Girl, Dance*, with Maureen O'Hara and Ralph Bellamy). Lucy played a gold-digging chorus girl in *Dance, Girl, Dance*, directed by Dorothy Arzner. In one sequence she did a modified striptease while singing "My Mother Taught Me." (Her voice was dubbed.)

Lucille was "almost box office." Producer Erich Pommer hailed her, somewhat belatedly, as "a new find." Orson Welles wanted to make a film with Lucille—but the studio was opposed.

The next important move in Lucille Ball's life would not be professional—it would be personal.

4

Desi Arnaz had risen from bongo-beating performer to Broadway stardom in a relatively short time.

While appearing in a Miami nightclub, he had been spotted by Xavier Cugat, superstar of Latin band impresarios. Arnaz was signed as Cugat's headline singer, but his salary was only thirty-five dollars a week. For a while Desi was "afraid to quit for a better job," but Cugat's band manager, Nick Niccolette, urged him: "Go out on your own. If you're good enough you can go to the top."

So, after eight months with Cugat, swelled by success and the desire to make it alone, Desi left the band and returned to Miami with Niccolette, who had also quit.

"We had only twenty dollars between us," Desi said, "but by the time we were down to our last five bucks we had made a connection with a man who was opening a nightspot. Nick and I accepted a job for 'our five-piece Cuban band.' Except for me, the leader, there wasn't a Cuban in the bunch.

"Three Brooklyn boys handled the piano, saxophone and violin. There was a Spaniard on the drums, an Italian boy on the bass. We sounded terrible."

According to Desi, the band had only played one set when they were given two weeks' notice. Luckily, radio personality Ted Husing was there and suggested the club owner reconsider. "The band isn't much but the young lead singer has something. If you'll keep him, I'll broadcast his music free every night on my radio program."

It was a big break for Desi. The band stayed, too, but Desi knew the score. "They were so lousy I had to figure something to drown them out. That's why I started the first conga line in the U.S."

Desi contends that the conga rhythm originated in his hometown, Santiago, during carnival time, and that he was the first to bring it to the United States.

The La Conga night club, on 52nd Street in New York, signed Desi and he played there for a year. The young, eligible bachelor was the hit of New York and Long Island café society; everyone important in town caught his act. And then Rodgers and Hart offered him a part in their musical *Too Many Girls*. Desi decided to take the plunge and try Broadway.

It was the right choice. Desi received good notices.

RKO bought the screen rights and cast their Queen of the B's, Lucille Ball, in the leading role. Desi was signed to recreate his conga-playing Cuban playboy role.

Lucy was filming *Dance, Girl, Dance* while George Abbott was conducting production meetings on *Too Many Girls*. The group at the studio had given Lucille a fantastic buildup to Desi.

In the placid nineteen-fifties, Desi remembered it this way: "The first time I saw Lucy was in a Hollywood studio lunchroom. Lovely, dazzling Lucille Ball was to be one of the stars of *Too Many Girls*. I was eager to meet her. Then she walked in. She had a black eye, frowzy hair and was wearing a too-tight black dress with a rip in it. She had been playing a dance-hall floozy in a free-for-all fight scene. I groaned, 'Oh, no!' That afternoon, when she showed up on the set where I was working, I said, 'Oh, yes!' She had fixed her hair and make-up and put on a sweater and skirt. She was a dream. I took one look and fell in love."

Years later, Desi phrased it more bluntly: "She looked like a two-dollar whore who had been badly beaten by her pimp." But, when he saw her out of costume: "She was dressed in a pair of tight fitting beige slacks and a yellow sweater, with beautiful blonde hair and big blue eyes."

He made his move. A group of the kids were going out to El Zarape, the current "in" Mexican night club. Desi, twenty-three, asked the twenty-nine-year-old Lucille to join them, "if you don't have anything else to do." She smiled. "I 'dunt' have 'anythin' else, and I'd love to." Arnaz was charmed by her playful burlesquing of his accent, a bit of business between them that they would later share with millions of loyal fans.

Ann Miller was there. "I was in the room when Desi and Lucy first met, and it was like love at first sight. When he first was introduced to her, her eyes just lit up. He was the cutest thing around. God, he was attractive."

That night the electricity between Lucille and Desi was undeniable.

Ann Miller (back at RKO for *Too Many Girls*) subsequently double-dated with Lucy and Desi. "I used to date Desi. But after he met Lucy I started dating George Abbott. The four of us would go to El Zarape, which was a night club up above an old market, way down on Sunset Boulevard. It was an all-Cuban place. Both of us gals really learned how to do a mean, mad rhumba."

Ann recalls that Desi "got around pretty good. He was always like a big, big kid. He was a great guy. I don't think anybody could play drums like Desi Arnaz. He would work hard all day long and yet he would be dressed and ready to go out to live it up at night—play his drums and dance up a storm, sing, whatever. And he was very nice. At night clubs if people wanted him to get up and sing and dance, he would do it—he would even lead the conga line."

The weekend after Lucille and Desi met, Eddie and Connie Bracken were having a house party in Malibu for the cast of *Too Many Girls*. Desi's date was a beautiful divorcée who had come out from New York to live with him. She was Arnaz's first real love and although, even today, he has fond memories of her and has not forgiven himself for abandoning her at this party, the attraction between him and Lucille seemed inevitable. He left the party not with the divorcée but with Lucille Ball, and they spent the night together. Obviously Lucy's attraction for Desi was equally intense, for she too changed her life overnight. She phoned Al Hall and said, "I'm moving out." She told Hall she would send someone to pick up her clothes.

In Hollywood lingo of the day, Lucille Ball and Desi Arnaz were "seriously dating." Press coverage of the day noted that the couple loved to argue, constantly contradicting each other.

About these early days and all the arguing, Lucy has said: "We couldn't have learned more if we'd been in college. His department was facts and figures and sports, especially horse racing. Mine was women—I taught Desi a lot about women."

Naturally, Desi was introduced to Lucy's family. Of Grandpa Hunt, Desi said: "Grandpa! A beautiful man. I loved him! Couldn't get in the door without his reading all those *People's World* editorials. I told him to cut it out or I'd teach him how to rhumba."

Lucy was crazy about Desi "in spite of the way he drove a car. The first time I drove with him," she recalled, "although he slowed to eighty miles per hour at corners, I thought he was a maniac. When I said, 'Mother wouldn't like this,' he slowed down. On another date he hit a low spot in the paving on a side street. Desi merely said, 'We dropped something,' and kept on going. I'll say we dropped something—only a fender and a bumper."

Their affair was in constant turmoil. "There was more than an undeniable physical attraction," notes a friend. "They were emotional dynamite to each other. Heated arguments all the time, their explosive temperaments clashing. And then there would be intense reconciliations."

Sheilah Graham, a Lucy-Desi observer, recounted: "Scott Fitzgerald and I watched them from the balcony of his apartment on Laurel Drive while Lucille, who lived in the same building as Scott, courted Desi Arnaz. She always seemed to be asking him not to drive away, to stay. We couldn't understand his reluctance and sometimes made bets on the outcome. No matter which of us lost, we were both pleased when Lucille won."

Lucille Ball wasn't the only leading lady in Hollywood who succumbed to Desi's charms. His other dates included Betty Grable and Ginger Rogers. Ginger was very interested in the studio's new "hot-blooded Latin," and as a far more important star than Lucille, she could have advanced Desi's film career. "Aside from being in love with Lucy, Desi was a man with strong personal integrity who wouldn't then—or at any time—use any woman that way," notes a close friend of his.

After *Too Many Girls* completed production, Desi went back on the road. It was the first of many separations Lucille and Desi would have to endure.

The studio put Ball into *A Girl, a Guy and a Gob,* the first movie Harold Lloyd produced in which he didn't star.

"Practically every morning," Lucy recalled, "Harold would hand us new pages of script. George Murphy and I would read them over and start arguing. To us it seemed no good at all. But Harold would say, 'Please trust me and give it a try.' At the end of the picture, I said to George, 'Too bad. We might have had a fairly good picture if things had been different.'

"You could have knocked me over with a feather at the preview. The audience just howled. It was a smash hit. That taught me not to argue too much with producers, which was probably the wrong psychology."

During shooting, Lloyd had given Lucy time off and she zipped to Chicago to spend a few days with Desi.

But when they weren't togther, they were on the phone arguing, he accusing her of sleeping around in Hollywood, and she accusing him of sleeping around on the road.

Dance, Girl, Dance was released in August 1940 and *Too Many*

Girls in October. *Gob* was scheduled to be released the following year. RKO sent Lucy on a cross-country publicity tour. One of the stops was Milwaukee, and, according to Arnaz, Lucy was supposed to stay only a couple of days but remained in Milwaukee for a week. His theory was that she was having an affair with Milwaukee's young, good-looking mayor, whom she had been photographed with.

When she arrived in New York late in 1940, her love affair with Desi resumed. He was winding up a band tour with an engagement at New York's Roxy Theater.

Lucy and Desi had courted in night clubs in Hollywood and now continued in New York's clubs. One night at El Morocco, he demanded, "Why wait around like this? Let's do it and get it over with."

According to Arnaz, Lucy wanted just to live together. "She was way ahead of her generation," Desi noted years later. But Arnaz wanted marriage and children, and of course she did, too. Perhaps her hesitation was because she was a bit more realistic about what they were letting themselves in for.

In any event, they eloped. On November 30, 1940, Lucille Ball and Desi Arnaz drove to Greenwich, Connecticut, to be married by justice of the peace John P. O'Brien. The ceremony was supposed to be in the judge's house but instead took place at the Byram River Beagle Club.

"Maybe it doesn't sound very romantic," Lucy recalled, "but actually it was. The judge took us there because he said all young people who were going to spend a lifetime together should start off in as romantic a setting as possible. He drove us out himself."

It appeared to many to be an unlikely match, doomed to quick failure. He was typically Latin: temperamental, hot blooded and at the same time rigidly conventional, with a double-standard attitude about women. He also was fun loving and his career meant only making enough money to live lavishly.

Lucy was career-oriented, and, though not a major star in Hollywood, she enjoyed a certain status which she had worked hard to achieve and had no intention of giving up. Desi was a bold man who "lived dangerously and appealed to women." Did the danger appeal to Lucille? "No," she said. "He frightened me. Marrying Desi was the boldest thing I ever did."

The Arnazes have always been accused of being press-conscious. A day after their marriage a magazine writer came to interview them in their hotel suite in New York. Lucille was alone. Almost immediately Lucy told the writer, "I'd love to let you copy the love telegrams we sent each other, but I'm afraid Desi would be mad if I made them public." But she couldn't resist displaying them.

Then there was the sound of a key at the door and Lucille swept the telegrams under a cushion as Desi walked in.

His first suggestion to the interviewer was, "Let's use those love telegrams for the article." The telegrams were promptly brought out of their hiding place.

During another interview, Desi turned to Lucille and said: "Darling, I love you more than Antony loved Cleopatra, more than..." Abruptly, he turned back to the reporter and asked: "Did you get that down? I'll repeat it. Darling, I love..."

Soon after the wedding Lucille Ball resumed her cross-country tour for RKO.

5

By movie colony standards of the day, Lucille Ball and Desi Arnaz were two fairly unimportant people. In fact, there were no movie roles at all for Desi. He had been typed as a Latin with a heavy accent who could dance, sing and play the drums.

Desi's shrewd business acumen was evident even in 1940. The newlyweds bought a five-acre ranch in Northridge, twenty miles from Hollywood in the San Fernando Valley. It was one of the best deals Desi could have transacted—complete with swimming pool, stables and a rambling ranch house. He got it for $18,000. They named the ranch Desilu.

RKO announced plans for a film with Lucy and Desi and radio superstars Edgar Bergen and Charlie McCarthy and Fibber McGee and Molly. But Desi was dropped from the cast. The film, *Look Who's Laughing*, was made and released in 1941.

Next, Lucy did a western potboiler, *Valley of the Sun*, with James Craig. Desi even went on location with Lucy to Taos, New Mexico.

If Desi had been content to stay home and be Mr. Lucille Ball, he could have remained in Hollywood. If he wanted to work and be independent, he had no choice but to travel with his band.

Lucy was appearing as a regular on Edgar Bergen's radio program. Desi was traveling, and he and Lucy spent a great deal of time on the telephone. (They later estimated they spent over $29,000 on long-distance calls during the years they were separated.) There was always an excuse to call—usually just to hear each other's voice.

"We spent a lot of money on the word 'what,'" Lucy recalled. "When Desi was calling me or I was calling him from little towns, the connection was always so bad we couldn't hear each other. That's why 'what' was so expensive."

When asked if she and Desi ever got jealous of each other, she answered, "Yes, we certainly do. That's all, sister—don't ask for particulars—we just do."

Desi was breaking box-office records all over the country. He was climbing towards that status of Dorsey, Shaw and Cugat as an in-person attraction. But Hollywood producers continued to see him only as "a Latin type."

In Hollywood, Lucille was thrilled because it seemed a *major* opportunity had presented itself. Her studio pal Carole Lombard had introduced her to Damon Runyon. Runyon realized Lucille would be perfect as the "heroine" of his story, "Little Pinks," which was going to be made into a film by the studio.

Runyon insisted Ball be cast in the lead—as a hard, bitchy, supremely egotistical night club singer crippled by her gangster boyfriend and befriended by a mild-mannered busboy who falls in love with her.

However, shooting was delayed and Lucille, between pictures, managed to work with Desi. Early in 1942, she appeared with him and his band in his stage revue at Loew's State in New York City.

Critics noted, "Miss Ball and Mr. Arnaz have created an act made up of singing, dancing, and amusing dialogue, and their presentation is entertaining. They sing 'South American Way,' 'You and I,' and 'Cuban Pete'; they dance the rhumba and conga, and Arnaz beats the conga drum and sings 'Babalu.'"

Lucy was in vaudeville at last. But she and Desi weren't able to tour together indefinitely, and Desi recalled feeling during this period that, "marriage is no good on a long-distance-telephone basis, and I thought if I got into another musical play it would help. So I hung around New York, eating at '21.' In a letter Lucy told me, 'The trouble with the "21" is if you eat there it means people think you're so successful you're not looking for a job. Eat at Sardi's.'

" 'Everybody is always reading his own reviews at Sardi's,' I argued, but Lucy insisted, so I went to Sardi's every night for a month. Nobody even said hello, and I went back to '21.'"

When Lucy returned to Hollywood, production on the Runyon film, tentatively titled *It Comes Up Love,* was not ready to begin. RKO wanted to lend Lucille to 20th Century-Fox for a Betty Grable-Victor Mature picture, *Strictly Dynamite.* Lucille would play the second lead, the star's wisecracking best friend.

Lucy refused the loan-out and went on suspension from salary. It was uncharacteristic of the girl who always played along, the staunch "family member" who considered the studio her family. Ball was off salary for four weeks. But the contention was that Lucy had refused the part not because it was secondary, but because she didn't want to lose the chance to be in Runyon's film at her home studio.

Finally, production went ahead on "Little Pinks," now titled *The Big Street.* The role of the busboy went to Henry Fonda. It was finally a top RKO film for Lucy. The cast also included Barton MacLane, Agnes Moorehead, Ozzie Nelson and his orchestra. (Lucy's singing voice would be dubbed by Martha Nears.)

Charles Laughton had once told Lucy, "If you ever play a bitch, play the bitchiest bitch who ever breathed." Gloria Lyons, the leading character in *The Big Street,* filled the bill: "A girl with a foolish, unhealthy obsession which made her more ruthless than Scarlett O'Hara. It was anything but a sympathetic part," Lucy noted, "but it was exciting because it was so meaty—so rich in humor, pathos and tragedy.

"I don't feel *The Big Street* was as fine a picture as it deserved to be. To some extent it was jinxed. The moment shooting was finished, Damon Runyon left the studio, the director joined the Army, and the editor dropped dead while he was cutting the picture. Thus, before an important phase of the work was finished, the three men who knew most about the picture were gone."

While *The Big Street* may not have turned out as well as Lucy felt it should have, it was still excellent and received good reviews. It was her best performance to date (many feel it still is her best dramatic performance). *Life* said, "The girl can really act." Respected critic James Agee wrote: "Pretty Lucille Ball, who was born for the parts Ginger Rogers sweats over, tackles her 'emotional' role as if it were sirloin and she didn't care who was looking."

The Big Street brought Lucy a contract offer from MGM. Lucy recalled, "During my time at RKO my pay went to $3,500 a week but I was only Queen of the B's. So I asked for my release and went to MGM."

Years later, though, Lucy admitted: "Charlie Koerner, who was general manager at RKO, said, 'Lucy, you should be doing better things.' And he sold half my contract to MGM. I almost had to be pushed out. I didn't care whether they were 'B' or 'D' pictures, as long as I was working."

While the move to MGM seemed to be a great opportunity— the biggest studio of them all, big salary, security—Lucy was, in effect, putting herself in direct competition with the leading young glamour girls of the day—Lana Turner (who was then twenty-two) and Hedy Lamarr. And she had unbeatable competition for straight dramatic roles at the studio: Katharine Hepburn, Greer Garson, Margaret Sullavan, Irene Dunne. While Lucy was capable of a wide range of roles, the studio initially saw her as a glamour girl and proceeded to give her that kind of build-up. Younger girls were also getting the glamour build-up—Kathryn Grayson, Donna Reed, Esther Williams.

However, Metro was pleased to get Lucy. With a studio full of problem children, Lucille Ball was a dependable, ambitious, steady, talented worker and Louis B. Mayer respected her. She was given the dressing room that once belonged to Norma Shearer. The studio's best make-up people were assigned to her and then came a "momentous" change in her appearance.

When they were color-testing Lucille for her first MGM picture, Sydney Guilaroff, Metro's chief hair stylist, dyed Lucy's hair a bright red. The wild carrot-pink shade became her trademark. When people protest that nobody ever had that shade of hair, she firmly says: "*I do.*"

"When I chose this shade, things began to break for me," Lucy explained. "It gave me just the right finishing touch before the cameras. Maybe I didn't look so good in person but I wasn't worrying about that."

Her initial MGM vehicle, *DuBarry Was a Lady,* co-starred her friend Red Skelton. The film was regarded as Lucille's "first real opportunity to become a big-time star." The thirty-nine films that had come before were described by *Life* as "honky-tonk" pictures.

Ironically, throughout much of *DuBarry* Lucy wore a huge powdered white wig covering her new hair color. The film was a typical Technicolor extravaganza of the day. The famed cinematographer Karl Freund was director of photography, and it was on this film that Lucy and Desi met him for the first time.

During these war years Lucy was one of a bevy of stars who went on bond-selling tours. Although Fred Astaire did not work with Lucy while they were both at MGM, he did make a six-week bond tour with her. "She had a lot of spunk, a lot of pep and she wasn't afraid of telling people what she thought," he remembers. "She was one of the busy workers. I know she resented being a leading lady in B films. That bored her to death. She wanted to be queen."

Astaire remembers that Lucy liked things her own way and would get angry if they weren't. "She likes to run things— period. That's it. And she doesn't care who she tells how to act or how to move or how to do anything. She's never done that with me, of course. I never worked with her like that."

Other friends describe Lucy during these years as "down to earth and refreshingly non-Hollywood." Once, at a celebrity-studded party, one MGM glamour girl was coming on "like she believed her own publicity." Lucy smiled at the girl's posing, sauntered over and said to her, "Aw, why don't you be yourself!"

During the war Lucy also worked some camp shows with Bob Hope. "It wasn't easy at first. He'd always offer to rehearse, but he never found time for it. He'd get off the plane, be swallowed by all the brass, then I'd wait for him to get back, but he never would. He'd turn up next on stage, and there I'd be, waiting in the wings, not knowing the answer to *one* joke!"

Although Lana Turner was originally cast in *Best Foot Forward,* she became pregnant, so the studio gave Lucy the starring role—a movie star who accepts an invitation to a college prom. It was in some respects a comedy part, and in every way an "A" production, produced by Arthur Freed and directed by Edward Buzzell.

Next came a cameo in MGM's star-filled wartime musical, *Thousands Cheer.* Lucy's old friend Ann Sothern (who was now Queen of the B's at Metro) and Marsha Hunt were in an amusing sequence in which, as prospective Waves, they were medically examined by Frank Morgan.

While Lucy's status and salary had increased, there were still no Hollywood roles for Desi. He stayed on the road much of the time. The relationship between the two volatile personalities became strained. Hollywood wags had predicted the marriage's demise from the beginning. "How could it last if she was a big star and Desi just a bandleader?" they asked. In Hollywood, an entertainer was nothing unless he was in pictures.

Desi got a big break when Louis B. Mayer saw him in a Hollywood revue, "Ken Murray's Blackouts." Desi's movie career had included such unmemorable films as *Father Takes a Wife, Four Jacks and a Jill* and *The Navy Comes Through.*

Mayer offered Desi a contract at Metro, but since the studio had no immediate film project for him, they allowed Desi to embark on a U.S.O. tour to the Caribbean.

But just as the tour started, MGM summoned him back for a big part in their major war epic, *Bataan.* It was a role tailor-made

for Desi and he had been dying to play it. Of course they needed
him immediately—if they need you at all in Hollywood, they need
you immediately.

Lloyd Nolan worked with Desi in *Bataan*. "He was a lot of fun,"
he remembered. "He had a death scene he was really counting on.
He was to get to say the Lord's Prayer when he died. He was
terribly disappointed, however, to learn he would have to say it in
Spanish and nobody understood what he was saying. But he was
good in the film."

Desi delivered a brilliant performance in *Bataan,* and at last
he and Lucy felt his movie career was launched. But the war
intervened. After refusing a commission in the Cuban Army, Desi
was drafted by Uncle Sam.

Even though in uniform, Desi was still Desi. He arranged to
buy a "hot" car. At that time it was almost impossible to get a
new automobile because industry was totally geared to the war
effort.

Lucy remembered the incident. "Our car was falling apart.
Desi was away, and I was home one afternoon when a stranger
rounded the corner. He asked, 'Is Deesee here?' I said, 'Do you
mean Desi?' and he said, 'Yes, Deesee.' I said, 'He's in Chicago,'
and he said, 'I've got his car here. He ordered it eight weeks ago.
You'd better make up your mind, sister. A lot of people want this
crate.'

"I looked at it. It was fire-engine red; it screamed when it saw
my pink hair. I said, 'I'm sorry, but we won't be able to take it.
You'll have to get another color, maybe blue.' He went away
mumbling, and when Desi called me that night I said, airily,
'Your car came today, but I sent it back.' He practically climbed
through the phone, and after a few husbandly remarks, I called
the man back at midnight and said, 'I hope you haven't done
anything with that car. I've just had hell bawled out of me.' So
we got it, and I kept my hair covered when I was in it."

During the war years Grandpa Hunt died. As he had gotten
older, he had become harder to manage. His socialist views and

moralistic attitudes had created many problems for DeDe and the family. One of his pastimes was to go down to the corner where the "hookers" hung out, lecture them on the evils of the oldest profession and offer them five dollars to "take the night off."

During the war Grandpa had been an air raid warden, but, since he had a hernia, by the time the family helped him into his truss the all-clear had usually been sounded.

Cleo was now married to Ken Morgan, a press agent who later became Lucy's press agent.

When Grandpa Hunt died the entire family—Desi, Lucy, Ken, Cleo, DeDe and Freddie—piled into a Cadillac and rode to the cemetery to bury him.

"It was wild," Morgan has recalled. "We kept topping each other's Grandpa stories, and before long we were laughing instead of crying."

By now, the fiery on-again, off-again, constantly-arguing-and-making-up Arnaz marriage had reached a breaking point. Special Services had assigned Desi to the Army's Birmingham General Hopsital near Van Nuys. He was not far from their Northridge ranch but he was still not living at home.

Lucy was an old-fashioned girl who believed in fidelity and "one man." Desi was an old-fashioned Latin who had the classic double standard.

Like most Latins, he would "fool around" and this would in no way affect his love for his wife. That relationship was sacred and had nothing to do with his indiscretions with women who threw themselves at him and who, in his eyes, were nothing more than tramps not worth more than casual intimacy.

However, this "arrangement" wasn't regarded too highly by Lucy. Friends asked Desi to be more discreet, but as one former pal explained, "He tried being careful but it just wasn't in his nature to sneak around."

Desi's extramarital interests, coupled with pressures created by their careers, made life a rather tense existence for the Arnazes. But they had something special going for them, emotionally and sexually, that up to now had welded them together and enabled them to weather all the heavy personal storms.

Suddenly, in September, 1944, Lucille filed for divorce, charging "extreme mental cruelty." "I couldn't believe it," said a friend. "I had a dinner date with them for that very night!"

No community property was involved in the divorce action and Lucille's attorney said, "We expect Sergeant Arnaz to waive his right to postpone trial of the suit until after he leaves the service."

Desi complied, and on October 15, Lucille was due to be awarded an interlocutory decree.

But at the last moment both had misgivings. Despite their adversarial relationship, they were still "nuts about each other." The day before the divorce, Desi phoned her and they agreed to get together for dinner. She had moved out of their Northridge ranch and into an apartment.

Sergeant Arnaz got an overnight pass, picked up his about-to-be-ex-wife, and after dinner the two spent a beautiful night together in bed. Nevertheless, in the morning, Lucille obviously felt she had to go through with the publicized divorce or look foolish. The judge was waiting, the lawyers were waiting, the court was waiting.

After being granted her interlocutory decree, Lucy hurried home and rejoined Desi in bed. She had testified at the trial, "He was spending too much money. When we argued about it, he became angry and went away. I never saw him for a week.

"That was a habit of his—going away whenever we had an argument. He always ran out on me rather than stay and talk the matter out. It left me a nervous wreck. I got no rest at night at all."

During the previous summer, when an interviewer had registered surprise that the marriage had lasted for almost four years, Lucy replied: "Me? I gave it a week."

The on-again, off-again relationship was on again. Years later, Lucy revealed: "I paid $2,000 for that divorce. I can show you the receipts." Desi added, "But it was never finalized, was it, baby? I could only stand to be away from her for a few weeks."

In the discreet nineteen-forties, Lucy's line was: "The day I got the interlocutory decree I went home and there he was."

Desi's recollections, thirty years later, were that Lucy divorced him because she said he was "screwing everybody at Birmingham Hospital." But even decades later Arnaz told her, "Well, honey, you were wrong." However, Arnaz has stated that under no circumstances, even if she had caught him in bed with someone, would he ever have admitted infidelity.

In any event, in the fall of 1944, Lucy took him back. They moved back into their ranch house and Desi was given a leave from the Army. Though he and Lucy were reconciled, their relationship didn't change much.

One day a friend ran into Desi sleeping in a big lounge chair in the lobby of the Beverly Hills Hotel. Rooms were very hard to get during wartime.

"Why don't you go home to sleep?" she asked Desi.

"I did," he said, "but Lucy had me locked out."

6

Lucy's career at MGM had reached a turning point. Although she had a starring part in Arthur Freed's top-budgeted *Ziegfeld Follies of 1944,* along with many of Metro's other stars, the film bombed in previews and would, for the time being, be shelved.

Ball hadn't quite caught on as a leading lady, so the studio cast her in a drop-gag role as the smart-aleck career girl opposite Keenan Wynn in the Spencer Tracy-Katharine Hepburn vehicle, *Without Love.* Lucy was billed below the title.

She was not pleased with her next film, a routine comedy, *Meet the People,* co-starring Dick Powell and bandleader Spike Jones. It was hardly an "A" effort and was indicative of the studio's new less-than-enthusiastic approach to her career.

Behind-the-scenes people at Metro remember Lucille as the court jester, "a good egg," not pretentious, always down to earth, always friendly with the crew.

A friend laughingly recalls a time when an interviewer, a

bosom-conscious male columnist, seldom bothered to glance above Lucy's chin. Lucy, at the end of the interview, totally unruffled by the columnist's steady stare at her breasts, casually reached into her bodice, plucked out the padding and elaborately wielded it as a powder puff, without missing a beat of conversation. "That writer damn near keeled over backwards."

Clowning was part of Lucy's nature. Another time MGM dance director Jack Donahue, a hard taskmaster, was assigned to work with Lucy on a number for a film. Jack put her through the paces the first day. The next day Buster Keaton pushed Lucy to the rehearsal hall in a wheelchair. She had one arm in a sling, blacked-out teeth, tousled hair and a bruised cheek—all done courtesy of the studio make-up expert. In her "good" hand she carried a sign: "I am not working for Donahue. Period." She had fun parading her fake injuries all over the lot before she suffered a sudden misgiving that the gag had embarrassed Donahue. Concerned, she asked him, "You don't think anybody took me seriously, do you, Jack?"

Buster Keaton, silent screen great and once as popular as Chaplin and Lloyd, was now under contract to MGM. But the studio felt he had "had it" and didn't assign him any films. Eddie Sedgwick, a director under contract to the studio, was considered "incurably old-fashioned" and was idle too. Keaton, Sedgwick and Lucy, who had time on their hands, became friends.

The comedian and the director recognized Ball's genius for comedy, slapstick comedy in particular, and comedy utilizing props—outrageous costumes, putty noses, mustaches, wigs, tooth work. They worked with her on developing her art, working with props.

In Lucy's own words: "I always wanted to do comedy. Buster spotted something in me when I was doing *DuBarry* and kept nagging the moguls about what I could do. Now a great forte of mine is props. He taught me all about 'em. Attention to detail, that's all it is."

While MGM was not interested in Lucille Ball doing slapstick or working with props, they did give her a chance to do broad comedy in her next film. She was cast opposite Keenan Wynn again, in *Easy to Wed*, which would star Esther Williams and Van Johnson. It was a remake of an old William Powell-Myrna Loy film, *Libeled Lady*, and Lucy had the role originally played by Jean Harlow, that of a dumb redhead. It was a far cry from *The Big Street* and, although it was a good comedy part, again it was a second lead with billing below the title.

Lucy was frustrated and unhappy. During her yearly layoff period at Metro, she went to New York and told the MGM publicity boys to book her on all the radio shows that couldn't afford to pay her any salary. If she didn't collect money for the appearances, the studio had no right to object.

"When word got out that I was available for free, Tom got calls from people and radio stations of which he'd never heard," Lucy recalled. "He'd tell me, 'I know you won't do this show, but I want to let you know about it.' I'd answer, 'Sure. That's exactly the type of show I want to appear on. Then I won't have to spend the next four years saying no when I'm asked to go on them.' Tom was confused. But I knew what I was doing. I wanted to reach all the people I possibly could in a short space of time."

When the war ended, Desi was quickly back on the night club circuit and the inevitable separations from Lucy continued. They were apart even when they were in Hollywood together. Lucy worked all day and Desi worked all night.

At the time, she explained the schedule. Work ended for her at six P.M. "Then I rushed for my car to make the twenty-mile trek to our ranch. I drove along Ventura Boulevard, and pretty soon Desi came along, driving the other way. We waved to each other as we passed. Then I had dinner and went to bed early, to be bright and rested for the next day's work, and he would stay up all night, playing."

Lucy said it was the same way in New York when she took a three-month vacation to be with Desi, "so we could be like married people." But she was busy all day, making personal appearances, "and he was up all night, playing. I had to get my sleep at night, and he had to get his sleep in the daytime. That's a married life?"

Desi's reputation as a lady's man hadn't dwindled, and this

was the cause of many of their continuing arguments.

Earl Wilson later wrote that Desi's pals advised him, "You should be more discreet. Stay away from girls that are known and recognized." According to Earl, Desi tried to heed this advice, but the next girl he had an affair with, although an unknown, rushed to a magazine editor and sold him her story. "I can't win," lamented Desi.

Arnaz broke his contract with MGM when he discovered the studio was planning to cast Mexican star Ricardo Montalban opposite Esther Williams in the swimming star's next vehicle. Desi realized that even though he was due $40,000 over the next forty weeks if he remained with Metro, it would be frustrating to know he'd always be second—or third—choice for Latin leads.

So he formed a new orchestra and booked himself into Ciro's. When Desi was performing in the Hollywood area, Lucy, despite her work schedule, made a point to spend some evenings with him. "That way," a friend recalls, "she made sure *she* was the girl at ringside."

Herman Hover, owner of Ciro's, later denied suggestions that Lucille was there to help boxoffice and confirmed that she was there *only* to be near her husband. Besides, according to Hover, Desi was a good attraction. "A good table-hopper—he knew everybody and they all knew Desi." But Hover also remembered that Arnaz was hardheaded and "always liked to have his own way."

Desi landed a recording contract with RCA Victor which stipulated that his band would be the only one recording Latin-American music for the company. Then he starred in a "B" vehicle for Universal, *Cuban Pete.*

Things continued strained between Lucy and Desi. She accused him of bedding down every girl that he met or worked with on the road. Desi discounted this as nonsense and retorted that her brother, Fred, who was his band manager at the time, got to the girls first anyway.

Back in Hollywood, Lucy had to maintain some semblance of social life, but it was difficult. In the first place, she found little pleasure going to parties or premieres without Desi. Secondly,

Desi, despite being in show business, always believed that a woman should never be seen with any man except her husband. He had never become *that* Americanized.

When Lucy had to make a public appearance, Ken Morgan, Cleo's husband, would accompany her. Usually the columns would begin to buzz: "Trouble between Lucille Ball and Desi? Desi's away—Lucille was out with a handsome man..."

Desi's "friends" would call him to report Lucille's "dating." More arguments.

"In those days," Desi has recalled, "we had plenty of battles. And every time we quarreled, I'd throw my clothes in a suitcase and move into a hotel room. The first thing I'd do was to send my clothes out to the cleaners, but by the time they were returned Lucy and I would be made up again. That was an expensive proposition, what with the hotel and pressing bills! So I decided to build a guesthouse in our back yard. Lucy's mother, who has a great sense of humor, wanted to know why. I said, "When that daughter of yours and I fight, I'll move out here. I can't afford to move to town every time we get mad.""

Though stormy, these were financially successful years for the Arnazes although the money was being spent as fast as it was being earned. Lucy was earning her MGM stipend, and Desi's earnings ranged from $75,000 to $100,000 a year. But Lucy later complained about these days. "They were getting us. Driving home alone after work, coming into an empty house—that's no fun. And always wondering, 'Is it going to be like this forever?' That sort of existence is all right when you're kids, when you're still working for that big break."

Lucy and Desi were no longer "kids." She was thirty-five; he was twenty-nine.

Lucy was understandably discontented at MGM. Her unhappy personal life only compounded the frustration of being stuck with acting roles that didn't begin to exploit her talents.

Lloyd Nolan, who starred with Lucy in her last MGM film, *Two Smart People,* said, "At this time, she was thought of as nothing but a beautiful leading woman. Well, at MGM there were

75

a lot of beautiful women, most of them with a lot of power. They were well established and she was just batting her head against a brick wall. And she needed the comedy to release her talents."

Lucy finally asked for her release from MGM. She began free-lancing. She did *Dark Corner*, a detective melodrama, at 20th Century-Fox. Then she starred opposite George Brent in Universal's *Lover Come Back*. The film opened in New York in July, 1946, when Desi was playing the Copa. Lucy came to town and they were together, in their usual he's sleeping-while-she's-awake manner.

Lucy and Danny Kaye were voted King and Queen of Comedy of 1946 by the Associated Drama Guild of America at their New York convention. The convention theme that year— "The emergence of sophisticated comedy on the American scene."

As a gag, at one of Desi's RCA sessions, Lucy made a recording, not intended for release. But RCA put it out and Lucy sued for $100,000. The disc, "Carnival in Rio," featured her singing in the background a falsetto version of the nursery ditty, "Peter Piper." The label on the record read: "Vocals by Lucille Ball." The suit was immediately settled out of court for an undisclosed sum.

Lucy and Desi wanted children. Desi had bought an anniversary gift for Lucy, a gold lapel pin in the shape of a key, set with nine rubies— "a $300 novelty." On the front of the pin Lucille's name was engraved and on the back was a significant inscription: "Nursery Key." When Desi reported the pin stolen, he was asked if the engraving meant that happy news was forthcoming. He answered, "Just hoping."

Lucy persuaded Desi to stay in Hollywood and he accepted the lucrative job of musical director on Bob Hope's radio program.

Lucy continued free-lancing. After *Lover Come Back* she signed with ex-MGM producer Hunt Stromberg to star in *Personal Column* (renamed *Lured*) for United Artists. It had a topnotch cast: George Sanders, Sir Cedric Hardwicke, Charles Coburn and Boris

Karloff. Directed by Douglas Sirk, it was a drama, with Lucy as a threatened beauty who offered herself to Scotland Yard as bait to trap a sex killer. Lucy was, as always, believable, and at, thirty-six, still youthful. However, *Variety's* critic commented: "Miss Ball registers best in comic bits as a wisecracking show girl and less effectively in the emotionally distraught scenes."

Lucy was earning good money free-lancing—about $75,000 a picture ($150-200,000 was the top price paid for free-lancing stars in those days), but her career was merely "treading water."

When Columbia Pictures, at the urging of producer Sylvan Simon, offered Lucy a film, she accepted, pleased with the studio's plans to star her in a comedy. *Her Husband's Affairs* had a screenplay by top movie writers Ben Hecht and Charles Lederer. Franchot Tone was her co-star and Edward Everett Horton was featured in this story of a husband-wife advertising team. Horton said of Lucy, "She's got more talent than these people realize. I loved working with her."

Critics liked the picture and began likening Lucille to Carole Lombard, but the film wasn't exactly a blockbuster and Columbia didn't have another good script for her ready for production. Lucy, never one to enjoy being idle, decided to give the legitimate stage another go.

Lloyd Nolan observed, "Lucille was always a puzzle during her Hollywood career. Her career never went really big and people couldn't figure out why. You'd never think of her then as being a slapstick comedienne. It was her main forte, but she never got a crack at it, and something was wrong. She was beautiful, she could act. I guess the biggest break for her was when she went on the stage in *Dream Girl* and suddenly people realized she was a comedienne."

Lucy toured in Elmer Rice's *Dream Girl* for twenty-two weeks at $2,000 a week. It had been June Havoc, one of the stars of the play when it was in New York, who suggested to Lucy she take the role. Author Rice later praised Lucille for giving the role just the right emphasis on comedy.

It was another tough experience, however. After the tour, Lucy explained, "You haven't been in show business until you've been on the stage, and even then you have to tour with a play to know what it's all about.

"I know what it is now to do one-night stands, and to act before audiences that aren't show-wise, as well as those who are. I know what it is to experience poor houses in remote sections and big audiences in major centers. And I've learned how you have to modify and key everything that you do to the public you're playing for."

In January, 1948, Lucy opened with her production of *Dream Girl* at the Biltmore Theatre in Los Angeles.

She had been determined to have *Dream Girl* play the Los Angeles area so that film producers could see for themselves the kind of comedy role she could handle. Naturally the other members of the cast wanted the Los Angeles engagement since it would be a showcase for talent scouts to see them as well. However, after twelve weeks in the east and a string of one-night stands on the road, bad luck struck.

Lucy recalled, "Our producer ran out of money. Some of the players got sick. I had to pay some salaries and hospital bills from my own pocket. It looked like curtains. But I promised the cast I'd get them into the Biltmore Theatre, come hell or high water, if they'd cooperate. I threatened to conk anybody on the head who failed to get the proper rest."

Lucy got the show opened in Los Angeles—and then collapsed herself. "I was delirious during one whole matinee and by the time I got out of the hospital, the play had had it. We folded shortly afterwards."

The critics, however, raved. Edwin Schallert in the *Los Angeles Times* prophetically wrote: "She is, in a sense, wasting her talents in pictures.... Miss Ball is a striking presence in the footlight world. She has efficiency as a comedienne. She can tinge a scene delicately with pathos. She has special facility in dealing with sharp-edged repartee. She apparently never overdoes the sentimental side of a role."

Dream Girl reinforced in the trade's mind Lucille's ability with comedy. CBS Radio signed her to star in the pilot of a new situation comedy, *My Favorite Husband,* opposite Lee Bowman. Ball and Bowman would play "Liz and George Cugat," characters made famous in two recently successful comedy novels. The pilot was such a success that CBS instantly wanted to go into series. Lucy signed, but Bowman was replaced by Richard Denning. The couple's neighbors, Denning's boss and his wife, would be portrayed by Gale Gordon and Bea Benadaret.

Two CBS staff writers, Bob Carroll, Jr., and Madelyn Pugh, were assigned to the series, and the initial producer-director, Gordon Hughes, was replaced the next year by Jess Oppenheimer (who wrote the *Baby Snooks* series for Fanny Brice), who became producer-head writer. It has been said that it was Oppenheimer's decision to change "The Cugats" to the more middle-American "Coopers."

In *My Favorite Husband,* Lucille portrayed a scatterbrained wife unendingly involving her poor husband in ridiculous situations. The show was a big hit and ran for almost four years.

Before doing the pilot for *My Favorite Husband,* Lucy went to Paramount for a Bob Hope starrer, *Sorrowful Jones,* a remake of Shirley Temple's *Little Miss Marker.* Lucy had worked with Hope on radio and camp tours, of course, and now in films they proved to be an extremely potent duo.

Director Melville Shavelson, then a screenwriter, worked on *Sorrowful Jones.* He remembers, "Most of the more serious moments were edited out, at least out of scenes detailing the relationship between the characters Bob and Lucy played. Lucy gave her role a whole new flavor. In those days she was very young, very pretty, very attractive. Her style was somewhat different than it is now."

Shavelson makes a very interesting point: "*Sorrowful Jones* rocked the whole boat in Hollywood for a while. At that time, production was a machine—you made three or four Bob Hope pictures a year and you knew how much money they were going to make. It meant you didn't have to pay much attention as long as you got a script the star was willing to do. And normally he didn't have much choice about that. If he didn't do it, he didn't get paid. And if he still insisted on not doing it, he would be put on suspension and couldn't work for anybody else. It was a real grinder operation.

"Well, Bob Hope pictures made a certain amount of money. *Sorrowful Jones* made *twice* as much money as any Hope picture that had been made before and it upset the whole thing. Obviously, there might be a difference in the quality of what was in the picture or who was in the picture, like Lucy, that determined this. And the producers had to stop and think."

Meanwhile, Desi was still nightclub king, but he was losing interest in that way of life. "One night, feeling lazy and self-important, I staged a poor show in a small club which wasn't paying the money I expected. Sloughing through the dance numbers, I quit early. Backstage, an angry man jabbed a finger into my vest and laced me up and down. 'Who do you think you are?' he demanded. 'In this business you never give less than the best of yourself. Just remember those people out there made you!' I took another look at him. It was Harry Richman. I humbly apologized to the veteran showman. And never again have I sloughed off a performance. There have been times when I have not been in tiptop shape, but I have tried to do my best."

Around this time, an actress, Yvette Taylor, sued Desi for $75,000, claiming she was struck over the head with a portable mike during one of Desi's engagements at Ciro's. Later, she dropped the suit, but the publicity reinforced the image of Desi as a hot-headed Latin. Desi's lawyer said, "We preferred to fight out the case as a matter of principle. We received offers to settle for $200."

Lucy returned to alma mater RKO to finish off an old commitment, and was lucky the commitment didn't finish her off. She played fourth lead—a secretary—in a story about pro-football, *Easy Living*, which starred Victor Mature, Lizabeth Scott and Sonny Tufts. The talk was Lucy had been offered the lead but turned it down, preferring not to work that hard, just wanting to finish off the commitment.

There was a renewed demand for Lucy's services. But though she was work oriented, Lucy was also more determined than ever to keep her marriage going. She and Desi hadn't been able to have children and didn't want to adopt. Friends said it was Desi who wouldn't consider it, but when asked, "I heard you were going to adopt a baby," Lucille replied: "Now *wouldn't* that be silly when I can have one of my own?"

Both Lucy and Desi had gone to doctors and been assured that there was no physiological reason they couldn't conceive.

Career-wise, 1948 was a bad year to be free-lancing in Hollywood. The bottom had suddenly dropped out of the annual boxoffice returns because of a new gimmick that "couldn't possibly last": television.

Lucy was fortunate. At producer-director S. Sylvan Simon's urging, Harry Cohn, head of Columbia Pictures, signed her for a three-picture deal at $85,000-per-film. Lucille's first was a comedy which took advantage of her zany quality and reinforced her radio show image. In *Miss Grant Takes Richmond* she played a dim-witted secretary who discovers the real estate agency run by her boss, William Holden, is a cover-up for a bookmaking parlor.

She and Holden hit it off, and in a couple of scenes in the finished film it was evident that he was stifling the urge to guffaw at some of Lucy's hijinks.

Desi also made a movie for Columbia, *Holiday in Havana*. The film included two songs he wrote—the title song and "The Arnaz Jam." They were both percussive Latin-type numbers and the critic for the *New York Herald Tribune* wrote, "Arnaz is boyishly enthusiastic about all this. His performance in front of the band has color and authority. This is not quite enough to redeem a mediocre Cuban-accented show."

At thirty-eight, after more than eight years of marriage, Lucille Ball became a June bride. Desi and his parents were devout Catholics although Lucy wasn't, and Desi's mother in particular had always been unhappy that her son hadn't been married in the Church.

A friend speculates, "Lucy and Desi hadn't been able to have kids and perhaps there was a psychological guilt because, according to the Catholic Church, they had been 'living in sin.'"

The Arnazes were remarried in a religious ceremony by Father John J. Hurley in Our Lady of the Valley Church in Canoga Park. Only their relatives and a few friends attended. Lucy was given away by Eddie Sedgwick and her mother-in-law was matron of honor. Ken Morgan was best man. Groucho Marx sent a telegram: "What's new?"

There was no second honeymoon for Lucy and Desi, since he was playing at a local night club and she too had professional commitments.

Lucy returned to Paramount to star again with Bob Hope, this time in a remake of *Ruggles of Red Gap*, titled *Where Men Are Men*. The movie received yet another title change, ending up as *Fancy Pants*, which proved to be another Hope-Ball hit.

In *Fancy Pants*, as in *Sorrowful Jones*, Lucy was used as a foil for Hope, and he got the laughs. "Lucille Ball...knows her small place and keeps it," wrote one critic. Another said, "Lucille Ball, handicapped by lack of comic lines, gives what help her pert presence can afford." Another critic noted, "She is a fine foil for the star, building up bits of business to a point where they are comically consequential even though they have next to nothing to do with the original plot."

Bob and Lucy were close friends and would work together often in the future. They had a lot in common. He appreciated her ability to deliver a gag or a wisecrack offscreen as well as on.

It was announced that Lucy was going to Broadway to take over Judy Holliday's role in *Born Yesterday*. Lucy later admitted that she wanted to do *Born Yesterday*, but only after the star had been chosen for Columbia's film version, because "I wouldn't want them to think I was auditioning." When asked if there was a possibility she might get the coveted role in the picture, she quipped: "Only if nobody else wants it!"

The Life of Lucille Ball

Lucille Ball had no reticence about appearing on the new medium, television. She and Desi guest-starred on Ed Wynn's TV variety show on CBS in 1949. In one sketch they played a husband-and-wife team.

But motion pictures were still the "prestige" medium. Lucy gave some candid, insightful comments on the workings of Hollywood studio politics. "You can't start at the bottom of this business and rise without running into trouble. I know the various steps of the ladder so well. At one studio you're expected to be a social butterfly and make command appearances at the boss's parties; at another you run smack into a political situation where your troubles never get to the head man, who could settle them with one word. At still another studio they leave your private life strictly alone provided your pictures make money.

"Well, I used to be the sensitive type. These things bothered me and I worried. Now I leave my worrying to my agent."

She pointed out that one of the aspects of her career she was proudest of had been the fact that she worked up to four figures a week from $50 at RKO. Seeming to forget the number of studios she worked at, Lucille noted, "Usually young actresses have to bounce around from studio to studio before they accomplish this. Of course I was at RKO for so long that I did everything, including sweeping up. If someone said, 'Ball, be there at four A.M.,' I was there. Or if someone said, 'For gosh sakes, Lucy, go home,' I would go home. Dutiful Ball I was, in those days."

Nineteen fifty was a harried year for Lucille. She was having her battles with Harry Cohn, tyrannical head of Columbia Pictures. She had even appeared in a cameo role, unbilled, in the studio's Rosalind Russell starrer, *A Woman of Distinction*.

But the studio seemed to find it difficult to come up with scripts that she wanted to do. Finally, S. Sylvan Simon cast her in *The Fuller Brush Girl* (he had produced the successful *Fuller Brush Man* with Red Skelton). Lloyd Bacon, who had directed *Miss Grant Takes Richmond*, would direct. Eddie Albert was co-star. Red Skelton agreed to do a cameo appearance in the film. This was the only one of Lucille Ball's movies, up to this point, that took generous advantage of her slapstick abilities. She played a cosmetics salesgirl who discovers a murder, uncovers a smuggling ring and dodges the police, despite the interference of her dim-witted boyfriend.

It was a strenuous picture and Lucy suffered some injuries during filming. She sprained both wrists while wrestling; displaced six vertebrae when she fell from a fence onto a clothesline; and pulled a muscle in her legs while walking with ankles bent, imitating a drunk.

Lucy told of one near-disaster. "I was a switchboard operator, and one of the gags was a wind machine hooked up to the board which squirted talcum powder out of the holes. One blast got me right in the eye. I didn't work again until every speck was out, four days later."

On the last day of shooting, she was suffering from a bad cold because of being drenched in several scenes. She had agreed to stop for a publicity shot to demonstrate a free-to-the-public X-ray machine. While she was posing, the X-ray technician gasped. "My God, Miss Ball! This shows you have pneumonia. Did you know?"

She didn't. But she went straight to the hospital.

Friends remember that things were still not peaceful in the Arnaz household. When columnist Sheilah Graham got wind of the dissension, she mentioned their "battles" on her radio program. Lucy, according to Sheilah, called in a rage, "I'm going to get you for this," she screamed, "and who told you?" Miss Graham replied that she could not reveal her source (but later admitted the source had been Lucille's own press agent).

Lucy became hysterical over the phone, according to the columnist, and said, crying, "You've got two children and you don't care. You say things like that about me and I will never have children."

Lucy told a friend, "I knew there was never anyone in the world for me but Desi and that we might have our ups and downs just as many people have. But I'd rather quarrel and make up with him than anyone else in the world."

Desi was almost constantly on the road with his orchestra. Lucy noted, "He'd fly to me when he could, and I'd fly to him, but our dream is to both be able to have our jobs in the same town at the same time."

Desi was still big box office for night clubs. When he next appeared with his orchestra at Ciro's, a typical review described his "pulse-pounding prancings with the conga and bongo drums.... Maestro's showmanship, tremendously improved over the years, is flashy, and even when he fluffs a line, which is often, he holds the ringsiders in his palm."

CBS was considering transferring "My Favorite Husband" from radio to TV and, naturally, the role was Lucille's if she wanted it. However, Lucy and Desi had decided that to make their marriage work, he would have to stop traveling and remain in Hollywood. Obviously, the only solution was for them to work together.

They tried unsuccessfully to persuade producers and talent agencies to co-star them in a film or a television series. "On screen, the public won't believe you're married to Desi," she was told. "After all, what typical American girl is married to a Latin?"

Lucy replied, "American girls marry them all the time, but not, I suppose, on television."

To prove that they were right and the producers wrong, Lucy and Desi put together their own vaudeville act and took it on the road in the spring of 1950. Lucy later said of the act, "It was mostly husband-and-wife situation comedy. Mixed in with it was a little music, dancing, gags and serious stuff." They also formed Desilu Productions, giving the company the same name as their ranch.

The tour proved to be a tremendous success, but it was a terrifically strenuous act. They did six and seven shows a day, playing such cities as Chicago and New York.

In one crazy knockabout sketch, Lucy wore a fright wig, played a cello and walked across the stage on her knees. Audiences howled, and obviously accepted the Arnazes as a married couple. Naturally, Lucy's radio show was a big hit at the time, and was instrumental in drawing audiences. So, in the act, she was playing an extension of her nutty "My Favorite Husband" character.

While in New York, Lucille jubilantly announced that she was going to have a baby. Friends suggested that she quit the tour and wait for the birth of the baby. But the commitments were made and the tour continued on to Buffalo and Milwaukee.

In July, Lucy and Desi returned to Hollywood, exhausted. Regarding her pregnancy, they said, "You can tell the world about it, but don't say child. We're hoping for twins." The couple displayed two baby sweaters which Lucille had knitted herself, one pink and one blue. Lucy explained that she always wanted a son and Desi hoped for a girl—hence their desire for twins.

Lucy was happy the tour was a success and thrilled about the expected baby. She planned to rest until its arrival, but the tour had taken its toll. She was rushed in a screaming ambulance to Cedars of Lebanon Hospital and for days doctors tried, unsuccessfully, to save the baby. The Arnazes were devastated and the doctor's consolation and promises that they would have more children fell on deaf ears.

According to the press of the day, Lucy was more determined than ever to have a baby and she was doing "everything the doctor prescribed."

"I've changed my whole program," she said. "I'm going to a gym to keep in good health and I'm not going to do any comedies that call for physical strain. You know, I was in bed for three weeks after I made *Fuller Brush Girl*. Now I'm going to do only two pictures a year, either very quiet comedies, or somber dramas. Nothing that will make me stand on my head or hang by my eyebrows from a chandelier."

Her friend Louella Parsons said, "... knowing her, I am convinced she will keep her word and get herself into perfect health and then concentrate on the hope of motherhood." Louella then scolded Lucille for having continued the tour after finding out she was pregnant.

Did Lucille agree that her strenuous tour was responsible for losing the baby? "I don't know," she said at the time. "I think sometimes things are just meant to be. Yet, I am not going to take any chances, and Desi is going to make it possible so I don't have to travel to see him. He is going to open a night club and bring his band to the Sunset Strip instead of going to the hinterlands."

Desi did not open a night club, but accepted an engagement at Ciro's. Meanwhile, Lucille still had a contract with Columbia Pictures. Since CBS would not remotely consider Desi for the lead opposite Lucy in "My Favorite Husband" if and when it ever made it to TV, the Arnazes had to come up with another idea.

The idea for their own series began to take form and shape when Lucy's arguments with Columbia Pictures about roles and money were reaching the breaking point. Lucy later admitted, "I wasn't happy at Columbia ever. Harry Cohn, who headed the studio...is so involved in the story of my quitting movies I can't leave him out. If he seems a heavy as far as I'm concerned, I'm not a hypocrite. He'd been asking me to do things I didn't like, which meant an impasse, because I wasn't about to do something I thought was bad for me. He was trying to break my contract, and I was all for letting him break it, but at the same time he was keeping me from doing a picture for Cecil B. De Mille on a loan-out."

De Mille wanted her for *The Greatest Show on Earth*. Lucy later claimed it was for the lead that went to Betty Hutton, but actually De Mille wanted Lucy for the supporting role of the wisecracking, red-headed "elephant girl," a role which eventually went to Gloria Grahame.

Lucy explained that she and De Mille had on the q.t. discussed the possiblity of her working for him. He knew she was under contract to Cohn, and asked Lucy, "How can you?" She replied, "I have no idea, but I will."

She later said, "I had several meetings with Mr. Cohn about it. But his idea was to outfox me. He kept saying, 'You don't have time. You owe me a picture.' 'That's ridiculous,' I said. 'You have nothing for me to do, and the De Mille picture is a great opportunity.'

"'We'll see,' he said, which meant he was going to hold out on me. In the meantime, the De Mille company was ready to leave for Florida and begin shooting, and I was so excited I couldn't breathe. To me, working with De Mille was the living end. I'd had some nice directors and some good ones, no super ones.

"I was getting nowhere with Mr. Cohn, so I said to him, 'I'm asking you again. Why can't you let me make this picture?'." According to Ball, "What really concerned him was trying to get out of having to pay me the eighty-five grand he would owe me if I made the one more picture for him.... If he'd asked me to let him out of that commitment, I would have agreed to forget the whole deal. But that was too simple. He wanted to outsmart me, so one day he sent me a script about the size of a small pamphlet, called *The Magic Carpet*."

Lucy's version of ensuing events was: "I read the script, and as I read I became hysterical with laughter. It was a Hymie Levin script. His name wasn't really Hymie Levin, but since he's a nice man and I wouldn't want to hurt his feelings, I'll call him that, because he made what were called 'the lease breakers.' If they wanted you out of your contract they sent you a genuine Hymie Levin script. He has made some fine pictures since, but at that time a Levin script was a short, hurried 'B' picture with any cast he could sling together. When I realized what was up, I was elated, although I didn't know what Desi would say to the idea that had popped into my head. When he got home, I said, 'I have a script I want you to read.' He read it, looked at me and asked, 'Are you cra-zee or something?' I said, 'All I have to do is appear in this picture and I not only get $85,000 but I've worked my way out of my contract and I can accept the De Mille role. I'm going to fool them. I'm not going to turn it down.'

"'You wouldn't dare,' Desi said.

"'Why not?' I asked. 'Hymie Levin is a likeable man, besides, it'll only take me five days to finish it.'"

Lucy never saw the finished picture. "I don't remember much

about it. As I recall, I was a harem girl, lying on a divan in lamé pantaloons, while slaves fed me grapes. I sent word to Columbia that I would be delighted to do the picture, then I checked in for my costume fittings. I tried on the muslin mock-up of my body they used for fittings when I wasn't around but I couldn't zip it. And I was puzzled. I'd made a picture only a couple of months before. The muslin figure had been perfect then, but now it missed closing by two or three inches. I didn't realize I'd put on so much weight. I must have been lying around eating too much. Then the next day I had a strange feeling.

"But I thought, *it couldn't be*. Desi and I had made up our minds that we couldn't have a baby. Nevertheless, the doctor said one was on the way. After that, the trick was to let nobody know. If Mr. Cohn had realized that I was pregnant, he could have refused to take a chance on an expectant mother in a film, and if I couldn't have done the Levin opus, it would have let him out of his commitment to me."

Although Turkish harem girls' middles were supposed to be plump, Lucy chuckled to a friend, "Not so plump as this Turkish girl's middle looked. I quickly found that pregnancy made me expand like a balloon, but, of course, I couldn't tell anybody, not even the wardrobe girl who was trying to tuck me into my lamé pants and my Turkish bra. I walked around all day trying not to breathe, and every night the wardrobe girl said, 'I simply don't know what's happening, Miss Ball. I let your things out last night myself.' And I said carelessly, 'Apparently you didn't let them out far enough. You're going to have to let them out some more.'

"I finished the picture, collected Columbia's money and, with Desi, went to see Mr. De Mille with tears streaming down my face. 'Why are you crying?' Mr. De Mille asked, and I said, 'I've always wanted to work with you, and this is the only opportunity I'll ever have, but I can't do your picture. I'm pregnant.' It was very sad. Even Mr. De Mille had tears in his eyes. He shook Desi's hand solemnly and said, 'I want to congratulate you. You're the only one who's ever crossed up Cecil B. De Mille, his wife, Paramount Pictures and Harry Cohn all at the same time.'"

There are other versions of this story. "Lucy knew she was pregnant *before* she accepted Cohn's lease breaker," says a friend. "Eddie Sedgwick told Lucy to tell Cohn she'd do the picture. 'It'll break Katzman,' Sedgwick said. 'His whole budget is less than your salary.'

"Sam Katzman tried to talk her out of the picture, but she would have none of it. She met the writers of the film when she bumped into them in the studio parking lot. They didn't even have an office. They were so thrilled to be working with a star of Lucille's stature they offered to write additional dialogue and scenes for her. 'Don't change a word,' she told them, 'I like it just the way it is.'"

After filming her final scene Lucille phoned Harry Cohn.

"Harry, this is Lucille Ball."

"Yeah, whaddya want?"

"I want you to be the first to know. I'm going to have a baby."

"Why you son of a bitch," Cohn screamed. "Why the hell didn't you tell me before the picture?"

"I just found out, Harry."

De Mille's reaction to Lucy's pregnancy, according to an informed source, was considerably more earthy than Lucille's recollection of it. De Mille was quoted as saying to Desi, "Congratulations. You're the only man who's ever fucked his wife, Cecil B. De Mille, Paramount Pictures and Harry Cohn all at the same time." Then the world-renowned director of Biblical spectacles was said to have suggested that the couple "do something" about the baby so that Lucy could appear in his movie.

The Arnazes were horrified. Their much-prayed-for and wanted baby was the most important thing in the world to them, and Lucy was determined to have it. After seeing De Mille, Lucy called Louella Parsons to give her the exclusive on the baby.

"This time," Lucy told Louella, "I'll rest all the time. I'm even giving up my role as the elephant girl in *The Greatest Show on*

Earth. I've just told Mr. De Mille that I cannot make the picture. As you know, I was very excited over the opportunity of working for C.B. But there will be other times, at least I hope so, and the baby is more important.

"We are already building a nursery," she said. "You know this happened in answer to our prayers. We both prayed so hard for another baby."

7

The year nineteen fifty-one was the most decisive and probably the most exciting year in the lives of Lucille Ball and Desi Arnaz, not only personally but professionally.

Television was eager for names but top movie stars shunned the new medium. Even if they wanted to appear, their movie contracts forbade it. Besides, it was beneath their stature to appear on television. Hence, television moguls had to turn to movie names who were beyond their peak and has-beens who couldn't get jobs in films.

But despite movie studios' disdainful attitudes, television had taken over as America's leading leisure-time activity. Jerry Lester's "Broadway Open House," the precursor of "The Tonight Show," was super-popular. Lester's busty blonde sidekick, Dagmar, enjoyed national popularity. Faye Emerson's cleavage was a national topic of conversation. "Howdy Doody," "What's My Line," Ed Sullivan's "Toast of the Town" were among the most popular shows. And the King of Television was "Uncle Miltie," Milton Berle.

But Uncle Miltie's "King" days were numbered. Soon there would be a new king and queen of television, and their success would far outlast that of any TV star that had come before.

In the spring, while Lucy was pregnant, the Arnazes decided to go-for-broke in their careers. Desi summed up their years together, and their future, when he said: "We had been married ten years. Each successful in our respective fields, movies and music. Yet we were almost total strangers. Our work pulled us far apart, east coast and west. We had neither home nor children. So we quarreled and talked of divorce. But deep down I knew that I couldn't live without Lucy, and she could not without me. We were on the edge of breakup when we hit upon a magnificent idea."

They were determined to play husband and wife on a television series. "From all sides we were told that the idea was ridiculous and were advised to give it up."

It was a gamble. Movie studios did not look kindly on movie stars who "deserted to the enemy." If the show flopped, Lucille would have no place to "crawl back to." However, Lucy noted, "There used to be this attitude that if you went into television, you must be starving. I made sure everybody knew I didn't *have* to do this."

In later years, both Lucy and Desi were irked by the oft-repeated story that the only reason they went into TV was because they were washed up in their separate careers. "Desi was making $150,000 a year," said Lucy, "and I got $85,000 from Columbia Pictures for my last picture, for one week's work. You think that's 'washed up'?"

Although CBS was interested in a television show starring Lucille Ball, they would not finance the pilot. With $8000 borrowed by Desi from his booking agency, General Artists Corporation, Lucy and Desi produced the pilot film themselves,

under their Desilu banner. They hired writers Jess Oppenheimer, Bob Carroll and Madelyn Pugh. Oppenheimer
would also produce. He hired Ralph Levy to direct. Levy was
producing and directing the Burns and Allen show for television, and Jack Benny's radio program. Though extremely busy,
Levy wanted to direct the Arnazes—he had already worked with
them when they had guest-starred on Ed Wynn's television
show.

With Lucy five months pregnant, they filmed the pilot and
sent it to CBS. Desi remembered, "The first script wasn't about
Ricky Ricardo at all. It was about a successful orchestra leader,
Desi Arnaz, and his successful movie star wife, Lucille Ball, and
how *Life* magazine loused up their anniversary celebration. I said
nobody could care less about a successful bandleader and a
successful movie star not being able to go out for their anniversary
on account of they gotta shoot pictures around their swimming
pool for *Life* magazine. Oh, it was funny, very, very funny, but it
was lousy. It was dishonest. It was wrong. That's how we happened
to invent Ricky Ricardo who was just making ends meet, and she's
a housewife."

While this is one of Desi's versions of the show's birth, there
are several accounts of how the eventual format actually evolved.
As with all collaborations, many people were involved and many
have taken credit through the years. The key players in the "I
Love Lucy" game were: Lucy, Desi, Jess Oppenheimer and the
writers, of course; Don Sharpe, the Arnazes' agent; Milton H.
Biow, Madison Avenue advertising executive; the Philip Morris
Company and its chairman of the board, Alfred Lyons; CBS
President William S. Paley; the network's vice president of
programming for the west coast, Harry Ackerman; Hubbell
Robinson, another CBS vice president; and a young director,
Marc Daniels, whom Desi hired after Ralph Levy decided not to
stay with the eventual series.

Biow has said that it was his idea to make the show more of a
situation comedy about a couple and less a show with vaudeville
routines, a band and guest stars.

Although Lucille Ball could portray a "typical" American wife with a zany side, Desi could never portray a typical American husband. The idea that evolved was that Arnaz would play a character basically like himself, a bandleader. Only he would be less successful, less hotheaded than the real-life Desi.

Ball has recalled that the writers gave them scripts to look at, "and asked us what we wanted our characters to be like. No one had ever done that before." She knew what she *didn't* want—she didn't want her character to be glamorous or wisecracking. She felt she had done all that before. She wanted to be an average housewife. "A very nosy but very average housewife, and I wanted my husband to love me."

Eventually, Lucy's character would remain basically the same as the role she had played on radio, only zanier, with ample opportunity for slapstick in the visual medium. The role also gave her the chance to wear a variety of costumes and utilize a wide range of props.

After the writers came up with the "Lucy and Ricky" characters, they realized they needed another couple who would serve as friends and foils for "The Ricardos." With these four characters in mind, the writing team created over a half-dozen scripts for the proposed series.

CBS approved the new scripts. Biow lined up Philip Morris as the sponsor, and the go-ahead was given. There was much discussion about the title of the show. Some reports claim that the network wanted it called "The Lucille Ball Show," giving Desi only co-star billing. Lucy rejected this. She also was not fond of an alternate title, "The Lucille Ball and Desi Arnaz Show." The story goes that someone at the ad agency suggested "I Love Lucy" and the Arnazes approved. Perhaps one of the reasons the couple liked the title was that Lucy was Desi's pet name for his wife. The rest of the world, up to this point, called her Lucille.

In any event, the on-screen billing would be "Lucille Ball– Desi Arnaz in 'I Love Lucy.'"

They had a network and a sponsor—"But." The first "but" was

Lucy at the peak of her young glamour girl days.
It was around this time she first met Desi Arnaz.

Katharine Hepburn, Lucille Ball and Ginger
Rogers in *Stage Door* (1936). Hepburn and
Ginger were the studio's "A" picture stars; Lucy
was on her way to becoming queen of the "B's."

Lucy visits husband Desi on
a movie set (1941). She was
thirty; he was twenty-four.

Arnaz on the set with (left) Max Baer and Jackie Cooper (1942). Desi's movie career never really took off.

Desi shows off his G.I. haircut to Lucy and Frank Morgan. Arnaz was leaving for the U.S. Army induction center (1943).

In their pool, in the early forties.

Servicemen clamor for glamorous
Lucille's and Gary Cooper's
autographs at the Hollywood
Canteen during the war.

Lucy's pretty mother, DeDe, visits her
daughter at work at MGM in the forties.

Lucy and Red Skelton in "Dubarry Was a Lady" (1943).

In *Ziegfeld Follies of 1946*.

A typical 1940s glamour shot.

With Bob Hope in their 1948 hit, *Sorrowful Jones*. Lucy was no longer selling glamour.

The happy couple celebrate a wedding anniversary.

With James Gleason and William Holden in *Miss Grant Takes Richmond* (1949).

With Eddie Albert in
The Fuller Brush Girl
(1950).

Lucille Ball as the public
wanted her: funny.

America's favorite couple: Lucy and Ricky
Ricardo, a.k.a. Lucille Ball and Desi Arnaz.

The world's most famous foursome in the most popular TV sitcom of them all, "I Love Lucy." The show premiered late in 1951. Lucy was forty.

the insistence that the show be done live from New York, which was then the emanating point for all network television programs.

Desi fought the decision. He wanted his show to emanate from Los Angeles. One reason Lucy and Desi had wanted to do television was they wanted to settle down, at last, in Hollywood and start raising their family.

Desi came up with the idea of doing the show on film. CBS countered, "Lucy needs a *live* audience." Hubbell Robinson and Harry Ackerman, who used to watch Lucille rehearse for her radio program, insisted that she needed a live audience.

Desi retorted, "So we'll film with a live audience."

Then there was the matter of cost: a filmed show would add $5000 a week to the budget and the sponsor wasn't prepared to go that high.

More negotiations. Philip Morris eventually agreed to put up $2000 a week more. CBS would put up an additional $2000 per episode. Lucy and Desi would take a $1000-a-week less in salary. Desi said, "Okay—less salary on condition we own the show." In effect, CBS bargained away fifty percent ownership of "I Love Lucy" to save a few thousand dollars!

"Everybody thought I was out of my mind," recalled Desi. "Bill Paley, president of CBS, thought okay, he'll do six weeks of film and lose every cent and be doing it live in six weeks."

One of the reasons the network gave Desi what he wanted was because no one, up to this point, had ever filmed a sitcom in front of a live audience and they didn't think Arnaz would come up with a way to do it successfully.

Within two days the deal was consummated, with Desilu to be paid $30,000 a week to produce each episode. Desi's long years of practical business experience with his band were invaluable during this period. Looking back, he remembered, "Innocent me. I thought all I'd have to do was act. Suddenly, because of a disagreement with the backers on where and how the show would be filmed, we became one hundred per cent owners of 'I Love Lucy,' and then thousands of shooting, casting, hiring and editing headaches rang in my ears.

" 'What do we do now, honey?' I inquired.

"Lucy said sweetly, "That's not the question, dear. What can *you* do?"

"Oh, boy, what headaches that first year! You need special mobile cameras for a fast action, filmed show like 'Lucy.' I didn't know one from a klieg light. I had to find a studio, dicker on rent, sign contracts, buy equipment, learn to cut and edit film, study scripts, boss costumers and set designers, audition, hire and reject hundreds of actors twice as talented as I. Lucy ('I'm a big dope about business,' she kept claiming) stood back while I learned private enterprise the hard way."

About the three-camera process necessary to film the show, Desi later said, "Man, I didn't have the slightest idea what I was talking about. But I knew Karl Freund, the first man to move the camera during the shooting of a scene. And I figured if anyone knew how to have three cameras working at once in a fully-lit studio and still have good close-ups of Lucy, he would.

"All I could pay him," Desi noted, "and remember, he had photographed Garbo and Dietrich, was scale. But he was intrigued by the idea, so he worked it out."

Desi leased a sound stage from an independent Los Angeles studio. Director Melville Shavelson credits Desi with being one of the pioneers in television film production by building a studio with concrete rather than wooden floors, enabling the cameras to roll noiselessly anywhere.

Filming on "I Love Lucy" would begin in September 1951. Now that the show was sold, Lucy could relax and eagerly await the birth of her baby. Lucy later said, "Looking back on that pregnancy, I can't remember that I was ever as difficult as women are supposed to be. Desi was an angel. He waited on me hand and foot, and I felt fine all the time. The only thing I remember, I had an aversion to smoke. I'd been puffing away on two packs a day, and, all of a sudden, I couldn't stand the smell of tobacco. I made everybody around me ditch their smokes, even Desi." (This aversion apparently lasted only as long as the pregnancy.)

The Life of Lucille Ball

On July 17, 1951, a month before her fortieth birthday, Lucille Ball gave birth to her first child, Lucie Desiree Arnaz, who weighed in at seven pounds, six ounces.

Desi was overjoyed with the birth of their first child. And simultaneously overwhelmed with preparing for the first season of "I Love Lucy." The studio was being rebuilt to accommodate Freund's new technique and they had yet to cast the roles of Fred and Ethel Mertz.

Neither Gale Gordon nor Bea Benadaret, whom Lucy and the writers had worked with for years, were available. So the hunt was on for two other great character actors.

The new "Lucy" director, Marc Daniels, and actress Vivian Vance were old friends from New York, where Viv had done Broadway. Daniels obviously cajoled Desi and Oppenheimer to check her out as an "Ethel" possibility. She was playing the role of Olive Lashbrooke, a sarcastic bitch, in *Voice of the Turtle* at Mel Ferrer's theater in La Jolla, a town about one hundred twenty miles south of Los Angeles.

After seeing Vance, the three men decided she was right for "Ethel."

However, Vance, at first, wasn't interested! She had just played a role in Jane Wyman's hit film, *The Blue Veil,* and throught her own film career was finally launched—why should she jeopardize it by doing TV? Fortunately for all concerned, they convinced her to sign for the series.

Character actor William Frawley had heard about the part of "Fred Mertz" and knew he was right for it. He also knew why it would be hard for him to land the role—his reputation as a heavy drinker. Frawley and Desi met and hit it off. They struck a bargain: Desi, a drinker himself, would be happy to drink with Frawley after work; but if Bill caused any production delays or couldn't function, he'd be out. According to Arnaz, in all the subsequent years they worked together, Frawley was never "even a few minutes late."

Frawley would prove to be the ideal "Fred Mertz." Movie audiences knew his gruff character from countless films, and his vaudeville background was perfect experience for what he'd be called on to do during the course of the show.

The elements were in place. The production staff had been assembled. In addition to his writing chores with Carroll and Pugh, Oppenheimer would produce, Daniels direct, Freund would be director of photography, Al Simon was production manager, Larry Cuneo art director and Lucy had lured make-up artist Hal King to join the show. These and a dozen other dedicated and enthusiastic professionals would form the Desilu "Family," and for the most part would stay together for years.

That summer and fall of 1951 were feverish days for all concerned. There were technical problems which had to be solved. Quick, and often harsh, decisions had to be made.

On Monday, September 3, rehearsals began for the first episode to be filmed. Vivian Vance met Lucille Ball for the first time. They got along fine. But there were numerous production delays, including Desi often being called off the set to make executive decisions. The show was filmed one day later than scheduled, Saturday, September 8.

A month later, on Monday evening, October 15, "I Love Lucy" premiered on CBS-TV. Despite the lore that has built up over the years, the program was *not* an overnight ratings success, although the critics, for the most part, liked it. However, in a matter of weeks, it was a huge hit.

The working schedule eventually settled into the following routine: Each Tuesday morning at ten, the director, cast and writers would meet for a first reading of the script of the half-hour sitcom. On Wednesday, they'd rehearse on the sets. On Thursday evening, they'd rehearse before the cameras. On Friday, rehearsal would begin at 1:00 P.M. with a final dress at 4:30. Then Friday evening at eight o'clock they would shoot before a live audience. It would take one hour to film the program, with brief stops between each scene. The Desilu company pioneered methods of production still used today.

By shooting in sequence and before a live audience, the "I Love Lucy" show had a spontaneity and sparkle heretofore unknown in filmed television. In the 1951-52 production schedule, there was a total of ninety-three actors, technicians and other personnel employed for each "Lucy" show. The production costs were between $23,000 and $25,000 a week, leaving an average profit of from $5,000 to $7,000 a week for Desilu.

The show utilized four permanent sets—two were the Ricardo's apartment, the third was the night club where Ricky worked, and a fourth was used for any other scenes the show might require. Desi noted, "We had real furniture, real plumbing and a real kitchen where we served real food. Even the plants were really growing."

He also said at the time, "Our 'I Love Lucy' program is a stage show on film. We don't stop the cameras every time somebody makes a mistake, but keep going and try to find a way out. Often this helps the comedy, particularly if Lucy is carrying the ball. I've never found her at a loss at such times. For instance, when her foot got stuck in a ballet practice bar, in a scene in which the fictional Lucy was learning to dance, Lucy made a big thing out of it."

Desi described Lucy as "the female Chaplin! She walks like Chaplin. There's nobody else that can do what she does with her face, with her walk, with her action. No other comedienne in the whole world. 'I Love Lucy' was designed for her, built for her. All the rest of us were just props—Bill, Vivian, me. Darn good props, but props. In a 'Lucy' show everything starts with Lucy and works backwards. The writer might decide it will be funny if Lucy gets in a wine vat with two or three fat Italian girls and starts a fight while stomping grapes in the third act. So the whole idea is how to get the world's greatest female clown in that predicament."

Vivian Vance described "I Love Lucy" at its inception. "Theoretically, our show consists of three miscasts and one case of perfect typing—Lucille."

Why did "I Love Lucy" find such an immediate, vast audience? It dealt essentially with the most universal situation: the battle of the sexes. Lucy's neighbor and friend, Ethel Mertz, represented the millions of women somewhat more disillusioned about husbands after years of marriage than the younger Lucy. Hence, Ethel magnified Lucy's occasional doubts, sowed seeds of suspicion and prodded Lucy to various misadventures.

One of the staples of the show was Lucy's crying jags. Her range of tears went from the simpering sniffles to calf bawls, the now world-famous *Wahhhhh!* And not to be overlooked was the fact that the Lucy character was essentially a likeable, lovable child.

For the next few years, there was never a divorce between the private and public lives of Lucille Ball, Desi Arnaz and their TV show counterparts. The program made the most of their seemingly extravagant devotion to each other and their extraordinary ability to find humor in situations.

The writers used competition between mates as the theme for many of the scripts. For instance, Ricky would say that modern women haven't the endurance and spunk of their grandmothers. Or Lucy would insist that men gossip more than women. They would inevitably bet on it and that week's program would revolve around comic situations when Lucy, allied with Ethel, and Ricky, allied with Fred, would try to win.

The fact that the Arnazes hadn't been major news-grabbers in the 1940s was now an advantage. Their separations and squabbles had never been page-one news and so the public now could accept them for what they appeared to be on "I Love Lucy."

The show saved their relationship and marriage. At work, a new bond formed between them. The "I Love Lucy" show was their baby, their challenge, and a chance to prove that two people could be fiercely independent in big-time TV.

"At night," Desi recalled, "instead of wrangling over little things, we plotted new ideas, ways to cut costs, funnier situations—things that enabled Desilu Productions to cover four square blocks and revolutionize television production."

On another occasion Lucy noted, "I am no marital expert ... but I have been through an experience that perturbs a large number of young married women. I have had to plot, scratch and connive to hold a husband. I lost him once and got him back. Both of us have been sickened and frustrated many times by conflicting careers. And we had been married more than ten years before we finally managed to have our first child."

What they didn't tell the public was that they spent their weekends apart. On Friday evening she would go to their ranch to be with the family. He would go to Balboa to be on their yacht with his cronies. Then they'd meet again late Sunday night to begin the tense work week together.

"I Love Lucy" was second in popularity only to Red Skelton, with an estimated viewership of thirty-five million. Milton Berle had dropped to eighth place. Lucille and Desi were household names. They were established not only as the country's top new comedy team, but as America's new sweethearts, symbols of the ultimate onscreen and real-life happiness in marriage.

And, for the time being, the Arnazes were genuinely happy. They had a beautiful daughter and at last they had managed to combine their professional lives to achieve stardom and financial security in tandem.

In February 1952, when Red Skelton received an Emmy Award from the Academy of Television Arts and Sciences as the Best Television Comedian of the Year, he said: "I don't deserve this. It should go to Lucille Ball."

Lucille's new-found popularity was evident that spring when she was asked to be a presenter at the annual Academy Awards ceremonies. (She presented the award for "Best Short Subject"). It seemed the motion picture industry might be wooing her back.

In May, Lucy and Desi's good fortune multiplied when Lucy became pregnant again. They were both delighted. However, no immediate announcement was made of the pregnancy.

Because of the huge success of "I Love Lucy," the Arnazes were in a position to command huge salaries for in-person appearances. They had been planning a summer tour, to include New York and Boston, which would have paid them, according to *Variety*, $57,000 for two weeks "plus overages on $100,000 weekly" at New York's Roxy Theatre.

During the year, expanding Desilu Productions not only

filmed "I Love Lucy" but the commercials for Red Skelton's show, the pilot films for a Leo Durocher and Laraine Day situation comedy series and Eve Arden's "Our Miss Brooks."

As Desilu began expanding, so did Desi's headaches. CBS liked the Eve Arden show, signed Desi to produce it and so the summer tour with Lucy was "postponed indefinitely."

"All my life," said Desi, "I've worried what I'd do when I got too old, too fat, too ugly to be in front of a band. Now I don't worry. We're learning to produce television films."

Desi once again proved his business genius when he found an error in the network's budgeting of their show. "Desi has a mathematical mind," Lucy has noted, "but he had never used it much up to that point. Then CBS sent over this budget, and he began to study it. He said to me, 'They've made a million-dollar mistake.' I said, 'That's impossible.' 'No,' he said, 'I know there's a million dollars more in here for us to spend on production. They've got their figures wrong.' The next day he took the papers in to CBS and said, 'You've made a million-dollar mistake.'

"They said, 'That's impossible. Look, Desi, stick to your acting. We'll handle the business details.' So then he spread their papers out all over their office. He proved to them that they were wrong; there was an extra million in there for production. From then on, when he talked, they listened. That gave him a boost of self-confidence."

Obviously, the Arnazes kept Lucy's pregnancy a secret as long as they could. But as they completed filming of the first season, important decisions had to be made. Over the years a minor controversy has surrounded who should get credit for one of the major breakthrough ideas in television history: to incorporate Lucy's pregnancy into the script.

Jess Oppenheimer has flatly stated that it was his idea, and there seems little reason to doubt him. Desi, on the other hand, has said outright that it was his, Desi's, idea. This disagreement and others—centering on credit for ideas—was undoubtedly the

basis for Oppenheimer's and Arnaz's eventual disenchantment
with each other.

At the time, however, Oppenheimer did not contest published reports in which Desi claimed credit for the brainstorm.
Arnaz must definitely be given credit for pushing the idea
through the ad agency, the sponsor and the network, who were
all vehemently opposed.

Desi went straight to Philip Morris board chairman Alfred
Lyons. Although Lyons never officially gave permission to
proceed with the controversial idea, from the moment Desi
contacted him for help all opposition vanished.

In retrospect it is incredible that this idea actually presented
problems! But in 1952, the mention of pregnancy, especially on
a family program, was absolutely *verboten*. It was unheard of.
Desi said, "We didn't want to do anything that would upset the
public. I called the heads of the Catholic, Protestant and Jewish
faiths in Los Angeles and asked them to assign representatives to
keep an eye on our shows. So for eight weeks a rabbi, a Protestant
minister and a Catholic priest checked every foot of film we shot.
There was nothing we had to throw out except the word 'pregnant.'
CBS didn't like that, so we used 'expectant.' CBS thought it a nicer
word."

There was a new director during the second season. During
the first season, Lucy had had creative differences with Marc
Daniels. Daniels had helmed thirty-eight episodes, three of
which were held over for the second season. (It was Daniels who
directed the now-classic episode in which Lucy does a TV
commercial as spokeswoman for "Vitametavegamin.")

Daniels was replaced by William Asher, but reports are that
Arnaz actually supervised direction from this point on.

Although Louella Parsons had broken the news of Lucy's
pregnancy in June, the Arnazes continued their plan not to
discuss the baby and to break the news on television when their
show resumed in the fall.

In September, Desi sat down in conference with a battery of
press agents, including men from the network and from the

sponsor. Their problem: how to squeeze the maximum amount of publicity from the fact that Lucy was going to have two babies: one in real life and one on TV. Suddenly one of the experts had an inspiration. Since Lucy's first baby had been delivered by caesarean section, her second child would have to be delivered that way too. Therefore, the date for her second baby could be pinpointed exactly. Why not, the group decided, have the real-life baby and the fictitious Ricardo baby born on the same day?

The press agents drew up a five-part confidential memo: "Various aspects of the Ricardo baby in the 'I Love Lucy' publicity and promotional campaign."

The entire group swore "that there must be absolutely no word about the baby released out of any office before December 8." On that date, forty million televiewers would be informed of the secret—Lucy Ricardo's pregnancy. Plans were made to tie the show in with a Columbia record of "There's a Brand New Baby at Our House" (a song Desi had co-written when Lucie was born) and on the flip side, "I Love Lucy," both songs sung by Desi and played by his orchestra.

The memo had a special section called "The Secret Gimmick About the Baby's Sex." This too required an inviolate pledge of secrecy on the part of all concerned. The memo read: "The Ricardo baby will be a boy regardless of the sex of the actual Arnaz baby. Of course, if the Arnaz baby does happen to be a boy, then all writers and editors can assume that the producers of 'I Love Lucy' are clairvoyant and possessed of sheer genius. If it happens to be a girl, the story (and the truth) is that Desi was so set on having a boy... that he went ahead and filmed the Ricardo baby as if it were, regardless."

Naturally, the matter of the baby's sex had to be decided right away because a number of episodes of the show would have to be filmed well in advance of the baby's birth to give real-life Lucy time to have the baby and recuperate.

Just as the public had become immediately involved with Lucy and Ricky Ricardo, they now became caught up in the excitement of both Lucy Ricardo's and Lucille Ball's expected baby. The public had come to identify completely the real-life Lucille and Desi with the TV characters of Lucy and Ricky.

The entire nation eagerly awaited the birth of the decade's most famous baby. On the morning of January 19, 1953, Lucille Ball gave birth to a son: Desiderio Alberto Arnaz IV, who weighed in at eight pounds, nine ounces.

That night on television, Lucy Ricardo gave birth to Little Ricky. The show garnered the all-time high Trendex rating for a regular commercial program: 68.8. CBS researchers estimated that over fifty million people watched the show, which had actually been filmed in November. Everyone connected with the program had been praying it would be a boy. Just as the television script demanded, the Fates complied. There was even a syndicated "I Love Lucy" comic strip at the time, and the day Lucy's son was actually born, the comic strip had Lucy Ricardo giving birth to a son. The real-life Arnazes were on the cover of *Newsweek* on January 19 as well.

Lucy, conscious during the delivery under a spinal anesthesia, constantly badgered her doctor, Joseph Harris, "What is it? What is it? Is it a boy?" He had to calm her several times and reply: "Wait a minute, honey."

Desi later said, "Nobody had to tell me it was a boy. I could tell by the expressions of the doctors and nurses." A few minutes after the birth, Desi burst into the corridor outside the operating room and, waving his arms, he shouted at the top of his lungs:

"It's a boy! It's a boy! Boy, do I love Lucy!"

Lucy's self-appointed godfather, Eddie Sedgwick, had the task of holding Desi IV up for friends to see. Sedgwick described the hospital drama as "a wonderful, marvelous, emotional, hilarious thing." Both grandmothers were at the hospital and each found family resemblances in the newborn. "He has a pug nose just like Lucy," said Desiree. "And black hair just like Desi," noted Mrs. Arnaz.

"God, this makes me the greatest writer in the world!" exclaimed Jess Oppenheimer.

That night, over the CBS network, when Lucy Ricardo gave birth to a boy, Ricky collapsed into a wheelchair at the good news.

Vivian Vance recalled, "The night we filmed the show in which Lucy tells Ricky about a baby coming, everybody on the set broke up. She cried, he cried, the propmen cried. We were so awash in tears that we prepared to do retakes on the show, but the audience stood up and yelled 'No! No! No!' The whole thing had been too real."

No modern child was ever ushered into the world with such attention. Years later, young Desi noted: "I'm probably the only flesh-and-blood human being ever brought into the world by a television network.... I'm told by my Hollywood friends— although I still find it hard to believe—that my birth attracted as much attention and news coverage as the presidential inauguration of Dwight D. Eisenhower, which—apparently through poor planning in Washington—took place on the next day."

Desi, Jr.'s information is correct. The night he was "born" on television the "I Love Lucy" show garnered a Nielsen rating of 71.7 per cent. President Eisenhower's inauguration scored 67.6 per cent.

That January morning of 1953 Desi Arnaz summed it up: "Now we have everything."

The world agreed.

Two weeks later Lucy was named Best TV Comedienne of 1952 and "I Love Lucy" received an Emmy as the Best Situation Comedy Show. (Other Emmy winners that year were "See It Now," "Dragnet" and "Robert Montgomery Presents.")

Lucille Ball and Desi Arnaz—biggest superstars in the entertainment world! Lucille was enjoying a success she had never known. When queried if she was interested in returning to films, she said she didn't care if she never made another movie. "I don't know if I'll every work again in a theater movie," Lucy yawned. "It doesn't interest me a bit. Though I might do one this summer. Just to see how I look in Technicolor. You know I've been in gray and black for a long time now."

The movie studios, which had shunned Desi and shuttled Lucy around for years, now sought them desperately. In an era when movie stars who were Lucy's contemporaries were tumbling or had been toppled from box-office favor, Lucille Ball returned in triumph to MGM. The studio signed the Arnazes to star in *The Long, Long Trailer*, at a salary of $250,000 for six weeks work. (Desi had tried to buy the film rights to the book, but Metro had beaten him to it.)

Pandro S. Berman produced; Vincente Minnelli, who had worked with Lucy in *Ziegfeld Follies*, directed.

CBS and Philip Morris were aware of how valuable Lucy and Desi had become. A new contract was immediately negotiated with Desilu Productions. The contract was for a staggering $8,000,000, the largest ever signed in TV up to that time. It covered the completion of the 1952-53 season plus an additional two years of "I Love Lucy." The agreement contained an incredible "no option" clause. "I Love Lucy" could not be canceled for the duration of the contract. The budget of the show went up from $35,000 to $50,000 weekly. Desilu now employed three hundred people. Desi and Lucy were the highest paid entertainers on television.

In April, they were on the covers of both *Life* and *Look* magazines. Discussing their new eight-million-dollar deal, Lucy said: "It couldn't happen to a nicer pair of kids—I mean our children, of course."

Though Desi's professional and home lives had changed somewhat, he still retained his fiery Latin temper, his flair for the dramatic, an eye for women and a love of excitement.

An observer was present at a typical poker game at the lush Beverly Hills Hotel. "In the game, which was seven-card stud, were Desi; Harry Chesley, a vice president of the company sponsoring 'I Love Lucy'; Larry Berns, who produced 'Our Miss Brooks'; David Jacobson, public relations director for CBS; and Jaime Delvalle, another producer.

"In the last pot, everyone was frozen out except Desi and Harry Chesley. Desi looked at his last card and gave Chesley an opportunity to look at his. Then he leaned across the table. 'You remember that eight-million-dollar contract we signed a little while ago?' said Desi. The sponsor was startled. 'Of course I remember it,' he said, 'who can forget a thing like that?' 'Well,' said Desi, 'I bet you that contract, double or nothing.'"

The friend shudders as he tells the story. "At first," he says, "there was complete silence. Then somebody giggled nervously. But everybody could see that Desi wasn't kidding. When the sponsor realized Desi was serious, he became pale. 'Cut it out, Desi,' he said, 'be reasonable.' Desi stared at him, then shrugged his shoulders and made a bet. He won the pot, I remember. But nobody can remember just what cards he held, because the shock was too great. Desi actually would have bet that eight-million-dollar contract, I'm convinced, and if he'd lost—I can just see him going home and saying, 'For the next two and a half years, Lucy, we work for nothing.'"

It seemed as if Desi and Lucy's luck was boundless. Then in the fall, Walter Winchell, on one of his Sunday night broadcasts, started a national furor. Winchell named no names. He revealed: "The most popular of all television stars was confronted with evidence of her Communist Party membership."

8

Few people knew that during the spring of 1952 Lucille Ball had secretly testified at a closed meeting of the House Un-American Activities Committee, discussing her late grandfather's political past. She thought that had ended it. But now, in the summer of 1953, she had been re-summoned for another closed hearing.

The Arnazes had finished filming *The Long, Long Trailer* and were relaxing at their home in the seaside resort, Del Mar. Lucy returned to Los Angeles for the hearing, but Desi remained in Del Mar. Obviously, they weren't unduly concerned. But then, a few days later, the Winchell broadcast. All hell broke loose.

It is almost impossible, in the 1980s, to comprehend the impact of being labeled a Communist in 1950s-America. Anyone who was accused of having Communist affiliations, loyalties or tendencies was instantly ostracized, in jeopardy of losing their jobs, friends, status.

Since 1947, various Hollywood elite, including studio chiefs Louis B. Mayer and Jack Warner, and director Sam Wood, had gone before the House Committee on Un-American Activities and denounced certain writers and directors who were said to be members of the Communist Party.

In December of 1947 the studio heads got together and decided to blacklist the now famous Hollywood Ten: Alvah Bessie, Herbert Biberman, Lester Cole, Edward Dmytryk, Ring Lardner, Jr., John Howard Lawson, Albert Maltz, Samuel Ornitz, Adrian Scott and Dalton Trumbo. Only one of this group—Edward Dmytryk—subsequently confessed to having been a member of the Communist Party and then abjuring it.

"Guilt by association" became the order of the day and it became a dangerous time to voice political opinions.

Throughout the late 1940s and early 1950s various Hollywood luminaries such as Elia Kazan, Clifford Odets, Robert Rossen, Budd Schulberg and Sterling Hayden came forward and voluntarily confessed to having had associations with the Communist Party. Others did not come forth voluntarily and would not supply the committee with names of friends and associates who at any time had been connected with "The Party."

John Garfield, at the height of his career in the late 1940s, couldn't get a job in the industry by 1951 because he had been denied "a clean bill of health" after testifying before the committee.

Fueled by the Korean War and anti-Communist feelings, the Red Scare was at its height in the early 1950s. Senator Joseph McCarthy had everyone quaking in his boots. In addition to the Hollywood Ten, many other actors, writers and directors were "unofficially" blacklisted, including Abraham Polonsky, Ann Revere, Gale Sondergaard, Larry Parks and Marsha Hunt.

That America's most beloved personality—zany, wildly comical Lucille Ball—would be involved in any way with even a long-past Communist taint seemed inconceivable.

September, 1953, proved to be the blackest month in the life of Lucille Ball. The night of Winchell's broadcast, Desi had rushed back from Del Mar to join Lucy, Ken Morgan and Howard Strickling, MGM's legendary publicity chief. (For the past twenty-five years Strickling had been the leading trouble-shooter in Hollywood, guiding MGM's top stars and executives through personal traumas and scandals.)

Strickling's advice to the Arnazes was to "lay low, don't make waves, it'll all blow over." This philosophy had worked in a surprising number of cases involving such notables as Louis B. Mayer, Jean Harlow, Clark Gable and Lana Turner.

For the next few days it appeared that Strickling's advice to Lucy and Desi was sound. After all, he pointed out, rumors about Lucy had been flying in the industry for almost a year and a half and nothing had come of them. The previous month, according to the *Los Angeles Herald-Express*, because "of the recurrent movie trade rumors that the biggest TV star was soon to be accused of Communist ties," Desi had cornered Senator Joseph McCarthy in the lounge at the Del Mar race track and at the time McCarthy assured Desi he had no information to Lucille's discredit.

Following Winchell's broadcast, Hedda Hopper contacted Lucille and Desi. According to Hedda, "Lucille herself came on the phone and denied that she was in any way affiliated with the Party."

Lucy and Desi proceeded with scheduled rehearsals for the next "I Love Lucy." But that Friday reporters swarmed around the couple's sprawling ranch home in Northridge. Lucy was in the house but reporters weren't allowed to see her. Desi told them, "Lucille registered for the first time last year with me as a Democrat and we voted for Eisenhower. I know that she never registered as a Communist. You can check with the Un-American Activities Committee. That will prove that she isn't a Communist."

A reporter countered that the newspapers possessed a photostatic copy of an affidavit showing that Lucille had registered in 1936 as a voter "intending to affiliate at the ensuing primary election with the Communist Party."

Desi, however, still flatly denied it. "What are you gonna do— spread it all over the country?" he snapped.

That's exactly what they did do. Hearst's *Los Angeles Herald-Express*, helmed by feisty city editor Aggie Underwood, came out with a special edition. A banner headline in red ink proclaimed: LUCILLE BALL A RED, and reproduced a copy of the registration card. Although the card had "Cancelled" stamped on it, in some newspapers it was reproduced so the word "Cancelled" was cropped out!

Desi quickly made some important phone calls. He phoned J. Edgar Hoover in Washington. Then, Frank Stanton, President of CBS, in New York. Then Desi called the most important man, as far as their future was concerned—Philip Morris's Alfred Lyons. Lyons assured Arnaz that they were behind Lucy and Desi. Arnaz tried to get through to Winchell, but without success. He did reach Hedda Hopper. Having her support was essential.

Lucy admitted to Hedda, "They found a registration card in the 1936 primaries. They asked me about it. They refreshed my memory. I didn't recall anything about it..."

Lucille's voice broke. "The reason we didn't tell you the other day was that the committee had asked us not to," Lucy tearfully explained.

"Did you register as a Communist or a Socialist in the election?" Hedda wanted to know.

"I don't know what they called the Party then," she replied, weeping as she tried to continue. After an emotional explanation, Lucy concluded, "I never had anything to cover up or be frightened about but they now have a sworn statement testifying..."

At this point Lucille could not continue and Desi came on the phone. "It's terrible, Hedda, that something the poor kid did in 1936 to please her grandfather can kick back in her face now. She has never in her life done wrong to anybody; has never had any sympathy for these Commies. You know, the girl has never even been connected with these pinks out here; she has never gone to meetings, never been a member of their party—this is terrible, Hedda. It was reported she was confronted with a Communist Party card. That is a lie. She never had a card."

"But why didn't you tell me this when I asked the other morning?" Hedda demanded.

"If I did something wrong to you the other day, please forgive me," Desi apologized. "When you get in a spot like this, you don't know what the hell you're doing."

One thing they decided they were doing was to go ahead with the filming of the show that night. The din and confusion in the Desilu offices were now caused by real events and not by production problems. Desi hopped around the room and loudly denied to one and all that Lucy had ever been a member of the Communist Party. She was not political, he declared. "You know Lucy. She doesn't even know who the hell the governor was last year."

Lucy, understandably distraught, was having her hair dyed, toning it down from an orangey-red to a softer shade. ("I just took some of the circus out of it.")

Lucy issued a statement through CBS vice president Harry Ackerman: "It is true I have talked to a representative of the House Un-American Activities Committee and have given full and truthful answers to their questions. I am very happy to have had this opportunity to reply to unfounded rumors and hope very much the committee will see fit to release a complete transcript of the information I gave."

Ackerman said Lucille was perfectly willing to stand on the statement she gave to the committee investigator. When reporters questioned Ackerman about Desi's statement that reports of Lucy's being a Communist were "ridiculous," Ackerman replied: "I think that the committee's report on Miss Ball will prove him to be absolutely right."

At the urging of Desi—inspired, apparently, by his conversation with J. Edgar Hoover—the House committee, through its member Donald L. Jackson, a Republican from California, would release for publication the transcript of her testimony to "present Miss Ball's status factually and officially."

Jackson hastily summoned a press conference at which he declared that the committee had no evidence that Lucille Ball had ever joined the Communist Party.

That night, on schedule, Lucille and Desi prepared to film "I Love Lucy." It was Lucy and Desi's first public appearance since the story broke. The studio audience, as always, was SRO— three hundred people. Before the show got under way, Desi addressed them: "I want to talk to you about something serious. Lucy has never been a Communist, not now and never will be." The audience let loose with a burst of applause that lasted a full minute. "I was kicked out of Cuba," Desi continued, "because of Communism. We despise everything about it. Lucy is as American as Bernie Baruch and Ike Eisenhower.

"By the way, we both voted for Eisenhower—so ladies and gentlemen, don't judge too soon—read for yourselves. Read her story. Don't believe every piece of bunk you read in some papers."

When Desi introduced his wife, he called her "My favorite redhead, and that's the only thing red about Lucy and even that is not legitimate."

The studio audience cheered Lucy as she appeared and both Lucy and Desi were teary-eyed as they acknowledged the applause and acceptance. An observer that night remembers that as the show progressed, Lucy cavorted as always. Her comedy showed no signs of the stress of that day. A doctor, however, was in attendance for fear she might collapse under the strain. But he was not needed, and when the show concluded, Lucy addressed the studio audience with a simple: "God bless you for being so kind."

The next morning, Saturday, newspapers declared Lucille was *not* a Red and carried the story of Jackson's press conference. With a degree of haste unmatched in the thousands of other cases investigated by the committee, the entire transcript of Lucille Ball's examination was made public.

Some members of the press felt that pressure to release the testimony had been brought from high sources. It was obvious that CBS, Philip Morris and MGM all had enormous investments in the careers of Lucille Ball and Desi Arnaz.

The public learned, from the testimony, that Lucille, her mother and her brother Fred had all testified before Committee

116

investigator William Wheeler. For Lucille, at first, it had been an unrecorded interrogation. But later Lucy was called in to give sworn testimony.

Although by today's standards the material is bland, at the time it was read avidly by millions of Americans and is therefore of historical interest. An example of some testimony:

MR. WHEELER: Are you under subpoena or are you appearing voluntarily?

LUCILLE: I am appearing voluntarily.

MR. WHEELER: Did you ever reside at 1344 North Ogden Drive?

LUCILLE: Yes.

MR. WHEELER: Who owned that residence?

LUCILLE: We rented it. I don't remember who owned it.

MR. WHEELER: When did you first register to vote?

LUCILLE: I guess the first time I ever did was in 1936.

MR. WHEELER: I would like to hand you a photostatic copy of a voter's registration and ask you if that is your signature.

LUCILLE: That looks like my handwriting.

MR. WHEELER: You will note that the party that you intended to affiliate with at that time was the Communist Party.

LUCILLE: In 1936?

MR. WHEELER: Yes.

LUCILLE: I guess so.

MR. WHEELER: You did register to vote then as a Communist or intending to vote the Communist Party ticket?

LUCILLE: Yes.

MR. WHEELER: Would you go into detail and explain the background, the reason you voted or registered to vote as a Communist or person who intended to affiliate with the Communist Party?

LUCILLE: It was our grandfather, Fred Hunt. He just wanted us to and we just did something to please him. I did not intend to vote that way. As I recall, I didn't. My grandfather started years ago—he was a Socialist as long as I can remember. He is the only father we ever knew, my grandfather. My father died when I was tiny, before my brother was born. He [grandfather] was my brother's only father.

All through his life he had been a Socialist, as far back as Eugene V. Debs, and he was in sympathy with the working man as long as I have known and he took the *Daily Worker*....

Lucille explained how the family considered her Grandpa's views a nuisance but humored him because of his age and health:

> LUCILLE: ... So finally there came a point where my brother was twenty-one and he [Grandpa] was going to see that Freddie registered to help the working man, which was, in his [Grandpa's] idea then, the Communist Party. At that time it wasn't a thing to hide behind doors, to be a member of that party.
> As I recall, because of this he influenced us. We thought we wanted to do him a favor. We thought we could make him happy. I at no time intended to vote that way. And I remember discussing it with my mother, how I could register and make him happy. When I go behind a curtain to vote, nobody knows who I vote for.
> MR. WHEELER: Have you ever been a member of the Communist Party?
> LUCILLE: No, not to my knowledge.
> MR. WHEELER: Have you ever been asked to become a member of the Communist Party?
> LUCILLE: No.
> MR. WHEELER: Did you ever attend any meetings that you later discovered were Communist Party meetings?
> LUCILLE: No.
> MR. WHEELER: Do you know whether or not any meetings were ever held in your home at 1344 North Ogden Drive?
> LUCILLE: No, I know nothing of that. I don't believe it is true.
> MR. WHEELER: How old were you in 1936?
> LUCILLE: I am forty-two now, twenty-four.

Wheeler went on to question Lucy about several petitions she had signed in the Thirties supporting Communist candidates and causes. More startling, however, was the accusation by former Communist Rena M. Vale who said her party indoctrination meeting had been held in Lucy's Ogden Drive residence. Lucy had no explanation and denied any knowledge of her house being so used. Neither did she have an explanation for being listed as a delegate to the Communist Party's state central committee one year.

When Wheeler continued questioning Lucille, and brought up events that occurred in the late 1940s, the record indicates that she wasn't intimidated by the questions—quite the contrary.

MR. WHEELER: Are you acquainted with the Committee of the First Amendment?

LUCILLE: Am I acquainted with it?

MR. WHEELER: Yes.

LUCILLE: Not to my knowledge.

MR. WHEELER: Or were you a member of the Committee of the First Amendment?

LUCILLE: Not to my knowledge.

MR. WHEELER: Well, your name is mentioned in the Daily People's World, the issue of October 28, 1947, page one, columns five and six, as one of the high personalities who were sponsoring or a member of the Committee of the First Amendment.

That committee was formed here in Hollywood to oppose the Congressional hearings in 1947.

LUCILLE: Refresh my memory on it. I can't imagine ever signing that. Did I sign that, too? Was it under an assumed name?

MR. WHEELER: That I don't know. There was a reference to it.

LUCILLE: What is the People's World? Is that like the Daily Worker?

MR. WHEELER: Yes, a Communist publication of the western states.

LUCILLE: In 1947? That certianly was not for Grandpa. Grandpa was gone by then. I can't imagine doing anything for these people. If I was hoodwinked into it, with one of those long democratic souped-up names, that is something else. Could I see that?

MR. WHEELER: I don't have a copy of the People's World for that date.

LUCILLE: Am I supposed to have signed something in sympathy?

MR. WHEELER: Your name was used as in—

LUCILLE: Was it used or did I sign something?

MR. WHEELER: I have no knowledge of your signing.

LUCILLE: Fine. Then I have no knowledge of signing it. However, I do recall I was at a studio, and I was working on a picture and I got a call in the afternoon. I don't know who called me. I assume now—I did then—it was the Screen Actors Guild, but I can be wrong. I don't know who called me now. It was something that was through a union or the studio wouldn't have felt compelled to send me off a set and hold up production until I got back. It had nothing to do with me.

I got the call to go to a radio station. As I remember, it was MGM—it may not have been. I remember an executive excused me and sent me to this broadcast.

I got down there and said, "What am I supposed to do?"

She said, "Dorothy Petersen"—whoever she is—"she is ill. We have to go on the air."

She said, "Will you read this?"

It was a long petition, or whatever you call them, as I recall. As I recall—I am not sure of this—it was about the Okies in upstate California, Fresno or someplace, about admitting the Okies. I read it. They thanked me and they sent me back to work.

I don't know how long after that it was that I was called downtown in an FBI office and asked why I did it. Apparently, it was wrong. It was my first knowledge it was wrong.

I had no answer at all, because I hadn't done it of my own volition. I had been sent there. It didn't seem wrong to go some place the studio had sent you.

I tried to explain why I had done it. I had no reason except I had been called....

She concluded the interrogation with the following:

LUCILLE: I am very happy to have this opportunity to discuss all the things that have cropped up, that apparently I have done wrong.

I am aware of only one thing I did that was wrong, and that at the time wasn't wrong, but apparently now it is, and that was registering because my grandfather wanted us to. I at no time thought it was the thing to do, nor did I ever intend to vote in the presidential election, I guess it was at that time, I don't know. To my knowledge, I didn't vote, but I did register. Since then I have never done anything knowingly against the United States.

I have never done anything for Communists, to my knowledge, at any time. I have never contributed money or attended a meeting or ever had anything to do with people connected with it, if to my knowledge they were.

I am not a Communist now. I have never been. I never wanted to be. Nothing in the world could ever change my mind. At no time in my life have I ever been in sympathy with anything that even faintly resembled it....

And Wheeler concluded with: "I have no further questions. Thank you for your cooperation."

Lucille's mother and brother also testified. They too explained they had acted to please and pacify Grandpa Hunt.

When asked about purported meetings in their Ogden Drive home, DeDe Ball testified, "Never, never." She went on to say: "We didn't question Daddy because, I mean, he was so firm in his beliefs and everything, that if he thought it was all right, we did it."

DeDe also said she didn't know whether her father had actually belonged to the Communist Party. But when he died she had gone through his wallet and hadn't found any party membership card.

Fred Ball told the committee much the same information but noted he had been discharged from the employ of Vega Aircraft after signing one petition.

Ball said he tried to get character letters from friends to get the job back because he didn't feel he had done anything wrong and was being accused of not being a good American.

He worked at other defense plants later without trouble, he said, and served fifteen months in the Army, getting an honorable discharge.

"Grandpa," he said, "died with the phrase on his lips, 'working man,' and that is all. That is all there ever was to it, in any sense of the word. All he cared about was the poor guy next door. That is why we went along with him. It is merely a matter of our loving Grandpa, helping him bide his time."

Now that the world had all the information, Lucy and Desi held a press conference at their ranch. She wore a white blouse with an embroidered "Lucille" on it, a pink hair ribbon and pink linen toreador pants. Desi wore an air of relief that it was all over.

Lucille remarked that she had never seen Congressman Jackson, but from his picture in the paper she concluded, "He's a pretty good-looking guy."

Despite her reiteration that her conscience had always been clear, Lucille expressed gratitude to the House committee for releasing all her statements promptly, as she had requested. She admitted she had been in the dark as to what public reaction would be, but said she took the attitude in the past two days, "If anyone is making more of this than they should, why—let 'em!"

Desi added happily that their TV sponsor, involved in their eight million dollars' worth of immediate future, already had telephoned its support.

A reporter asked: "Didn't you think then, back in 1936, that this might hurt your career?"

"Career?" quipped Lucy. "I didn't have any career. I was a stock girl at RKO. Down in the small print it said I had to sweep out the office if they wanted me to."

"How old were you then?"

"I don't even know how old I am now!"

Discussing the previous night's show and the heartwarming reception they received, Lucy said: "I was pretty numb. But I was thrilled the way the audience acted. It was sensational. Unbelievable. More than you could hope for."

Lucy insisted to the reporters that she was "glad the whole thing has come out. We asked them, begged them to bring it out."

Two or three times during the afternoon Lucy's saucer eyes watered up, but she held her tears back. Lest anyone think they took the situation lightly, Desi kissed her on the cheek from time to time and muttered, "This has been terrible, terrible."

During the press conference Lucy was only occasionally her usual saucy self. "In the last couple of days," she noted, often dabbing her perspiring forehead with an embroidered hanky, "I've realized this is nothing to laugh about."

Lucy expressed total confidence in the public's understanding of the entire incident. "Hurt me?" she said. "I have more faith in the American people that that. I feel that any time you give the American people the truth they're with you."

While Lucy visited the powder room, Desi took a dip in the pool. He climbed out smiling, dripping and cool.

"You know, Desi," remarked a reporter, "yesterday was one of the hottest days of the year."

"You're tellin' me!" he exclaimed.

He went on to tell the press, "We're tremendously happy and grateful to everyone all over the country for their support. We've had thousands of wires and telephone messages and they're still pouring in." He added that he and his wife were grateful to the press for its complete handling of the facts.

The following night Walter Winchell, who had started it all, coolly reported that Lucy had been cleared "one hundred percent."

9

THOUGH EXONERATED by her public, Lucy gave information in her testimony which angered the right wing press. They felt that some radio broadcasts she had made in the 1940s, which she claimed were at the request of her studio and about which she recalled little, obviously had nothing to do with Grandpa and were difficult to explain.

Those who criticized her did so for three reasons: first, they contended that a twenty-four-year-old woman certainly *was* responsible for her actions; secondly, they implied that she had registered as a Communist because it would further her career, since in the 1930s many Communist sympathizers were in positions of power in the movie industry and people who did not sympathize suddenly found that they couldn't get jobs at the studios; thirdly, Lucy was criticized because she hadn't come forward voluntarily "to confess her past actions" but had waited until she had been "ferreted out" before "baring her soul to the public."

Columnist Ed Sullivan made some pertinent comments about the affair. He expressed the views of many when he wrote: "It's a singularly fortunate thing for Lucille Ball that she's been a weekly visitor to millions of American living rooms. In those Monday night visits, people have come to know her well. TV cameras being as revealing as they are, so the jury of Public Opinion is an informed jury as it renders a verdict on a silly thing she did seventeen years ago."

But not all columnists defended Lucille. Ultra-right-winger Westbrook Pegler became infuriated with the "kind" treatment of her in the press. He devoted his entire syndicated column to "the Lucille Ball Case" soon after her committee appearance. Pegler wrote: "In some published comments on the affair of Lucille Ball... I detected a threat that any loyal American who does not forgive this woman will be punished. I do not react favorably to threats and I would not forgive her anyway, because she did not come clean but had to be tracked down and exposed. The propositions that she was 'only twenty-four years old' and that her grandfather was a family tyrant, a Socialist who made her do this, have no value at all with me."

To read Pegler today presents a penetrating view of how vociferous anti-Communists thought and wrote in 1953. Pegler went on to say: "I hate Communists. I wish it were possible to round up all those who are reasonably known to be Communists, including all who have invoked the Fifth Amendment, and put them into concentration camps as austere as the Arizona State Prison, where relatively harmless and morally stupid criminals of the common sort must dip water from the john if they get thirsty in the dead of summer nights in the desert...."

It was Pegler's opinion that "This Ball woman knew what she was doing when she registered with the Communists, and I can tell you that the poor devils out there in Hollywood who fought the traitors in the movie business took terrible persecution. They suddenly lost out at the studios, never knowing why. They got threadbare. They got drunk and despondent, and the Reds sneered at them and snubbed them. Their friends were afraid to be seen with them.

126

"They could have done the same thing that Lucille Ball did, but they were too courageous and loyal. Some of them have died. Did Lucille Ball ever send any of these brave, lonely men a note of confidence or encouragement? Did she ever call up Jimmy McGuinness or Pat McNutt and admit that they were right and that she had been wrong?

"Socialist grandfather. That is a new variant of the whine of the crooked White Sox player who did it for the wife and kiddies."

Even considering the source, these attacks horrified the Arnazes. Of course, most newspapermen were in their corner and some even wrote rebuttals to Pegler. Syndicated columnist Royce Brier said:

"It appears to be high time for the American people to pause in a moment of self-questioning, relative to the case of Lucille Ball... The Ball case is preposterously simple, and so the more easily examined by the people to determine if they want this public stock to be continued in its current indiscriminate use."

Brier defended Lucy as vigorously as Pegler had denounced her.

"Surely every middle-aged citizen of this country (Miss Ball is forty-two) is not under moral obligation to arise publicly and confess his or her manifestations of immaturity or ignorance at twenty-five. And surely no committee of Congress is going to save the nation from subversion by operating permanent machinery for such a confessional."

Brier voiced the opinion of many liberal thinkers of the day when he concluded: "Our freedom is in peril if this pillory for the exhibition of peccadillo and casual dissent is permitted to stand indefinitely. But it is up to us. The congress cannot filch our liberty. Only we can from ourselves filch our liberty."

Through the month of September and into early October, the attacks against and defenses of Lucy's actions dragged on. A group of war veterans in Indianapolis protested against her appearance on television. The group, which included two former American Legion post commanders, sent a petition to the Philip Morris Tobacco Company which said that the signers would "switch to another brand of cigarettes" until she was replaced.

The petition also said, "we intend to use our memberships in veterans' organizations to combat the appearance on TV, stage or screen, of anyone supporting or belonging to any party supervised by the Soviets."

Isolated unpleasant cases such as this certainly didn't reflect the country's thinking, but they did crop up and create bad publicity, anguish and tension. However, *Variety* summed it up: FANS LOVE LUCY—TAKE HER SIDE IN RED AFFAIR. After a wait-and-see period it seemed her network was satisfied, her sponsor was satisfied, and Lucy's TV ratings remained in the stratosphere.

There was no doubt that America had forgiven and forgotten the whole affair. Someone who was then on the scene notes, "You have to keep one thing in mind here. Revealing Lucille Ball to have Communist affiliations was tantamount to saying the same thing about your favorite relative.

"Lucille *was*—still is—middle America. As far as the public was concerned, she was—is—like a favorite neighbor. She was not an offbeat 'Hollywood type' or a New York 'stage type' who had been spouting social-oriented causes. She was the housewife next door. She was *loved*. The idea of her being a Communist sympathizer at any time was so preposterous in the minds of most Americans that Lucille's explanation to the committee was eagerly accepted and the entire episode was quickly dismissed."

Lucille didn't forgive Walter Winchell. When asked how she thought he had discovered her secret she replied acidly, "Walter Winchell knew I was pregnant before I did myself."

The ordeal had taken its toll on Lucy's health, emotionally and physically. There were visits to a psychiatrist. But according to statements made by Lucy, the female analyst only saw the actress a few times, saying that there was nothing psychologically wrong with Lucille. She was just worn out.

However, the analyst counseled her, in effect, to be less outgoing, more guarded in social situations—to keep her emotions to herself at such times. It seems to be advice Lucy adopted readily.

The Arnazes had weathered the greatest storm they had yet

faced. Their success had been on the line. Now that it was all over, Desilu's future was brighter than ever. In ensuing years, the entire communist episode would be completely ignored by Lucille and Desi. The matter was never again written about in a single interview over the next twenty years.

In November, 1953, the B'nai B'rith named Lucille "Woman of the Year." It was the first time the award had gone to an actress and it was presented for her "untiring efforts for charitable causes—Community Chest, March of Dimes, Red Cross, YMCA, Cerebral Palsy, American Cancer Society, City of Hope, Sister Kenny Foundation" and many others.

The day after the awards, Lucy and Desi flew to Washington for "Dinner with the President," a special telecast honoring President Dwight D. Eisenhower.

10

LUCY AND DESI went back to work selling America's best-known commodity—marriage—to their millions of fans. They appeared to live the roles offscreen as well. Lucy often attributed the success of their show to their "ideal" private lives. "I always felt our show was so successful because somehow, through film and over the air, we communicated the fact that we were excited about each other. It wouldn't have been the same had we just been playing married."

The real Arnaz home in Northridge was a far cry from the modest "Ricardo" apartment in Manhattan. The ranch had undergone considerable change after the children were born . . . $22,000 worth of change (a good deal of money in the early 1950s). The gray and yellow nursery, housed in a separate wing from the main house, had its own workroom, patio, play area, nurse's bedroom and an intercom with a direct hookup to Lucy's and Desi's bedroom. But by Hollywood standards the ranch house remained very informal. The great financial wealth that "I Love Lucy" brought them did not change the Arnazes' lifestyle a great deal. Lucy's mother lived nearby, as did Desi's.

However, Lucy and Desi had little time to spend at home. The new TV season had begun. It was their third year on the air, and, as with any television show in the top spot, they began to be the object of sneers and snide forecasts: "Lucy and Desi on the Downgrade?... Comedy Couple Finds It Hard to Maintain Terrific Ratings..."

Some guessed long before the Communist headlines broke that Lucy was in for a slide in popularity. Not a big slide, just some sort of leveling off. After all, the show had racked up the most amazing ratings ever, and it seemed logical that it would subside.

One critic wrote: "The opening show was pretty funny. Just pretty funny. Last year's opening, as I recall, was a riot. This one wasn't... the Lucy shows, let's face it, are beginning to sound an awful lot alike. Miss Ball is always trying to bust out of the house; Arnaz is trying to keep her in apron strings. The variations on this theme are infinite, but it's the same and I'm a mite tired of it. I don't think I'll ever get tired of Miss Ball, though; she's a joy to watch."

Though the critics were getting a mite tired of "I Love Lucy," the public wasn't. The show was one of the few comedies on TV in which husbands were not portrayed as children. While the show had no monopoly on the humor inherent in marriage— certainly the idea was as old as time—what the imitators lacked was the extraordinary discipline and intuitive understanding of farce that the "I Love Lucy" scripts provided and the four members of the cast projected.

Lucy and Desi always knew what they were doing. Every episode of "I Love Lucy" began with a logical and believable premise. The groundwork was laid for the essential situation: Lucy vs. Ricky.

"I Love Lucy" was, in other words, marriage projected in larger-than-life size. But still believable, in order to communicate with the viewer. By exaggerating marriage they helped put it in sharp focus. And, most importantly and holding it all together, was the character—and person—of Lucy, possessing wifely patience, always the regular gal and the good sport. She was *real*.

Also real were problems between the four leading actors on the show. Press agents and columnists painted a rosy picture of four people who got along famously. In fact, however, "Mrs. Mertz," a/k/a Vivian Vance, was often quite unhappy. Contractually, she was forced to remain twenty pounds overweight and to wear dowdy clothes on the show so that her character would appear older than Lucy's. Vance was actually one year younger than Ball. There were even a few verbal battles between the two female stars.

To Desi's dismay, Vance's high-powered agent would hold him up for giant salary increases each year. Frawley and his agent never dickered with Arnaz about salary. They didn't have to— Desi always matched, for Bill, whatever he was forced to pay for Vivian. But Bill Frawley was often disgruntled about having to work with Vivian, whom he considered " a no-talent fat-ass bag of bones." She was not enchanted with him either. Over the years the discontent would grow.

But they were all great actors and, on film, none of this tension showed. Few outside the industry knew that other members of the Desilu family were disgruntled. Through the years a few of the cast and crew have revealed that Desilu was, in certain cases, inordinately cheap when it came to salaries.

On November 30, Desi surprised Lucy with a thirteenth wedding anniversary party at Mocambo, a Sunset Strip night club. Lucy had expected a quiet dinner with Desi and their friend Vincente Minnelli.

Along with a special anniversary cake Mocambo owner Charley Morrison provided a television set for the party. The highlight of the evening was tuning in to the regular Monday night broadcast of "I Love Lucy."

As a matter of fact, people all over the country were pausing from 9 to 9:30 P.M. on Mondays to tune in America's favorite show. There had been nothing like it since radio's "Amos 'n' Andy," which, in the 1930s, had brought America's home life to a halt every night for fifteen minutes. Chicago's mammoth Marshall Field department store changed its evening shopping hours from Mondays to Thursdays because so few customers showed up on "Lucy" night. Even the telephone company reported that fewer calls were made during that time period.

The New Year brought more riches to Lucy and Desi. MGM released *The Long, Long Trailer,* which was a huge and immediate success. The Arnazes were not only king and queen of television but of the big screen as well, and they were the only television superstars who could draw at the movie box office!

To publicize *The Long, Long Trailer,* Lucy and Desi visited New York. Metro announced plans to shoot another Lucille Ball-Desi Arnaz film and Desilu reached an agreement with MGM, promising it would not release the theatrical film version of "I Love Lucy" —three episodes strung together for showing abroad—until *Trailer* had completed its overseas bookings.

Offscreen, Lucy and Desi were always questioned about their children. Although Lucy had admitted "I am no expert on babies..." she was adamant in telling the public that she had not had her caesarean because of fear of pain or vanity. "I believe word has gotten around that some Hollywood actresses have their babies by caesarean because they are afraid of pain or because they fear normal delivery will do something to their figures," said Lucille. "Other girls may regard this method with envy, lacking the necessary cash to finance it or, bitterly, despising the actresses for cowardice. I know this: doctors do not encourage caesareans unless they are necessary. At least one prominent pediatrician tells me that normally born babies, even when they arrive after long labor in a condition he calls 'beat up,' are usually stronger than the unexercised caesarean babies. My first baby had to be born by caesarean and so my second, weighing eight pounds nine ounces and strong as a tractor, was also delivered by caesarean, because normal delivery would not have been possible. I shouldn't like to be accused of saving my figure. Because of young Lucie and her new brother, I've hardly had a figure for the last few years."

The children, only toddlers, were already celebrities. With their parents they had appeared on the cover of *Life* magazine in a story about TV's First Family. Although their parents were working much of the time, Lucie and Desi, Jr. were surrounded by loving grandmothers, other relatives and, of course, nannies.

After the release of *The Long, Long Trailer* Desi remarked, "We can make pictures any time we like. But we'll concentrate on television. But if either Lucy or I want to do a movie, we can always pile up a backlog of TV films that will tide us over."

Lucy, however, had specific thoughts on the subject. "I'm not particularly interested in going back to movies." Discussing the TV show she noted, "We work four days and rest three. You can't do that in picture making."

Being a successful businessman was changing Desi. When Lucille was asked what she thought was mainly responsible for the excellence of the program, she quickly replied: "Desi does it all."

In a revealing statement he admitted, "I found that bringing 'I Love Lucy' to home screens was ninety per cent desk work, ten per cent acting. Soon I developed an eye twitch, headaches and my first gray hairs. I was worrying myself sick trying to be everywhere at once. My pal Bill Frawley remarked, 'Remember when you led a band? You just waved a stick, and the boys took it from there.'"

"I Love Lucy" rolled along, topping the ratings. However, the sponsor wasn't happy! For some unknown reason, though millions were watching "I Love Lucy," the show wasn't selling cigarettes.

Philip Morris was going to drop their sponsorship of the program at the conclusion of the fourth season, marking the end of the famed $8 million contract. However, CBS had already lined up other sponsors and the network was pressuring the Arnazes into signing a new longterm deal.

"Carefree" Lucy and Desi, as they were painted in the press, had reached a major turning point in their lives. They were spending little time with the children—in fact they had had to steal a few days around Christmas, 1954, to be with the kids in Palm Springs before rushing off to fulfill a commitment for a highly lucrative in-person stint with Vance and Frawley in Las Vegas.

With CBS's backing, Desilu had bought Motion Picture Center, the small studio where they were now shooting the program. They had beat out Lucy's nemesis Harry Cohn, who was also after the property.

Lucy and Desi were set to co-star with James Mason in *Forever Darling* for MGM. The script was originally written in the forties for Lucille and William Powell. *Forever Darling* would be directed by Lucy's boyfriend of two decades earlier, Alexander Hall. Desi's new company, Zanra Productions (Arnaz spelled backwards) would produce.

Desi was overworked and realized that the situation wasn't going to improve. Important decisions had to be made. For one thing, it was impractical for them to continue to live in Northridge—it took too long to commute. They'd have to move closer to the studio and assume a different lifestyle. Desi wasn't looking forward to this.

According to Arnaz, he and his wife had a serious discussion. He suggested that after shooting *Forever Darling* and completing the current commitment to CBS, they sell the library of "I Love Lucy" shows to the network and semi-retire. They'd be multi-millionaires. Lucy could work when and if she chose and Desi would be free to run Desilu unencumbered by keeping "I Love Lucy" going.

Lucy opted for keeping "Lucy" going, and as the cliché states, the die was cast. They signed the new contract with CBS (which included the network buying 179 episodes of "I Love Lucy"). One of the new sponsors was General Foods. Lucy would now be selling Jell-O, as she had on "My Favorite Husband."

In November, 1955, Lucy and Desi celebrated their fifteenth wedding anniversary. To reporters they continued to give the expected responses. Desi attributed their happiness to "a sense of humor and the ability to laugh." He told the press, "Often when we've had words, one of us sees the absurdity of it and starts laughing. If people would laugh more, marriages would last longer."

Lucy also acknowledged the marital spats, adding that "before we know it one of us will interrupt a disagreement to say, 'What a perfect situation for the show.' That's how so many of our marital problems have been incorporated on film."

Press agents for the show claimed that a psychiatrist had written the Arnazes, saying that a half hour of watching their show on TV often solved problems that ordinarily might require weeks of treatment.

As Desilu began filming the 1955-6 season, there were some changes on "I Love Lucy" —but behind the scenes, not on screen. Bob Weiskopf and Bob Schiller joined the writing staff. Director Bill Asher left and was replaced by James V. Kern. And Jess Oppenheimer announced that he would leave at the end of the season to join NBC.

As "I Love Lucy" progressed, the writers had expanded the Ricardos' horizons. They had taken them out of their usual setting via a cross-country motor trip to Los Angeles, where Ricky was to make a film. That stay in Los Angeles had enabled the show to have movie stars as guests.

Then the writers sent the Ricardos on a trip to Europe with the Mertzes. On these various jaunts, Lucy and Ricky left "Little Ricky" with Lucy's mother (and, in real life, too, the Arnaz offspring were often left with a grandmother).

For three and a half seasons after "Little Ricky's" birth on "I Love Lucy," the baby had not been integral to the show's story lines. Desilu had hired a set of twins to alternate portraying the infant. But then, in 1956, a creative decision was made. "Little Ricky" was to become the show's fifth main character. For story purposes, they would make the child's age five. Desilu held casting calls for a month, but found no suitable youngster.

Desi Arnaz later claimed he saw Keith Thibodeau, a five-year-old, on television. But another version of the story is that Thibodeau's father took the boy to the casting department at Desilu. In any event, little Keith was a great drummer. And since the child actually resembled Desi, and had musical talent, he seemed a natural for the part. The boy's name was changed to Richard Keith, and as "Little Ricky" he made his debut on the premiere episode of the 1956-57 season.

In the public's mind, from this point on, "Little Ricky" and the real-life Arnaz son were one and the same. Behind the scenes young Keith was integrated into the Arnaz family. He spent a great deal of time with Lucie and Desi Jr. And little Desi emulated the older boy, even to the point of learning to play the drums.

On "I Love Lucy," Ricky Ricardo displayed husbandly dignity. Ricky never flirted seriously with other women, for example. He was firm with Lucy, but always fondly tolerant of her feminine illogic. As an actor, Desi had evolved from the rather awkward young Latin of early "Lucy" shows into a polished foil for his wife's wacky style of TV comedy.

Lucy remarked, "I believe that Desi is a better actor than he gets credit for being. I take note, and many another professional are taking note too, that against my wide, sweeping style of comedy he is doing a deft job of quiet underplaying, mighty good, I think. Even 'mushin pitchers' have finally come to look on us as a team."

The Long, Long Trailer had been a big hit and all were hoping to hit again with *Forever Darling*. To ballyhoo the picture, released in the spring of 1956, Lucy and Desi went to her hometown, Jamestown. It was a gala "Welcome Home" for the girl who was at one time snickered at as being "one of the fastest gals in town." On this return visit, Lucy reminisced: "I get so emotional realizing this is where I learned about life."

Lucy and Desi went on to New York City where the *New York Herald Tribune* invited them to be marriage counselors at its 1956 seminar for brides. The questions at the seminar covered just about every aspect of what Desi termed "the sea of matrimony." With her famous sharp wit, Lucy parried the more personal questions. She warned the ladies not to try and change their mates: "They never change," she observed with the voice of experience. "You just get more tolerant and more tolerant," she added with a resigned grin.

By now the Arnazes had sold their Northridge ranch and were living in a $90,000 mansion on Roxbury Drive in Beverly Hills. Their neighbors were Jack Benny, José Ferrer and Rosemary Clooney, the Oscar Levants, and Ira Gershwin. The new house was not the typical flamboyant home of a superstar. It was a dignified setting for successful business people.

One month a year Lucy and Desi would take the children to Del Mar. On weekends, they would often go to their home in Palm Springs. The Arnaz house stretched along the seventeenth fairway of the swank Thunderbird Golf Club. There Lucille would supposedly spend every waking moment as Desi's playmate and as camp counselor and game supervisor for Lucie, Desi Jr., Richard Keith and a half-dozen moppets from neighboring luxurious homes. She would make home movies and tape-record mock interviews with the children.

However, Lucy later revealed that as early as this, "I noticed the change in Desi. When I felt fatigued, I could relax at home with the children...When he found he couldn't relax, he would go out on the town. Desi had a tendency to play even harder than he worked.

"At the beginning, he would go off on long fishing trips, which were perfectly all right with me. I understood a man's need to be alone occasionally. But then it dawned on me that Desi was seeking more than solitude."

Desi was not discreet in his pursuit of other pleasures, and it was hard for Lucy to stand by silently and even harder for her to save face among friends. "It is a horrifying experience to watch someone you love, someone you think you know, turning into a stranger," she later noted. "We saw it happen. Then we hardly saw him anymore."

People on the scene observed that it wasn't that Desi couldn't relax; he simply couldn't turn off business pressure and transform himself into the part-time homebody that Lucy wanted. Desi's idea of relaxing was playing hard; Lucy's was to stay home and "be a family." "But Lucy had no desire or intention of curbing her professional life, despite anything she said," observes an ex-colleague.

In June, 1956, Desi was hurt while filming an "I Love Lucy" episode with Bob Hope. In one scene Lucy was thrown into the air by Bob and Desi. When she came down, she leaned too heavily on Desi, tearing ligaments in his back. Desi kidded that Lucy must have been gaining weight; she retorted that maybe he wasn't as strong as he used to be.

Forever Darling was Lucy and Desi's last movie together. It was not the commercial hit that *The Long, Long Trailer* had been, and though other film projects with the Arnazes might have been contemplated, they never materialized.

When queried on why "I Love Lucy" was still flourishing in its fifth year, while other situation comedies weren't, Lucy answered: "I really don't know why. We just sit back and enjoy it."

She noted, "Desilu produces 'I Love Lucy' and 'December Bride.' It films 'Our Miss Brooks,' 'Make Room for Daddy,' 'Line-up,' 'Wyatt Earp,' 'The Jimmy Durante Show,' 'The Red Skelton Show.' The new Orson Welles show is being produced by Mr. Welles and Desilu. We also produced *Forever Darling*, 'High Tor' and a new potential series, based on helicopter pilots, 'Whirlybirds.'"

Did Lucy participate in production matters? "I handle personnel relations, such as planning the annual picnic and matters of that sort."

Lucy also commented on a persistent rumor. "People keep saying that I am the real power behind the Desilu throne, that I make the big decisions. No myth could be further from the truth. I don't make one bloody decision! My job is at home with the kids. Desi does ask my opinion once in a while, but only on personnel problems or the very biggest matters. Even then, the decisions are always his."

Did she look forward to retiring one day? "I don't think any actor or actress actually looks forward to retiring, any more than anybody else 'looks forward' to it. Let's face it, why should I? I spend four days a week working, but the early mornings and evenings are spent at home with my husband and children. We might someday work on a schedule that is less regular than once a week."

How would she spend her time if "Lucy" folded? "I don't even want to talk about that."

By now Desilu Productions was a giant, grossing around fifteen million dollars a year and using up more raw film per year than MGM and 20th Century-Fox combined. Eight hundred people were on the payroll. Though Lucille was vice president, she "kept her hands off the business transactions."

President Desi was by now portly and quite gray, wore tortoise-shell spectacles and smoked a Cuban cigar. He presided with authority over Desilu.

On screen, of course, he was still dark-haired Ricky Ricardo. The last (and 179th) episode of the original half-hour "I Love Lucy's" was shot in the spring of 1957. Lucie Arnaz, now five and a half, and Desi, Jr., four, appeared in a crowd scene in this episode.

After this last show—titled "The Ricardos Dedicate a Statue"—Desilu dropped a bombshell when it announced that "I Love Lucy," in its half-hour filmed version, would be discontinued. The decision was no last-minute maneuver. It had taken Lucy and Desi almost two seasons to persuade CBS and the sponsors to abandon the half-hour format in favor of a monthly one-hour show.

The stars were deluged by protests from an outraged public.

Lucy was candid. "Sweetie," she told a reporter patiently, "we've loved our work and we've loved being pioneers but the time has come to let somebody else 'enjoy' it. We're a little brain-weary, you know. How do you make people understand that? In letters, viewers tell us they're sad because of our plans, but I don't think they understand. As I say in the return correspondence, we're not exactly quitting. There'll actually be as much of 'Lucy' around next season as they'll want to see. Even the kids will be able to see us next season. CBS is going to show our reruns in a 7:30 P.M. time slot, so the whole family can watch to their heart's content. Then, there'll be the five one-hour shows we're going to do for Ford. Ye gads, isn't that enough?"

They were slated to begin production shortly on the first of her big monthly shows, each of which would have a huge budget of $350,000.

Impresario Arnaz announced a spectacular business deal in 1957. Desilu already owned the huge lot once known as Motion Picture Center, which had seven acres and nine sound stages. Now Desilu bought the old RKO Studios in Hollywood, which had fifteen sound stages and fourteen acres, and RKO's Culver City facility, with eleven sound stages and a twenty-nine acre backlot.

Lucy was aware of the ramifications. "When he decided to buy the RKO Studios for Desilu's expanding business, I knew this would mean more pressures on him than ever before," she noted. "Some columnists wrote that both of us had been fired from RKO in years past and we were now taking revenge. That was ridiculous. Neither of us was fired from RKO; our association had been peaceful. I, for one, certainly never thought of buying the studio. In fact, I never dreamed of owning anything. I never had such high aspirations.

"Desi had high aspirations, but I can't believe they included buying RKO. It just happened. We needed more space and it was available there. Someone asked, 'Why don't you buy RKO?' and he said, as usual, 'Well, why not? How much do they want for it?' He went to the bank and said, 'Can I buy a studio for $6,150,000?' and they said, 'Yes. You have excellent credit.'"

It was reported that Desi's purchase was a fantastic bargain. "Actually, he got the studio for a song," insiders said. Howard

Hughes, who had bought the studio in the 1940s, sold it to General Tire and Rubber for twenty-five million dollars in the mid-Fifties. General Tire had planned to reestablish RKO as a major film producer but failed. The tire company then decided to retain most of the company's assets (TV and radio stations, film library, etc.), but divest itself of the physical plant. There weren't many buyers for motion picture studios in 1957, and Desi got his bargain with the aid of a loan from the Bank of America.

In addition to RKO and Motion Picture Center, Desilu's holdings included a music publishing firm, a prospective record company, Desi Arnaz's Western Hills Hotel in Palm Springs, and a considerable amount of real estate.

Lucy and Desi remained sole owners of Desilu, despite hints that key members of their permanent staff would be awarded percentages.

In a time of crumbling motion picture studios, Desilu was flourishing. It was responsible for almost fifteen percent of the entire filmed output for television.

For the first Lucille Ball-Desi Arnaz one-hour special, they had signed guest stars Cesar Romero, Hedda Hopper, Ann Sothern and Rudy Vallee. They filmed, as always, before a live audience. Only this time they utilized four cameras instead of three. The first show was seventy-five minutes long, and the network balked at running it.

"It was funny about that first film we made in the new series. In the middle of rehearsals, everything went like this," Lucille told a friend, snapping her fingers. "Suddenly Desi slowed down. I thought, 'This man has finally forgotten a line after seven years.' But no, he had suddenly got the idea the script was so good it had to be extended another fifteen minutes!"

The network flatly refused to telecast a seventy-five-minute show. Desi was told by network head Bill Paley to either cut it down or pad it by fifteen more minutes.

"Of course I asked him why we couldn't run it like it was," recalled Desi. "I didn't want to cut anything, because that would weaken it. And I didn't want to pad it, because that would spoil the show too.

"'Now let me tell you something, Cuban,' Paley said to me. 'We do half-hour shows, hour shows and hour-and-a-half shows. There's no such thing as an hour-and-fifteen-minute show.'"

Desi pointed out that the U.S. Steel Hour, which followed "Lucy" on CBS, had been taking a beating in ratings. Why not ask U. S. Steel to do a forty-five-minute show just that one week? Paley told Arnaz he was crazy to think anyone would stand still for cutting an hour show to forty-five minutes.

"They'll love it," Desi told Paley. "They'll get a tremendous holdover audience from our show."

Paley said no.

Desi said he'd call the head of U.S. Steel on his own. He did, and, astonishingly, the time cut was agreed to.

"After I told him, Paley just smiled and said: 'You crazy son-of-a-....' Well, the result of it all was that we got our fifteen minutes and U.S. Steel had the highest rating they ever got."

Although the public still loved Lucy and Desi, some of the critics were not happy with the longer format. The initial seventy-five-minute show culminated in a wonderfully funny drunk scene between Ann Sothern and Lucy. TV critic John Crosby noted, "Operating within half-an-hour, Lucy has always managed in the nick of time to get her feet out of the wet cement... This [drunk scene] was well worth waiting for, but I don't know why they had to add forty-five minutes to the normal running time to work it in."

In addition, Crosby noted, "Somewhat hesitantly I point out that the accumulated ages of the participants in this romp [Lucy, Desi, Cesar Romero, Ann Sothern, Hedda Hopper, Vivian Vance, Bill Frawley] would add up to a very impressive statistic indeed and I wonder if it might not be wise in the future to leaven the roster with somewhat younger actors, if only to spread the work around."

They didn't. Later specials included guests such as veterans Tallulah Bankhead, Betty Grable and Harry James, Danny

Thomas, Milton Berle, Bob Cummings and Maurice Chevalier.

The Arnazes became the official owners of RKO in 1958. Lucy took over the dressing room formerly occupied in the studio's salad days by Ginger Rogers. Lucy had it redecorated from Ginger's pink, peach and black to white and yellow. The "dressing room" actually included a sitting room, kitchen, make-up room and full bath.

One of Lucy's initial projects at the new studio was to set up the Desilu Workshop. She hadn't forgotten the days when she had benefited from acting experience gained at Lela Rogers' RKO Little Theatre.

Desilu aide Maury Thompson was assigned to help Lucy with the workshop. Lucy spent six hours auditioning the first batch of sixty-two people. She not only watched them perform, but met each one personally. In all, 1700 were auditioned, from which Lucy eventually selected twenty-two.

Discussing her students, Lucy said, "We don't take any money from them. We pay them sixty dollars a week—the Actors' Equity minimum—and they're free to work anywhere they want. They're not tied to us at all."

She added, "I understand the old agency trouble these kids have. It's the same old vicious circle: you can't get a job unless you've acted, and you can't act unless you've had a job. We're just trying to give them exposure!" Lucy wasn't interested in exposing them too young, however. "We won't pluck them out of high school or college. We tell them to finish what they're doing and then to come see us."

In 1958 the *Los Angeles Times* named Lucille Ball "Woman of the Year."

The Desilu Workshop was hailed by many Hollywood observers as the only practical workshop to come out of television production.

Lucy had had another motive for setting up the workshop: it would keep her mind off other things. The situation between her and Desi had reached the breaking point.

11

The Arnaz children were aware of their parents' unhappiness together. Desi Jr., years later, disclosed: "I learned pretty early to relate to 'I Love Lucy' as a television show and to my parents as actors in it. I *had* to learn that, because there wasn't much relationship between what I saw on TV and what was really going on at home. On TV, my mother was overplayed and my dad was underplayed. Those were difficult years—all those funny things happening each week on television to people who looked like my parents, then the same people agonizing through some terrible, unhappy times at home, and each of them trying to convince my sister and me separately that the other was in the wrong."

Although Lucy was constantly denying rumors of any rift, insiders knew that things were drastically wrong. People told Lucille that it was her career that was standing in the way of her happiness with Desi. If she would retire, they said, the rift would be healed. Lucille was in total disagreement. "No one

147

who really knew me would say that," she said. "Desi never asked me to retire. It meant something to him, having me work. He always was proud of my work and still is. He respects what I do as a performer. It was he, as the guiding genius of 'I Love Lucy,' who presented me in the best possible light.

"Whatever his faults, he is not one of those men who automatically assumes that all career women are competitive. He knew me too well for that. The first lesson I learned, as an actress, was how to take direction. Only a stranger could imagine me competing with Desi."

Competition was not the problem between them. The continuing problem was not work but how they would spend their non-working hours.

"Sometimes I went out with him on the town. But I am an eight-hours-of-sleep girl, and his hours were a little long for me. He did nothing in moderation. He never does. Naturally, I went through a long period of being positive that I was the one to blame. It was hard to keep working, to keep on being funny, when I was condemning myself. I became so depressed I couldn't go on alone. I had to get advice."

Lucy later revealed that she had even gone to psychiatrists to help save her marriage. "When it was pointed out that what was happening to Desi was not my fault, at least I could live with myself. I began to understand my situation."

On another occasion she noted, "When I married him, I knew that Latin men expect their wives to take a secondary role. I was all for it. I think one of the reasons Desi wanted to marry me was that I felt this way about him. I wanted him to be the boss. He knew I adored him. That's a hard thing for a man or woman to resist."

Desi's drinking increased as his unhappiness and pressures at the studio mounted. He began "playing" harder than ever. There were a number of separations which were never made public.

Lucy set up a trip to Europe for the family in an attempt to save their marriage. Observers recall that she was determined to take the children along. A close friend advised, "Why don't you try it alone, just the two of you?" But Lucy was stubborn. "I won't go without them."

It was a gala trip. Lucy bought tons of clothes and a magnificent full-length sable coat. It would be summer in Europe, so why take a fur coat? She told a friend, "I've bought it and I'm going to take it. Besides, Desi hasn't seen it."

When they returned, Lucy was scarcely speaking to Desi. They had quarreled constantly and he never saw the sable coat. Lucy later said, "I used it on the ship as a blanket for the kids."

For the outside world, however, the Arnazes kept up their image of being happily married.

Although through these years Lucy contended it was Desi's obsession with business which was their main problem, years later Desi, Jr. revealed that his mother's ambition was as strong if not stronger than his father's. "Even when we were young, my mother was never really able to turn off from whatever it is that drives her in her work. Ever since I can remember, she has talked about 'getting away,' and when she does, she's great—for about three weeks, then she has to get back to work."

As Desilu flourished, Lucy and Desi were driven farther and farther apart. It was an ironic situation, because their marriage had weathered years of shakiness, struggle and separation, and now, as Lucy later stated, "We came apart only when it looked as if we finally had smooth sailing ahead."

In May, 1959, Lucille Ball received the first bad publicity she had had in years. She went to Oklahoma to appear at a youth rally, but refused to perform because of what she termed "a small crowd." The Kiwanis Club Youth Rally to combat juvenile delinquency was being held in Oklahoma City's Taft Stadium, which seats 12,000. Only 2,000 showed up, and Lucy refused to leave her air-conditioned Cadillac for a scheduled comedy routine and a talk on delinquency. One young boy had a dozen roses to present to her, but when she wouldn't leave her car he kept the roses, saying he would give them to his mother for Mother's Day.

The program chairman, Fred Daugherty, told the audience

that Lucy was "disappointed with the crowd and declined to perform." The show went on without her and later Daugherty said, "The crowd didn't seem too disappointed."

Lucy drove to the airport to return to Hollywood. She told newsmen, "I didn't go on because of the small crowd. I believe in youth rallies, but there weren't enough there to do any good."

The following day, she told the Hollywood press that only 325 people appeared in a stadium built to seat 14,000. The Kiwanis apologized and everybody apologized, but somebody goofed and forgot to tell the people.

"I've played to thirteen people in a dugout. It doesn't matter to me how many there are. But when they don't care enough to publicize the affair, it's high time they stopped asking people to go thousands of miles to perform."

The publicity about Lucy leaving the stadium in a huff continued for several days. Daugherty contradicted Lucille, claiming that plenty of publicity preceded the event. He added: "I don't know what kept them away. Maybe she is too easy to see on TV."

That same year Desilu Productions announced that its gross for the year was $20,470,361. Its profit for 1959 was almost a quarter of a million dollars, up from only $90,000 in 1958. However, future profits would be enormous because of the reruns of films it was currently making. Desilu had about 560 half-hour TV shows to be rerun; by the end of the year it would have almost a thousand.

Desilu was involved in twenty-seven shows and rented studio facilities to three others. In addition to its other successful programs, "The Untouchables" was about to be launched. It would become an enormously successful series about the FBI fighting organized crime in the 1920s. It also proved that Walter Winchell had obviously made amends with Desi, since he was signed to narrate the series for an astronomical $25,000 a week.

"In Hollywood, business is business," notes an ex-associate of Desi's. "Winchell provided an authenticity for 'The Untouchables' that Desi considered extremely important. He was willing to let bygones be bygones despite Lucy's objections."

Desilu stock had gone public, starting at ten dollars a share. It shot up to twenty-nine and leveled off at between sixteen and eighteen. At one point, before the public offering, Desi encountered Texas oil millionaire Clint Murchison at the Del Mar race track. Murchison casually, but sincerely, offered Desi $11,000,000 for Desilu. Supposedly Desi, just as casually, replied, "Not enough."

Years later Arnaz revealed that he had wanted to sell Desilu at this point, and that in addition to Murchison, MGM had made an attractive offer. But, once again, Lucy didn't want to sell.

An observer at the time remembers that the Arnaz seen on the Desilu lot bore less resemblance than ever to the "Ricky Ricardo" fans knew. On television, he still appeared reasonably dapper with black hair and also wore suits and ties. At the studio he dressed casually, appeared burly, broad-chested and had ruffled gray-white hair.

Some thought he looked like a Latin-American dictator relaxing in sports clothes, and that he acted like a dictator on the lot—a hard-working and determined dictator. Desi's temper tantrums grew legendary. A fifty-four-year-old character actor, David O. McCall, alleged that Desi had attacked him without provocation while "grossly intoxicated" on a day in July. He later brought suit against Desi for $100,000 claiming back injuries and numerous bruises. The suit never came to trial.

The only similarity between Desi offscreen and on was the thick Cuban accent. In real life the accent was liberally sprinkled with American epithets for emphasis. His accent was so thick that there were times when even Lucy couldn't understand him.

Desi was still a dynamic force on the lot, shouting orders. "His movements were almost acrobatic," says one observer. When he had a problem that required concentration, he would drop his chin to his chest and rub his thinning hair. Or he would slouch into a director's chair and bury his face in his hands. But these periods would only last for a few seconds. Then he would jump up, throwing his arms about like a Latin windmill, shouting orders, muttering to himself. One time, throwing his arms open wide to direct something, his hand hit an electric fan, cutting his fingertips.

When he was directing actors he would hop in and out of the action, moving them physically, showing them where to walk. He was noted for planning every detail of production and he would often learn the lines of all the actors.

Milton Berle was a guest star on one of their hour-long specials. Berle and Lucy had one bit of business that would only last about thirty seconds on screen. The rehearsal for it took about a half hour. Desi had them rehearse the bit numerous times. Then he said, "Now we go through it one more time."

"Ah, c'mon now, Des," Berle said.

"No," Lucy said flatly. "We're not doing it again."

"C'mon," Desi said. "We do it one more time."

They did it again.

"He was manic in rehearsal, but downright frantic during shooting," recalls one who was there.

He often skipped lunch. While other people were eating, he conducted business conferences. It was not unusual for him to consult with the casting director, talk to the propman, set designer, the script editor and listen to some salesman, all within a matter of ten or fifteen minutes. He handled them all with executive ability and efficiency.

"One thing about him, though," notes an ex-associate. "He always listened to your advice. You could discuss anything with him. But the final decision was always his."

Milton Berle said about Desi, "I was so struck by the way he handled everything on his own show that I asked him to direct a show for me. He's got a tremendous flair for comedy; there's almost nobody like him around. He's a driver, a perfectionist, and he usually knows ninety-five per cent of what he wants."

Another Desilu executive remembers that Desi was loyal to all his workers. "He didn't like to fire anybody."

During this period Desi was rarely away from work. He did get a chance to play golf sometimes with friends like Phil Harris and Bob Hope. He was a good golfer, with a handicap of only nine. He also loved the races and would go to Del Mar as often as he could. And he was an avid Los Angeles Dodgers and Rams fan.

Although Desi had changed radically, the one carryover from his pre-mogul days was his churchgoing. He still attended Mass regularly, whether in Hollywood, Del Mar or Palm Springs.

In the summer of 1959, for the first time in ten years, Lucy and Desi took separate vacations. Of this period, Lucy said, "I had three months off, but I spent most of it working with the kids in our training program in the Little Theatre, helping them put together a revue. And I spent as much time as possible with our children—I took them to Del Mar a couple of times, to Disneyland, Marineland and helped them with their French lessons."

It was a tense time for the children. Though only eight and six and a half, they knew what was going on. Their father, too, was concerned about the negative effect his and Lucy's arguments were having on the children. It troubled him deeply. He flew to Florida to consult with his father and get the elder man's advice. (Although Desi's parents had been divorced for years, he had remained very close to both of them.)

Arnaz explained the dilemma to his dad: He was discontented remaining in the business; it infringed on his freedom to be the person he sometimes wanted to be. He knew that whether he stayed with Lucy or split with her, the children were going to be affected. Desi wanted a happy home life—what the hell was he going to do?

The senior Arnaz commiserated with his son and simply told him not to do anything until he was *sure* of what he wanted to do.

At this point Desi still didn't know. One thing was clear—he had to return to Hollywood and continue with all his contractual commitments. Production problems at Desilu were staggering.

Then one night in September Desi was picked up by police "on a simple drunk charge." He was seen "weaving down Vista Street." Two plainclothesmen saw him and went over to offer assistance. According to the police, Desi denounced the officers with offensive language. Desi didn't believe they were police, but Desi's chauffeur, parked nearby, called two uniformed officers who convinced Desi that the plainclothesmen were "authentic."

The mêlée wound up at the police station. Desi was released on twenty-one dollars cash bail after spending half an hour in a cell. But he failed to appear in court the following week. When Desi's lawyer said, "He's out shooting," the judge misunderstood and thought Desi was hunting. It was explained that "shooting" meant making a film, but the judge still noted: "This courtroom is filled with people who had to leave work."

The lawyer asked for a week's continuance, but the judge ordered Desi to appear the following morning. Desi did not appear, forfeited bail and the episode came to an end. For some unexplained reason the judge later said that there was no necessity for Desi to appear in court.

Desi's drinking problems and the Arnazes' less-than-ideal marital situation could no longer be kept from the public. She was embarrassed by his public behavior and wanted him to act in a more refined and dignified manner, one befitting the position they had attained in the industry. He wanted her to accept him exactly the way he was, as she had always done in the past. He simply was not concerned with "other people's opinions" about him—and she was.

Hedda Hopper was appearing on a TV show for Desilu. Lucy was making her debut as a director. The cast consisted of a dozen players from her Workshop. Hedda recalled, "Desi was back from Europe and he and Lucy were arguing." Vivian Vance, Bill Frawley and Hedda all took cover from the storms between Lucy and Desi.

Hedda warned her, "You can't insult him before the entire company. You're partly responsible for this show too, you know."

Obviously Lucy's directorial talents left something to be desired. "It seemed we were doomed to have a flop on our hands," noted Hedda.

During dress rehearsal Desi calmly asked, "Lucy, dear, will you let me see if I can pull this thing together for you?"

Lucy snapped back, "Okay. Try it!"

Hedda recalled that while Desi might not be winning medals as a husband, he was a great producer-director. In ten minutes he had whipped the program into shape.

People in the Arnaz inner circle knew, of course, it was a marriage in name only and had been for some time. Lucy would accuse him of meeting his needs elsewhere, and he would accuse her of the same thing. Arnaz later admitted that they had not slept together during the last year they lived together.

One night, after a bitter confrontation, Desi moved out of the house. He had done this many times before, but this argument proved to be the final one. It was over. But for public appearances and the sake of the children, they would both continue to lie.

Amid loud rumors of a marital rift, Lucy told a friend, "I believe he is going to Europe for a month." Her friend was nonplused: "She said it as though she were speaking of some casual acquaintance."

Lucy was again talking of leaving television and going to New York to star in a Broadway play, heightening rumors of the split. She shrugged when confronted with the reports. "Some people live on rumors. Desi and I have been in this whole thing long enough to be accustomed to them. We got through that kind of thing before, and we'll get through it again. Maybe it's good for some couples to be separated for a time. Maybe it can renew and refresh a relationship."

When Desi sailed in October, without a bon-voyage visit from Lucy, there were more printed reports of the rift. Desi pooh-poohed the rumors: "We're working too hard. That's the only trouble. Probably someone heard we had an argument. But we have lots of arguments. When a redhead and a Cuban get together, we argue pretty good."

This time there were not only reports of a possible divorce, but it was said that Desilu was up for sale.

Lucille countered with, "We have had many offers from many corporations in the last few years, but we haven't considered any of them. We are a going concern and everybody wants to buy in." She added, "When there is a sale, we will be the first to announce it." Was this the editorial "we"?

About a divorce she sharply noted: "Desi is in Europe on business. When he returns to this country around December first, he will come home and live here with his family as he always has."

But Lucille was putting on a good front, as she had so many times in the past. At Christmas time, she packed up the kids and spent the holidays in Sun Valley with Ann Sothern. Desi went to Palm Springs alone, for a different sort of vacation.

No one could ask them what was really happening. But a witness on the scene noted that their business relationship was a definite tip-off. "There was no sign of unpleasantness. At the studio they acted with deference and courtesy to each other. In the old days, their relationship had been marked by an easy give and take. They used to kid each other unmercifully. Now they were being *too* nice to each other. We all knew something was wrong."

Lucy later confirmed this. "Strangely enough during the last few months, I didn't have the same problems at work. The set was one place that was fairly good humored."

The last Lucille Ball-Desi Arnaz television special was filmed before the end of the year. It was called "The Redhead Meets the Mustache," and co-starred Edie Adams and Ernie Kovacs. The plot revolved around Lucy Ricardo masquerading as a chauffeur in order to get Ricky a TV job with Kovacs.

Edie Adams recalled, "Every time they wanted to film a funny scene, Lucy would break down and cry. Nobody could stand to watch it." The final scene had the Ricardos embracing and kissing.

At the end of the filming, an air of unhappiness hung over Lucy, Desi, Vivian Vance, Bill Frawley and the other members of the cast and crew. The 209th show with "Lucy and Ricky" was the last.

12

Lucille's version of the breakup: "When our problems began affecting our children, I had to act. With Desi away from us most of the time, I knew they felt deserted. Kind, as all children are, they never said a word.

"One night, as I stopped by little Desi's room for the nightly tuck-in, I heard him uttering whimpers of anguish. Lucie, normally a sound sleeper, was tossing and turning in her bed when I looked in there.

"Their grades in school went down, and I was called in and told that my children were showing symptoms of 'a troubled home life' in their attitudes. The experts said to tell them, so I did.

"I took Lucie aside first, because she is the older. 'Lucie,' I said, 'I have to tell you that Mommy and Daddy are not getting along and I know that the unhappiness you see is affecting you. And I want you to know that it has nothing to do with you. We love you very much. I want you also to know that we are trying to work things out.

"And she said 'You wouldn't get a divorce, would you?'

"And I said, 'What do you know about divorce? What is a divorce?'

"She stammered. 'W-well, it's—well, you wouldn't get one, would you?' She didn't quite know what it was.

"So I told her: 'I am only planning on being separated from Daddy, and I just want you to know that it has nothing to do with you. We will probably see much more of Daddy, actually.'

"After I confided in Lucie, she perked up. I'm sure it was because she knew what was going on and didn't worry about her own part in it any more. She relaxed and stopping having nightmares. She was safe.

"Shortly afterward, I had to tell little Desi, because he was taking Daddy's absences even harder than Lucie. He adores his daddy. I said to him. 'You know how you and Lucie fight over your games or something. Well, mommies and daddies have their problems, too. They get angry with each other. It takes time to work these things out, and then everybody's happy again.' He just nodded."

Despite the insistent rumors for over a year, it was still a shock to the public when Lucille filed for divorce in early 1960. Few marriages were more famous. Few Hollywood marriages had seemed so perfect. But though the public thought of Lucille Ball and Desi Arnaz as Lucy and Ricky Ricardo, they discovered it was an illusion. Lucille Ball was not erratic, extravagant, always-inventing-wild-schemes Lucy; she was conservative, concerned with public opinion and slow to accept change.

Desi was hardly the level-headed Ricky, slow to anger, a steadying force on his scatterbrained wife. Though a successful business tycoon, Desi was noted for being pleasure seeking, impulsive and hot headed.

Desi's drinking and temper tantrums were said to be the reasons for Lucille's finally making the move. "But what irked her most of all," believes an ex-Desilu employee, "was Desi's continued interest in other women—women considerably younger than Lucille."

In later years, when discussing Desi, Lucy said: "It was romance—out of step. It was romantic and fun, occasionally. It was emotional. But our sense of values were different."

With the final break, Lucy and Desi had to tell the children. They drove to their home in Palm Springs, specifically for that purpose. Lucy asked Desi to tell them.

He did, while she sat there. In Lucy's own words, "He began by saying that Mommy and Daddy were not getting along. Lucie again said, 'But you won't get a divorce?'

"Desi explained that perhaps we would. They got very quiet, put their heads down and didn't want to look at us. He said a little more about how we would see each other often and that he loved them very much.

"Finally, little Desi looked up and said, 'But, Daddy, a divorce? Isn't there some way you can take it all back?' That was almost more than we could take."

The divorce affected the children more than Lucy and Desi wanted to admit. In Desi, Jr.'s words: "They were divorced when I was seven, and I stayed home at my mother's for several days hoping the public attention would quiet down. I still remember the first day I got on the bus to go to school; the other kids couldn't wait to question me about what had *really* happened. But when you're seven years old, you can roll with things like that, and I did. Those days upset me much more later when I thought back on them than when they were happening."

After Lucy filed for divorce, Desi, Sr. was mum on the subject. And for the next sixteen years he allowed Lucy's version of the story to become the official one. Lucy, in a public-relationsy statement, explained, "I feel success had been difficult for Desi to take because he gave up the goal we shared. Security was only one of them. Prestige still another. But happiness—the mature happiness that comes from making other people happy, the laughter that follows the comedian's custard pie—this was our principal goal, and it was abandoned by Desi somewhere along the way." She added, however: "It's still my goal, without Desi."

Lucy announced she would leave Hollywood and return to New York to accomplish a long-time ambition: to star in a Broadway show.

"I assume that Desi will come to New York, so that the children will see more of him than they have during the crisis that affected all our lives," she remarked. "I know that my attitude toward him will be friendly, so that we won't disturb the children.

"I know better than most people how much the 'I Love Lucy' legend was built around the marriage of Desi and me. Now that I have to go it alone, I am not frightened. I know it will not be as satisfying to me, because I loved the legend while it lasted." Giving deep insight into what makes her tick, Lucille concluded: "But I am a performer, and when I perform, I perform with all my heart. As long as I can make people happy, that is all I want to do."

Though the Lucy-Desi divorce trial revealed a seamier side of Lucy and Desi's marriage than the public could have imagined possible, by Hollywood standards it was as amicable as could be expected.

Lucy arrived at the Santa Monica hearing with her cousin Cleo, her corroborating witness. Outside, Lucy clowned for photographers in her usual manner. But her composure seemed to vanish when she took the stand before Superior Court Judge Orlando H. Rhodes. When her attorney, Mickey Rudin, started questioning her, Lucy's chin began to quiver and she only nodded her answers about Desi's alleged cruelties. The judge told her to make her replies vocal.

Lucy was smartly dressed in a black-and-white tweed silk suit, and she carried a jeweled black umbrella. During the hearing Lucy wiped her teary eyes several times as she told the judge:

"We could have no social life for the last three or four years.... I couldn't bear to be at parties when he would blow up. I preferred the privacy of our home when the battles started."

She also stated, "It was a Jekyll and Hyde thing. He would frequently have fits of temper in front of everyone, including the children. It got so bad that I thought it would be better for us not to be together. These tantrums would happen everywhere. They happened at home, they happened at work. It could be anything that sets him off."

As an example, Lucy told of a time when the water pipes burst in their Beverly Hills home. "He made himself sick for two days over it. He blamed everybody and everything. By count there were sixteen people he blamed. He was hysterical and screamed and raved about it. There was no discussing with him in such violence."

Lucy said it had been difficult working with Desi for the past nine years "with this sort of thing going on."

She told Judge Rhodes that because of Desi's frequent outbursts she felt "for the sake of the children it was better for us to be apart."

Rudin asked her, "Did you try to work things out?"

"There's no discussing anything with him," Lucy answered. "He doesn't discuss very well."

Cleo confirmed Desi's "completely irrational behavior."

Both Lucy and Desi gave out official statements to the press. Desi's was: "We deeply regret that after long and serious consideration we have not been able to work out our problems and have decided to separate. Our divorce will be completely amicable and there will be no contest. Lucy will pursue her career on television and I will continue my work as head of Desilu Productions."

Lucy's official statement: "I'm sure our separation will come as no surprise since every columnist in the country has hinted at it for months. I've tried so hard to be fair and solve our problems—but now I find it impossible to go on."

Lucy said she and Desi had agreed on joint custody of the children. "We both love them very much," said Lucy, "and Desi can see them as often as he likes."

The financial arrangements of the divorce were simple. Everything was split fifty-fifty, with their Palm Springs hotel being turned over to a trust fund for the children. Lucy kept the Roxbury Drive house, Desi the forty-acre ranch and stock farm which they had bought in 1959. They each got 282,800 shares of Desilu stock, which was worth approximately twelve dollars a share at the time. Desi would also pay $450-a-month child support for each of the children.

Lucy was asked whether there could possibly be a reconciliation, as there had been with the 1944 divorce. Her simple reply: "Nope."

If friends were saying, "Poor thing, without Desi her life will be so empty. What will she do now?" they got an immediate answer. Lucy had contended that they had been working too hard and that Desi wouldn't stop to relax and enjoy everything they had, but after the divorce Lucy continued her professional activities at the same pace.

She signed for her first film in five years, a comedy with Bob Hope called *The Facts of Life*. "She didn't even wince at that title," notes a friend.

Desi had a rough siege during the divorce. While Lucy was testifying, he was in Las Vegas brooding and having one too many Scotches on the rocks. It was a tough period in his life. He was asked to leave the Desert Inn because the manager decided his language was offensive to the other guests.

But Desi's ability to bounce back from disaster was as strong if not stronger than Lucy's. Shortly after the divorce, he checked himself into a Los Angeles hospital for a ten-day "rest" and friends noted that that was apparently all he needed. He returned to work cheerful, relaxed and full of energy.

Later a friend met Desi while he was playing in a golf tournament at his Palm Springs club. "He had two eggs, ham, three pieces of toast for breakfast—the same Desi who used to start with tomato juice laced with Worcestershire sauce and a chaser of Scotch and then no food till noon. He'd been 'on the wagon' for three weeks when we met and thinks the ride will be permanent."

Although it was Lucy who had always pleaded for Desi to slow up, she was the one who now set an exhausting schedule of work for herself, while he appeared to be taking her advice for the first time and enjoying some of the results of his undeniable dynamism.

While he summered at Del Mar, combining business with two of his favorite forms of pleasure, golf and horse racing, Lucy was shooting *The Facts of Life* at Desilu. But in the film, the ending was a happy one, even though it was the story of two unhappily married people.

In it, Lucy and Bob Hope were each married to loving spouses, but the spark had gone out of their marriages. Lucy was married to Don De Fore, who was concerned with business; Bob was married to Ruth Hussey, who was devoted to her home and children. Bob and Lucy decide to have an affair, but, needless to say, comic situations intervened "in the nick of time," preventing them from committing adultery.

Mel Frank, director of *Facts of Life,* said of Lucy: "She may be the single greatest talent I've ever worked with. She is one of the really superb actresses of our time. I just say 'Action!' and all the magic comes out."

An associate recalls that while Lucy was filming *Facts* she was busy negotiating for rewrites on her upcoming Broadway play. There were also phone calls about television business. During these calls, Lucy talked in terms of $50,000 and $100,000 as casually as the average woman might discuss the price of tuna fish.

"How does it feel to be Hollywood's richest woman?" a production assistant once asked her. "Nyah!" was her only reply.

Lucille Ball was, for the first time in twenty years, officially "eligible." An observer remembered an occasion when Lucy received a call from a show business friend, asking if she would like to go out that night. Lucy seemed bored as the man chattered on. He apparently had made plans to attend a young night-club singer's act.

"I've seen him twice already," said Lucy into the phone, "and his press agent is now saying I've been there eight times. If I go again the kid will be saying I'm in love with him. He's two-feet-six and nine years old. I don't want any part of it." The voice on the phone pleaded with her to change her mind. Lucy held the phone away from her and looked to the sky for help. She finally hung up.

"I go out because people ask me to," commented Lucy. "I have no love for night clubs, unless there's an act I especially want to see. And I don't especially want to see this kid's again."

During filming of *The Facts of Life* she had an accident on the set and was rushed to the hospital. Desi, immediately notified, hurried to the hospital to console her. Then he accompanied her to their beach house at Del Mar. The obvious question was, now that they were living under the same roof again, did this mean a reconciliation? Desi wouldn't answer, but Cleo and her husband Ken Morgan did. "We see no way of their being reconciled at this time."

Romantics wanted to believe that America's sweethearts would indeed be reunited and everything would be all right. But it wasn't going to happen. Lucy and Desi had split permanently.

In the beginning, Lucille Ball and Desi Arnaz had come together like two speeding trains colliding head-on. They had experienced an excitement that few people know. It had been thrilling and challenging at first, but now, after the heat had long since subsided, they viewed the wreckage. Each would piece together his life and go on. But it would never be the same for Lucille or Desi.

BOOK II

13

"And now it is time to start a fresh page," Lucy said characteristically. "I have always wanted to do a Broadway play, but kept putting it off because of my Hollywood commitments. Starting this fall, I will have none. My divorce had nothing to do with my decision to move to New York," she fibbed, "but I will be grateful for the change of scenery as I cross this new bridge."

It was generally agreed that Lucy was running away from Hollywood, Desi, the continual reminders of their life and careers together.

Under no circumstances would there be any more Lucy-Desi specials. "Even if everything were all right, we'd never work together again," Lucy said with finality. "We had six years of a pretty successful series and two years of specials. Why try to top it? That would be foolish. We always knew that when the time came to quit, we'd quit. We were lucky. We quit while we were ahead."

Years later, Lucy admitted that breaking up her marriage to Desi was "wrong." They were America's most beloved couple and Norman Vincent Peale used to remind Lucy that they were everyone's idea of the perfectly married pair and if they admitted they were fallible they would betray the faith of millions.

Lucy later said, "I received eight thousand letters at the time of the divorce announcement and read most of them; I couldn't answer them all, of course. They asked me not to get a divorce. They said, 'Why isn't there something you can do?' They didn't know I had been trying to do it for years."

After divorcing Desi it was, according to Lucy, many years later, "the worst period of my life." She said in retrospect, "I really hit the bottom of despair—anything from there on had to be up. Neither Desi nor I have been the same since, physically or mentally, though we're very friendly, ridiculously so.... I did everything I could to right that ship, trotting to psychiatrists. I hate failure and that divorce was a Number One failure in my eyes.... Anything in excess drives me crazy. He'd build a home any place he was and then never be around to enjoy it. I was so idealistic. I thought that with two beautiful babies, a beautiful business, what more could any man want? Freedom, he said, but he had that. People don't know what a job he did building that Desilu empire, what a great director and brilliant executive he was, yet he let it all go... maybe Latins have an instinct for self destruction...."

Was *that* the conflict, a Latin temperament married to an old-fashioned American female? "No, the *machismo* didn't bother me. I like to play games too."

On the rare occasions when she reminisced, friends recalled Lucy would often stop to wipe her teary blue eyes. But she would always quickly change moods, preferring to look ahead.

A few months after the divorce, Lucy's reaction to it was beginning to set in. "I get tired too easily," she confided to a friend. "I've had pneumonia twice in a year. That's not good."

Desi still looked out for Lucy's professional interests. In fact, after their divorce their relationship improved considerably.

Although Lucy supposedly wanted financing for her Broadway show handled by outsiders, Desi suggested that Desilu pick up the tab. Hence they wouldn't have to share the profits and they would also own the movie and television rights.

According to Lucy, there were "many friends who were all too willing to invest in it." But she also noted, "The Desilu stockholders weren't too happy about my stepping out of the TV picture after eight very profitable years. But, by making Desilu the backer of the show, there is a continuing relationship, and I am still working for them with the possiblity of bringing in more profits."

Was she happy, at least? "No," she admitted frankly. "Not yet. I will be. I've been humiliated. That's not easy for a woman."

It was on to New York and Broadway. "I intend to devote my time to the stage from now on," she said. "We'll keep our home in Beverly Hills. My mother will accompany us to New York to help me get things started, then she'll return to California to live in our house. But I am selling the house in Palm Springs that Desi and I built five years ago. We've been suffering from an excess of houses for some time. Desi is building a new house for himself. He enjoys building houses; I prefer living in homes."

"Every spare moment I get, I want to concentrate on my children," she stated on another occasion, observing that "They've had too many servants, too many people hovering over them. They haven't been called upon to do all the things they could. They should be more independent than they are."

During filming of *The Facts of Life*, Lucy had also suffered from a leg injury, necessitating a minor operation. Along with the gash in her leg she picked up a stubborn staphylococcus infection. Antibiotics eventually cleared it up, but the drugs lowered her resistance to virus infections—and Lucy's health was about to undergo its severest ordeal.

After *The Facts of Life* was completed, Lucy moved east. Her New York apartment was on the twenty-third floor of Imperial House at Lexington Avenue and 69th Street—a luxury apartment with seven rooms and a terrace. Lucy took along a nurse and a maid. She furnished the apartment in a contemporary California style, with bright fabrics, light woods. She loves vivid colors.

Lucie was enrolled at the Marymount School, a branch of the same school she attended in Los Angeles. Little Desi was sent to St. David's. Both schools were Catholic.

"They are homesick for California," admitted Lucy about her kids, "but my work is in New York and I want them with me."

They wouldn't lack for reminders of home. "I brought all the terrace furniture from Palm Springs, five TV sets, a piano that was sitting out there doing nothing, the toys for my daughter Lucie, little Desi's bongo drums, all my paintings and all my books," noted Lucy. "Plus a limousine with chauffeur, and a big package of courage."

In New York, news stories turned from the divorce angle and the end of the "I Love Lucy" series to Lucy's Broadway debut.

At forty-nine, Lucille Ball was going to tackle the roughest physical experience of her professional career.

Lucy didn't have any illusions about herself. "I'm not beautiful, not sexy and don't have a good figure," she told Hedda Hopper. Hedda concurred. "She knew she couldn't sing, admits she was too old to dance, but for her Broadway debut she would sing, dance and have to hold the whole show together."

As a vehicle, Lucy chose *Wildcat,* a comedy with music by Richard Nash, author of *The Rainmaker. Wildcat* had many elements similar to *The Rainmaker,* and the lead character was described as a sort of Annie Oakley of the oil fields. The score was by Cy Coleman and Carolyn Leigh. Michael Kidd was signed to direct, co-produce (with Nash), and choreograph the show.

"Professionally, I exchanged Desi for Michael Kidd," noted Lucy. "I needed someone I could depend on. I love people who know their business. I bow down to talent."

"I'm terrified too," she admitted. "I've never really been on the stage before, except years ago on the tour with *Dream Girl.* It's a challenge. I'd gone as far as I wanted in TV. I know I'm sticking my neck out—but I stuck it out in TV, too. It won't kill me

The Life of Lucille Ball

if the play flops, but I'm not anticipating failure. My contract runs
eighteen months, and I've leased an apartment for five years, but I
hope the play doesn't run *that* long."

She said that if the show is a hit," I naturally will stay with it to
the end of the run." Referring to Kidd and Nash, "we three make
the decisions. Right or wrong, this way it's faster. I like people
who know what they want. I have no qualms—this way I don't
have to check with forty people. One reason for the success of 'I
Love Lucy' was that Desi didn't have to check with anyone."

Lucy began arduous singing lessons. "Why, I haven't even
been in the habit of singing in the shower. Naturally, I've been
taking vocal training like mad. I have a marvelous coach, Carlo
Menotti, and by the way, he's not Gian Carlo Menotti, the opera
composer.

"I'm not going to do any of that talking-off-a-song stuff the way
some nonsingers do in musical shows these days. Seems to me
that that is harder than actually trying to sing. I'll just have to
take my chances by rearing back and letting go. Fortunately, I'll
have mostly funny or action or character-type songs. That means
I'll be doing a lot of cavorting around while I'm singing, and
maybe that will keep people from paying too much attention to
the quality of the voice."

About a leading man, Lucy said "I want an unknown. He has
to be big, husky, around forty. He has to be able to throw me
around, and I'm a pretty big girl. He has to be able to sing, at
least a little." (Keith Andes, hardly an unknown, got the role of
"Dynamite Joe.")

Discussing her role: "It's a sort of tomboy type of role," Lucy
said with relish. "I get into the oil business because my father
was in it, and there is the incentive of trying to make good
because I have a crippled sister to look after. The romance angle
is a continual fight with the leading man. I'm the sort who
always thinks and talks big without any substance to back it up. I
guess you'd say I'm sort of a con woman in the oil business."

The "con woman" aspect of the character bothered Lucy. But
she went along with it—for the time being.

169

"Rehearsing is a seven-day, seven-night deal. Out in Hollywood, I worked four days a week and could spend the rest of the time with my two kids."

But doing *Wildcat* was, in concept at least, a labor of love. Lucy told an observer. "I've always wanted to be on the Broadway stage. It's a new medium for me, my first time on Broadway. Sure I'm scared and I get butterflies when I think of the opening night. But I'm also excited about it. I chose *Wildcat* because it's close to the character I play in 'I Love Lucy.' It's comedy, and, while comedy is harder to do than drama, I thought I'd better do something I'm known for. Later on, if Dorothy Parker's 'Big Blonde' story is still available, I'd like to do that on the stage in New York. It's a wonderful story. But for my first Broadway appearance, it's too morose."

As rehearsals for *Wildcat* progressed, Lucy began to feel uneasy. At least there seemed to be a genuinely friendly relationship among the principals of the show. Michael Kidd called Lucy "an outstanding combination of naivete and self-consciousness," intent solely on "living the character. What she felt was real for the character became her own feelings."

Lucy had to be convinced of several things during production. "I can't do it," she told Kidd about one of the songs. "It embarrasses me." Kidd noted, "We tried to show her that she was a con woman who would say such things." The song was dropped.

She also had an altercation over costumes. When designer Alvin Colt showed her the sketches, she was horrified and insisted upon wearing her rehearsal clothes—an old denim shirt and blue jeans.

"We had a horrible time convincing her," Kidd said, "that on the stage a certain artificiality is accepted. I told her someone in real jeans and a torn shirt doesn't generally appear on a lighted stage in make-up, in front of painted scenery before an audience and sing songs accompanied by an orchestra, or strike oil that comes out of a scenic artist's oil well."

The show began its tryout in Philadelphia, where the *Wildcat* heroine was an attractive but tough, raucous, profane and two-fisted girl equally adept at bringing in oil wells and bringing down men. It didn't go over very well and thereafter bits of business and references that television viewers associated with the "Lucy" character were added. One observer noted that these "Lucy" additions "were inserted like maraschino cherries in a tuna fish salad."

Lucy was deadly calm opening night in Philadelphia, but later said, "Of course I flipped three weeks later after all the changes."

Director Kidd recalled how inadequate Lucy felt as a singer. He said he was convinced that it was this feeling of inadequacy that made her forget the lyrics midway through a song every once in a while. But he also noted that she turned these lapses to her advantage. During performances she would raise her hand, stop the music, tell the audience what happened, ask the conductor to start from the top again and the song would still end up with rousing applause.

The show still wasn't going over as expected and Lucille wanted even more of the "Lucy" character written into it. Author Nash objected violently, but the public obviously was paying to see the Lucy they knew, and Nash later admitted: "We found out the audience had come to see 'Lucy,' not Lucille Ball playing in *Wildcat*. She became increasingly unhappy. Should we run against audience demand and her increasing unhappiness, which might have kept her from opening? I had a responsibility to $400,000. I was writing against my own views as a writer, but I had to."

Director Kidd had his hands full. And Desi was a frequent visitor. "They finally got around to making the changes he suggested and they're still making them," Lucy noted while the show was in previews.

It was a trying time for all concerned. A friend recalls accompanying Lucy to a local restaurant. " 'Goddammit,' Lucy said, 'why don't they make tables so you can put your legs under them?' The proprietor quickly brought another chair. She hoisted her feet up on it, made herself comfortable and ordered a Chianti on the rocks."

About her personal life during this hectic period: "The children are completely adjusted to their changed mode of living. They see their father a lot more these days and so do I. Everybody's happier."

This may have been what Lucy wanted to perceive—but events would prove, and the children themselves would later confirm, that they were not happier and certainly not adjusted.

While *Wildcat* was in Philadelphia, Lucy's mother brought Lucie and little Desi from New York every week to see the show and visit their mother.

Wildcat opened on Broadway at the Alvin Theatre on December 15, 1960. By this time the character had been furiously rewritten into a reasonable facsimile of Lucy's television self.

"It's fine with me," Lucy said at the time. "I love 'Lucy,' love doing her. Love the mugging. Saying to a character onstage, 'Say, you know a fellow named Fred Mertz?' They eat it up. I have a ball. Do what I like.... Little Mousie, the Yorkshire terrier we use in the show, made a, well, a mess on stage one night. I stopped the show, grabbed a mop and pail and cleaned it up. Told 'em I'd read the small print in my contract. They loved it."

Lucy's personal notices were enthusiastic, but the show was panned. Walter Kerr said: "Naturally, in the case of *Wildcat*, what you really want to know about is Lucille Ball. So do I.... Miss Ball is up there, all right, doing all of the spectacular and animated and energetic and deliriously accomplished things she can do...."

Although Lucy's worst fears about the play were realized, she was determined to make the show a success. Other stars had carried Broadway turkeys for long runs—Ethel Merman and Sammy Davis, Jr., for example. There was no doubt that people would flock to see Lucille Ball no matter what she was in.

Her film with Bob Hope, *The Facts of Life*, released only the previous month, was a tremendous hit. Critics called it the best of the films Lucy and Bob had done together. But she couldn't really enjoy its success. *Wildcat* was wearing her down tremendously. "That role would have knocked out a girl twenty years younger than Lucille," notes a friend. "She was incredible, the way she delivered her performances. But she wasn't a kid, and the ordeal took its toll."

Officially, Lucille remained optimistic. She had said, "I want to devote at least five years to the Broadway stage, now that they'll have me." After all, she had achieved one of her girlhood dreams by starring on Broadway. "When I roamed around New York as a struggling young actress, I couldn't *buy* a job on Broadway. Now here I am prancing around in my first show, and it's even more fun than I thought it would be."

But she candidly told a chum, "How long can you have a ball saying the same things and dancing the same steps?"

And her health was failing.

Bill Frawley came to see *Wildcat* one evening, and created a minor sensation. "It's Fred Mertz," the audience buzzed. Another visitor was Dr. Norman Vincent Peale. He stopped backstage one night and told Lucy, "I hear you're very ill and working too hard." "Work never hurt anybody," Lucy protested. But he reminded her she had two beautiful children to bring up. "If I was in bad shape, how could I do it?" Lucy realized. "I've learned you don't rake more leaves than you can get into the wheelbarrow. I've always been moderate, but I was too spread around, trying to please too many people. You don't become callous, but you must conserve your energies."

Lucy had become a follower of Dr. Peale and his "power of positive thinking." Dr. Peale's philosophy calls for bringing God and the teaching of Jesus Christ into one's life. Lucy also became an advocate of *The Art of Selfishness.* "I ran across the idea in a decrepit old book when I was at a very low ebb. It said don't worry about the whole world. If you do it will overwhelm you. Worry about one wave at a time. Please yourself. Do something for you and the rest will fall in line. This idea appealed to me. The theory said, pin up a sign: IS THIS GOOD FOR LUCY? The point was, 'to thine own self be true.'"

Lucy's personal life seemed at a standstill. She was, in fact, dating at the time, but declined to mention any names. "The only plans I have," she said, "are to make no plans. Marriage? Who needs it? I had it."

She wasn't too happy with her New York existence. "I hibernate in New York," she observed. "Can't go out in the daytime, you get recognized. And I'm not much of a night club kid. I enjoy going to Sardi's, and at the risk of sounding corny, I enjoy being with show business people."

Lloyd Nolan's last encounter with Lucy was in Sardi's during the *Wildcat* run. "There had been a muck-up with Lucille's reservation," remembered Nolan, "and they didn't have a table for her and her party. I asked her to sit at my table until they got her one. She was so damned mad she could hardly speak. I don't blame her."

Also in town during *Wildcat* was Busby Berkeley. Lucy invited him over to her apartment and they talked about old times.

Around this time she hinted that she might retire after the run of the show. "I'm signed for eighteen months and then I have a commitment to do another movie with Bob Hope. After that, what I'm going to do is take the children out of school and get a tutor for them and then go and live in different places, wherever we choose to go."

"She probably meant it when she said it," says a former associate. "She was tired and the idea of retirement couldn't have been all that depressing at that time in her life. For the first time, she was working but not having fun."

The Alvin Theatre could seat a total of 11,200 a week at eight performances. Tickets were priced so that weekly capacity was a then hefty $65,000. The average weekly gross for *Wildcat* usually ran above $55,000. It even surpassed that figure during one week of February snowstorms. There was no doubt that Lucy was a huge draw. But in February the show had to close for two weeks because she was suffering from a viral infection, physical exhaustion and bursitis in her right leg. She spent the two weeks recuperating in Miami.

174

On her return the show resumed, but Lucy's health never quite recovered. Over the next few weeks there were a couple of occasions when she fainted on stage.

It was obvious that she would not be able to continue, and her physician ordered her to take a leave of absence from the show long enough for her to recover from her "severe respiratory infection complicated by exhaustion."

It was announced that the musical would go on vacation and reopen in August. But the show closed. "It just about broke my heart," she said after the closing. "And some day—when I get time and if I can still walk—I want to do another Broadway show."

In addition to the show closing and her failing health, Lucy had been named one of the worst-dressed women of the year by the fashion world's flamboyant "Mr. Blackwell," who described her taste in clothes as "a sense of turmoil." Lucy was in good company, however. Blackwell also rated Brigitte Bardot, Kim Novak, Anne Baxter and other luminaries as "worst-dressed." But Lucy headed the list.

By September, Lucille had returned to California. (Her divorce from Desi became final months before.)

Years later she candidly summed up the post-divorce and New York-Broadway experience. "That was a terrible time in my life.... I hired the best people in the business (I *thought*) to do what they do and they didn't do. I should have shouted some and maybe it would have been a better show, but I was tired. It was the first time in years I had been free. I had my divorce and I wanted to move bag and baggage away from trouble. I backed the show with my own money, sank thirty grand in an apartment and settled down for a long run. It was never anything more than a female *Rainmaker*, but nobody told me how bad it was. Except the gypsies in the chorus. They knew everything. Finally I began to listen to them and they were right. But you know we were SRO from the time we opened and when you're a hit, the powers-that-be are inclined not to change anything. But I was fixing and changing *Wildcat* up to the night I closed. When I left the show, I was so sick they almost carried me out in a coffin. I had to give them back $165,000 outta my own pocket for ticket refunds—the most money ever refunded, they said.

"Now I don't think I'll ever do another play. The loss of the days and contact with the outer world is terrible. You don't sign up to do a flop, you sign for a long run, and I don't have that kind of time anymore. But I learned something good, even from a horrible experience like *Wildcat.* I learned the people came to the theater to see the Lucy they knew and I didn't give it to them."

A TV special had been planned, called "Lucy Goes to Broadway." It was called off because "there really was no time to do it," noted Lucy. "Desi, who was to produce it, has not been well and I certainly wasn't in any shape to do it." Viv Vance and Bill Frawley were also scheduled to star in the special.

What would Lucy do after *Wildcat?* "Who the hell knows?" she said.

What she did do after *Wildcat* was the most surprising thing she could have done—she got married again.

14

Gary Morton, who started out life as Morton Goldapper, was a relatively unknown comedian whom Lucy met in the summer of 1960, while rehearsing for *Wildcat*. At the time, Gary was a stand-up comic at Radio City Music Hall, working seven days a week.

They were introduced by one of Lucy's *Wildcat* co-stars, Paula Stewart, who was then married to comedian Jack Carter. The Carters felt that Gary and Lucy would hit it off, and one night after the show the four went out for a pizza.

Morton was forty-two, almost ten years younger than Lucy. A big, amiable, sexy man. He was struck with Lucille's gaiety as they shared that first pizza. But he claims he had no idea he would wind up marrying her (he had been married once before).

"The first thing I noticed about Lucy was her warmth," Morton has recalled. "The second was her carriage. I mean, she's like a thoroughbred. When she walks into a room, you know she's there."

Gary and Lucy had "a lot of fun" on their first date, and they followed it up by exchanging kidding telegrams. Then, "one date led to another, and, without realizing it, we were going steady," Morton said.

After *Wildcat* had closed and she was about to go to Switzerland for a vacation, she was asked if she intended to marry Gary Morton.

"Oh, don't talk marriage to me," she said. "I've had it."

"I'll bet Gary will be in Switzerland to see you while you're resting," noted a reporter. Lucille didn't say yes and she didn't say no. The reporter pressed onward: "I'd like to make a bet that you will marry Gary Morton."

"You'll lose your money," said Lucy. "Don't bet. It's nice this way."

She later explained, "I didn't intend to get married again. I didn't think I would find a mature, adult person like Gary, a really understanding guy who is wonderful to be around and uncomplicated. He has none of the worrisome characteristics I lived with. I learn from experience. I wasn't going to walk into the same trap."

Gary and Lucy had more in common than people realized. "We both came up the hard way," Gary said. "I got started in World War II, clowning for USO shows. I've been in show biz for thirty years and can appreciate what she goes through."

Professionally, Morton was noted mostly for his work in the "Borscht Belt," the famous string of Jewish hotels in the Catskill Mountains. But he had also played some top night clubs, including the Copacabana in New York. When he appeared at the Copa in the spring of 1961, Lucy was often at ringside.

Gary's background was strictly New York. He was born in the Bronx. His father, a truck driver, and mother, Rose, lived on Long Island.

When Lucy returned to California, Gary followed. He met Lucy's friends, and she noted, "He knew more people there than I did. By the time he was here for a while, everybody was saying 'Why don't you marry the guy?'"

Lucy had met Gary's mother and was especially thoughtful of her. "She often called from California to see how Rose was," said a friend. "The first time she called was to wish her a happy birthday."

Friends noted that Gary's style of comedy changed after he met Lucy. "Lucille influenced him tremendously," an associate pointed out. "Once he was like all comics—throwing lines constantly—always 'on.' Then he became almost distinguished. You could say he got 'class.'"

"He's just a wonderful guy," Lucille said. "A great guy. I like to make someone happy and I guess he was a candidate since he made me and my children happy."

In California, Gary was introduced to Desi, Sr. They liked each other. "It's all set," Lucy told a friend. "He accepts Gary." She later told Earl Wilson, "Desi has been very sweet and very nice about the whole thing—he certainly has given his approval."

Lucy and Desi would, of course, retain joint custody of the children if Lucille remarried.

Lucy and Gary decided to be married in New York. They set the date for November 19. The wedding was performed by Lucille's friend, Norman Vincent Peale, at Marble Collegiate Church on Fifth Avenue. Lucille wore a gown she bought at Bergdorf Goodman's. Paula Stewart was matron of honor and Jack Carter was best man. Lucille's close friends and family, including DeDe and the children, were present. The wedding was followed by a small reception for about fifteen people at Lucille's Imperial House apartment.

"We've had a beautiful year together," said Gary, "and we want to continue having beautiful years together."

After the reception, however, Gary had to leave for Palm Springs and a night club engagement. Lucy had to remain in New York to rehearse for a TV special, "The Good Years," with Henry Fonda.

Lucy had told Earl Wilson that she wouldn't go to Gary's night club openings. "I'll frequently be busy, but even if I weren't busy, I wouldn't go. Because if you go people mistake the reason. They don't think you go because you want to be with somebody you like. They think you go to help business."

Lucille admitted that she had made some attempt to coach him in his work. "Yes, I'm guilty of that. I heard him do his act one night at the Concord. One word bothered me. I didn't say anything for weeks. Then he did it again and I said, 'Guess I'll tell him about the one word he's dropping.'"

Gary said, "Criticism of that kind is like coming from the Queen. And it worked. I wasn't pronouncing one word clearly. When I corrected it, what was a snicker became a scream—"

Lucille cut him off. "It was just a set up for a joke," she noted.

Christmas, 1961, was a happy one for Lucille. She was rested and in good spirits, kidding and joking on the set of "The Happy Years" with Fonda, director Franklin Schaffner and producer Leland Hayward.

Gary's marriage to Lucille didn't hurt his career. For the first time, he was booked on the "Ed Sullivan Show."

"Poor Gary," remembers a friend. "Millions of 'Lucy' fans all over the country were horrified that she had remarried. They had all preferred to believe that Lucy and Desi's divorce was nothing more than a temporary separation. But now Gary was going to appear on national television and there'd be a huge audience sitting in judgment on the new man in Lucy's life. Boy, he had better be funny *and* attractive, both at the same time."

Gary was a pro, and he came off respectably. However, in the opinion of critics, he was "nothing out of the ordinary." Unfortunately, the public concurred and his career as a television comic was short lived.

But Lucy hadn't married him for his comic talents. She found in Gary exactly the qualities she had been looking for. "I didn't make the same marriage mistake twice," she repeated. "Gary digs what my life is. Why I have to work. We have tranquility. We want the same things, to take care of what we have."

About his hobbies, Lucy commented, "My husband is a clothes and car nut. [His cars included a Model T Ford, a Mercedes-Benz 300SL, an Astin Martin, a Rolls convertible.]

But it's a harmless vice. Better than booze or chasing women, right?" One didn't have to be an expert in psychology to conclude that Lucy had chosen Gary as the antithesis of Desi.

Naturally, when Gary married Lucy the major question was how he would get along with the children. "They didn't exactly welcome him with open arms at the beginning," notes a friend. But Gary understood and so did Lucy. "After all," Lucy later explained, "they were only seven or eight when this strange man showed up. Gary was a nice man, but he was no father figure, and my children weren't about to accept him without a battle. They'd seen *The Parent Trap*, the movie where Hayley Mills tries to get her parents back together after they separated. They thought that if they took me to see the film often enough, I'd get the idea. I must have sat through that picture five times! But I kept telling them that their daddy was happily married, and so was I. Eventually, mostly thanks to Gary's patience, it all worked out."

Later Lucy remarked, "I wouldn't even call it an adjustment. The children really dig him. Gary gives them the kind of discipline they have never had before, and they love it. I can be strict—for about sixty seconds. Then the children can wind me around their little fingers. You can depend on the person who disciplines you, because he is always the same way; he's dependable."

Gary and Lucy continued to pursue their individual careers. "We have no plans or even thoughts of working together," she said shortly after their marriage. "In the first place, he works in another area of show business—the supper clubs—and has not thought much about TV."

Even if Morton wanted to transfer to TV, it was felt by some observers that Lucy would be careful to keep their careers separate. But long-time Lucille watchers knew that she believed in nepotism. Her family had always been closely involved in her business activities. The feeling was that Lucille had the same plans for Gary. However, Gary's move into her professional life had to be gradual so no one would be embarrassed—especially Gary.

The special with Henry Fonda was broadcast in January and

Lucy was on the cover of *Life* with the caption: LUCY'S BACK ON TV.

She had a commitment for another film with Bob Hope, and the plans for the "Lucy Goes to Broadway" special were reactivated by Lucy and Desi.

Desi was still running Desilu as efficiently as ever. He wasn't as frantic and temperamental as he had been and he was on the wagon. He continued to be involved in controversies. The year before, he had had a fight with Frank Sinatra and Sinatra moved his film company off the Desilu lot, objecting to the portrayal of Italians as hoodlums on Desilu's long-running "The Untouchables."

Hedda Hopper said that Frank told Desi, "The boys don't like it." Desi didn't care what "the boys" liked or didn't like.

By the end of the year, however, Sinatra and Desi had reconciled. Frank said, "C'mon, Cuban, let's make up. I don't remember what we fought about." They contemplated several television ventures, but none materialized.

Instead of a special for Lucille, Desilu formulated a new series, "The Lucy Show," starring Lucy and Vivian Vance, even though Lucy had said she would never do another TV series. And Vivian had ostensibly left the business. During the Lucy-Desi specials, Vance had made a pilot for Desilu, which hadn't sold. She had divorced her first husband, Philip Ober, and had recently married John Dodds, a literary agent and editor (seven years younger than Vivian).

Viv was living in Connecticut, but Lucy convinced her to come back to Hollywood for the new series. One stipulation: Vance insisted the character's name in the series be "Viv." She had become nationally famous, but only as "Ethel Mertz." She was intent on having an identity of her own. Also, in the new series, she would wear tailored clothes and contemporary hairdos.

The new show would be produced by Desi, written by the old "Lucy" writers and filmed before a live audience at Desilu.

About the new series Lucy said, "I don't think I'd be doing

this if it hadn't been for Viv. The studio had the idea, and the offers were fabulous. But the thing that jelled it was Viv."

What would the series do to Ball's new marriage? "Nothing—I hope. Gary will work and I will work. We have our own careers. And Gary is adult about it. His work is mostly out of town. But he'll be home some of the time, too."

Before production started on "The Lucy Show," Lucy completed her new film with Bob Hope, *Critic's Choice*. Then she turned all her energies to the new TV show. She loved the character she was portraying and noted, "Even when my marriage to Desi was falling apart I never got tired of 'Lucy.'"

In announcing her return, James Aubrey, Jr., president of CBS, said: "We are delighted that after her record-breaking run in 'I Love Lucy' she has decided to return to 'active duty,' and we are certain that her millions of devoted fans will welcome her back with deep affection."

Looking back now, it seems ridiculous that the question then asked in the TV industry was, "With millions of dollars riding on the answer, can Lucy come back?"

Lever Brothers and General Foods were the new sponsors. Desi announced that the show would be adapted from a book, *Life Without George,* by Irene Kampen, an account of a divorcée's life in the suburbs.

Insiders predicted, however, that Lucille Ball would never be presented as a divorcée and they were right. The part was written with the Lucy character a widow with two children, a son and a daugher. Vivian Vance played a divorcée. Dick Martin, of the Rowan and Martin team (who, with "Laugh-In," would be Lucy's toughest competition in a few seasons), was cast as their bachelor neighbor.

When the series debuted in October, 1962, one critic noted: "Ever since her retirement, television comediennes have been competing for the crown of Lucille Ball. Last night, that contest was decided. Miss Ball herself is back."

Jack Gould, television critic for the *New York Times* wrote: "Lucille Ball is back in her first weekly series since 'I Love Lucy' and she is as remarkable a gal as ever. Put her in the wildest half-hour of improbability, the sort of far-fetched doings that so regularly trip up many TV notables, and she makes it all seem not only quite likely but diverting fun in the bargain."

About the situation of Lucy and Vivian being husbandless, Gould noted that the arrangement was "entirely incidental to the show's primary purpose, which was to provide a serviceable situation in which Lucy can display her zest and craftsmanship in broad clowning."

More important than critical acclaim were the ratings. Lucy's devoted fans hadn't deserted her.

When Lucy and Gary, married a year, came to New York, Lucy expressed how happy she was with her new husband. When Gary entered the room during one of Lucy's interviews, writer Kay Gardella observed, "Almost too politely, he took a seat opposite Lucy. His manner indicated he did not want to intrude. Frequently, he had to be prompted by his wife to talk.

" 'Tell Kay about your plans,' she directed."

Gardella noted, "Briefly and reluctantly, Morton mentioned two ventures: a plan for a golf center in California's San Fernando Valley and a production company to make offbeat short films for art theatres."

Gary, who had just finished an engagement at the Copacabana, told Miss Gardella that night clubs were dying. Kay observed, "He no sooner had said this than the phone rang. It was for Morton. After the conversation he turned to Lucy and said lightly: 'That was an offer for a job in Milwaukee.'

" 'Forget it,' replied the redhead with a wave of her hand. Morton did."

The new "Lucy" series was a success, but it was overshadowed the following month by a decision Lucy made. She and Desi had remained together professionally after their divorce, so many assumed that the business relationship would continue indefinitely. It was a surprise when Lucille bought him out, gained control of the company and assumed a new role—business tycoon. She bought Desi's shares of Desilu stock "at a price considerably in excess of the current market." The stock was selling in November for about seven and a half. The high for the year had been twelve, the low six and a half.

It was initially reported that Lucy paid Desi two and a half million dollars for the stock, but *Variety* later reported the figure was three million.

Although three million dollars was a lot of money, many in the industry felt Desi had sold out "cheap." Certainly Desi's share of the land, alone, was worth twice what Lucy had paid him. Westinghouse had sought to buy Desilu just a couple of years before this, and the fixed selling price was in the area of twenty million dollars.

"Desi wanted to get out," according to a former associate. "He had had enough of the pressures. He was sick of life being one continual emergency and felt that, if the time ever came when he wanted to build another empire, he would. He wanted to spend his time at other activities, like his thoroughbred breeding, golf, his Palm Springs hotel."

Another associate says that Desi had wanted out for some time, but didn't want to leave when the studio's fortunes were at a low ebb. Now that "The Lucy Show" was a hit, as well as "The Untouchables," things were supposedly in good shape financially. At the stockholders meeting in August, Desi had painted a rosy picture of the company's future prospects. The studio was running at eighty-seven per cent capacity, and Desilu's first feature film, *The Scarface Mob*, which was actually the first two one-hour segments of "The Untouchables," was ready for release. Desilu Sales, Inc., the company's syndication subsidiary, had passed $1,750,000 in sales.

At the time Desi sold out, the company was producing three series and nine other shows were being filmed at the studio.

Lucy succeeded Desi as president, but all other officers of the company remained the same: Edwin E. Holly was administration and finance vice president; Jerry Thorpe, programming vice president; W. Argyle Nelson, production and studio operations vice president.

Desi had hand-picked all the executives. He had a knack for perceiving executive ability.

Arnaz resigned as director of the company and as executive producer of "The Lucy Show." Lucy became the first woman in show business history to be president of a major production company and studio.

Although "I Love Lucy" reruns still appear throughout the world and new generations associate Lucille Ball and Desi Arnaz as husband and wife, Lucy's takeover of Desilu marked the final professional split between America's "most famous and beloved couple."

Since her days as an aspiring actress in Jamestown, Lucy had faced and overcome many problems. Now, at fifty-one, she was embarking on still another career.

At first almost no one outside the industry could visualize "Lucy, America's beloved scatterbrain," as a Hollywood tycoon. Supposedly, neither could she: "I never expected to be president, but Desilu was, in a way, our baby. It seemed only right that one of its parents should, after all this time, accept custody."

At this early juncture Lucy was modest about her new role. "The place was running nicely and had been for some time," she said. "I didn't have to jump in and worry."

Despite all her efforts to make light of her new position—"It's still all in the realm of comedy," she quipped—there was no doubt that it was no laughing matter and Lucy was firmly in charge. "She *was* the president," an associate remembers. "She ran the place."

She moved the president's office to her three-room dressing-room suite. Discussing the formal president's office in the administration building she noted dryly, "I've seen a total of eleven presidents in and out of that office. I wouldn't know how to behave in a place like that. I'd see a lot of ghosts. In fact I still refer to this place occasionally as RKO. I'm sure an analyst could find something Freudian there someplace."

Lucy contended that she would have been happy to continue

the business relationship with Desi, and she flatly denied that her marriage to Gary had been instrumental in breaking up the business partnership. She also insisted that Gary would not become an executive at Desilu.

Some believed that Desi's sellout had been triggered by the marriage situation. Others said that the "final straw" came when Lucy and Desi had a showdown over 'The Untouchables." Desi had announced a week before he sold out that he was "restoring violence" to the series, which was sagging in the ratings.

"We made one mistake this year, eliminating too much violence from 'The Untouchables,'" Desi had said. "The show has suffered by it. I'm going right back to the Mafia, the gangsters, the machine guns. I'm not going to let any senator talk me out of it." He was referring to the extended Senate investigation into violence on television.

Leonard Freeman, executive producer of the series, had already left Desilu because of "differences of opinion" and Lucy too was against continued violence in the series. However, the most talked-about reason for Desi's departure—and the one Lucille stressed—was his desire to be free from day-to-day responsibilities.

Her explanation of the details of buying out Desi was simple. "When we started this operation, Desi and I were in charge of it together. Our marriage was going well.... But we set it up so that if anything ever happened, if he wanted out or if I did, one could buy the other's stock. It was always that way. And even if we hadn't had trouble and broke up, he was planning to retire long before I was going to."

Lucille said that when she decided to go into her new TV series, Desi said, "If you're going to do that, how about buying me out now?" Lucy said, "Fine."

A friend remembers that during this period a note of pride crept into Lucy's voice when she spoke of Desi. She told friends she thought he would marry again soon.

Now that Lucy was on her own and "running things," it was inevitable that people would accuse her of "turning into a man."

Lucille Ball was saddled with the "boss lady" image.

A top director says: "The whole purpose of Lucy's career from this point on was to show Desi she didn't need him. She had gotten herself a new husband; her new TV show was a hit; and now she was out to prove that she could run the studio as well as Desi could."

"Listen, honey," Lucy herself told Rex Reed a few years later, "if I was going to turn into a man I would've done it a long time ago. I've been in awe of most men all my life.... Life takes guts. If you don't take chances, you'll never bathe because you might get dirty again; you'll never eat because you might get sick. So I took on all our responsibilities, but I ran my studio like I ran my home, with understanding for people."

Lucy claimed to Reed that she hadn't liked being a woman executive. "I hated it," she said. "I used to cry so much—and I'm not a crier—because I had to let someone go or make decisions I didn't understand. There were always two sides to every question and the trouble was I could see both sides." Lucy had her own "side" of the story about the Desilu buyout. "No one realizes how run-down Desilu was. The finks and sycophants making $70,000 a year, they were easy to clear out....

"I wanted to go to Switzerland with the kids, anywhere to run away, but Desi wanted out. Then I found out that for five years, our empire had taken a nose dive and if I wanted to get my money back, I had to rebuild it first. For the first time in my life, I was absolutely terrified—I'd never run any show or a big studio. When I came back from doing *Wildcat* I was so sick, so beat I just sat in that back yard, numb, for a year. I'd had pneumonia, mononucleosis, staph, osteomyelitis. Lost twenty-two pounds. Friends told me the best thing I could do physically, psychologically, was go back to work."

Naturally, there were many headaches to be faced as president. To begin with, Lucy was unhappy with the time slot for her new show, and there was some question whether she would renew for the upcoming 1963-64 season. As the trade was fond of noting, Lucille Ball was the only star who annually renewed the network, rather than vice versa.

This hesitation on Lucy's part to renew was the start of a yearly ritual which would continue for the next decade. "Lucy was using her own show as a wedge to try to sell some of Desilu's other products," explained an ex-network executive. However while her demands for herself and her "Lucy" show were always met, she was relatively unsuccessful in persuading CBS to buy other properties.

For the 1963-64 season, Desilu did manage to sell to CBS not only the "Lucy" show, but a new situation comedy, "Glynis," starring Glynis Johns. The studio also sold a one-hour weekly dramatic series, "The Greatest Show on Earth," starring Jack Palance, to ABC.

But there were a number of Desilu shows that hadn't sold. Lucy's greatest disappointment was the failure to sell a series starring Ethel Merman. Lucy later said that during the Aubrey regime at CBS, "I couldn't sell the new pilots. . . . I couldn't sell anything but me."

As Desilu's fiscal year ended in July 1963, the company wound up with a loss. Although income was up to over $21,000,000, the loss exceeded $650,000, for which special write-offs in the fiscal year were deemed responsible. The stockholders were not happy.

At the annual meeting, President Ball stressed that the write-offs were in line with the firm's "hard, conservative policy."

It was interesting to observe Lucille's "hard-as-nails" attitude when she was presiding as an executive versus Lucille Ball, actress. "Eventually," an associate says, "those two attitudes meshed into one."

Lucy's professional life for the next few years was concentrated on her show and coping with Desilu's corporate problems. She did double duty as president-actress and ran "a tight ship."

Lucy's personal life, of course, concentrated on her children and her new husband. After the takeover, although she was keeping the same rigorous work schedule, starting rehearsals on Monday and working through a late Thursday night shooting, her home life was considerably different than it had been with Desi. Gary was always within easy call.

Shortly after selling out to Lucy, Desi married again. His wife was forty-five-year-old socialite Edith Mack Hirsch, who had just received a Juarez divorce from her millionaire husband, sportsman Clement Hirsch. Hirsch, who had made his fortune in dog food, and "Edie" had been Lucy and Desi's Del Mar neighbors for years. They all shared an enthusiasm for horse racing.

Edie and Desi had been dating for several months. Lucy had even predicted to friends that marriage between them was likely, and she had described Edie as "a friend of ours for years. She's a real doll."

They were married on Desi's forty-sixth birthday at the Sands Hotel in Las Vegas. Only a few close friends were on hand, including the Jimmy Durantes and Van Johnson. Edie wore a "knockout" net lace cocktail dress. Margaret Durante was maid of honor, and Dr. Marcus Rabwin was Desi's best man. Edie was described as "a Lucy look-alike," with the same red-gold hair.

Lucy sent the couple a horseshoe-shaped floral display, with a note: "Congratulations on both of you picking a winner."

"Despite Lucy's happy façade, Desi's remarriage had its effect on her," speculates a close friend. "Sure, she had remarried first, and Lucy's relationship with Desi was a hundred per cent calmer and friendlier. But the guy had been the one big love of her life."

Though she tells friends today that she and Desi have a better relationship than they ever had before, she once frankly stated that since their divorce, "Neither Desi or I have been the same."

Lucy's working day left no time to dwell on the past. Decisions all day long; meetings, day-to-day production emergencies and just plain problems calling for a consultation with the president. Work. Work. Work. She was working harder than ever and that's the way she wanted it.

Lucy was trying to do her best for the children. At the time she said, "They attend Catholic school, in Beverly Hills, where they mingle with many other youngsters of celebrities." She claimed, "They are not singled out for preferential treatment."

Lucy had tried sending little Desi to a military academy.

190

"Actually, it was his idea," she said. "He had seen the uniforms and the band and the drums, but soon he had nightmares when he came home and, boy, I got him out of there fast. I didn't dig all those thirteen-year-old generals. And those disciplinary rules! Once he got a demerit for bending down to tie his shoelace when he wasn't supposed to."

An extremely bright boy, Desi, Jr. has summed it up. "My school years were chaotic. I went to seven different Catholic schools and a military academy before I settled down. I spent the second grade in New York. The real trouble started when we got back to California. I really wasn't cut out for the military academy—a point on which the people who ran it would agree— but I also found out when I went back to Catholic grade school that I wasn't cut out for that either."

Little Lucie, almost twelve, and Desi, Jr., almost ten, began making brief professional appearances on their mother's TV show. Lucy said, "This is something they have been asking about for the last three years...since they were really very tiny. The roles aren't much but they are a start and I don't see any reason to say, 'Oh, no, you can't,' because there are thousands of 'Why nots.'"

Richard Keith, who had portrayed "Little Ricky" through the Lucy-Desi specials, was now a regular on "The Andy Griffith Show," playing "Johnny Paul," best friend of "Opie" (Ron Howard), Griffith's television son. Keith was working, the Arnaz offspring could point out, why couldn't they?

Ball later said that she allowed her kids to perform at this point because she wanted them to see it was hard work which took concentration. She also hoped the experience would prove to Desi, Jr. that he didn't "know it all."

Late in 1963, Lucille Ball made her dramatic TV debut in a segment of Desilu's by-then-floundering "The Greatest Show on Earth." Titled "Lady in Limbo," it was broadcast before Christmas amidst much publicity hoopla. Lucy had finally appeared in "The Greatest Show on Earth," although it was not directed by De Mille.

She had only done it, of course, to bolster the show's failing rating. "It isn't the perfect dramatic spot for me," said Lucy honestly. "The ideal serious role will pop up sometime in the future."

The critics agreed. The show was panned. "She shouldn't have gone to the trouble," one critic noted. "She is much better at provoking yoks than putting on a long face for most of an hour, miscast as a lonely circus performer who falls for—and wins for adoption—a small, orphaned boy."

As renewal time for her own show rolled around, Lucy was supposedly entertaining notions of retirement. But this merely meant that the network had better give careful thought to Lucy's other wishes.

CBS wanted her to extend her show to an hour. Lucy repeated that she was not sure she would continue her series at all for the 1964-65 season. Associates said she felt she must devote more of her energies to Desilu, since the company hadn't sold any of its ten series pilots to the networks.

The firm had plowed a great deal of cash into development of new properties since Lucy had taken over, and insiders said she was shocked when none of the new shows were picked up. She was especially rooting for a Dwayne Hickman series, "Mr. Hannan and the Little People," about a grammar school teacher, and "The Hoofers," with Donald O'Connor and Soupy Sales as turn-of-the-century vaudevillians.

The O'Connor series had been Lucy's own idea, and she said, "Television needs a talent like Donald. For his versatile talents to be fully appreciated, he needs weekly exposure."

The networks didn't agree. And Lucy had been disappointed that "Glynis" had been dropped after its first thirteen weeks. "She's a great performer," said Lucy about Glynis Johns, "and it was a wonderful show. But if things aren't good, they start breathing down your neck and what are you going to do?"

Lucy noted that many hit series didn't start out as such and had to be given a chance to build an audience. "Listen, do you know how we all begged the sponsors to keep the 'Dick Van Dyke Show' on when it was just starting?"

The happy couple at a Hollywood
Press Photographers Costume Ball.

With beloved daughter Lucie.

Desi Arnaz, Jr.
and his adoring parents.

Lucy and Desi in their smash-hit big screen comedy, *The Long, Long Trailer* (1954).

The Mertzes, the Ricardos and Fred MacMurray in one of the hour-long Lucy-Desi specials.

Two legends, similarly
garbed.

"Lucy," solo.

On the set of *The Facts of Life*.
It was after the divorce from Desi.

With Hedda Hopper. The powerful columnist
was a big fan—and pal—of Lucy's.

With Jerry Lewis.

In the early seventies,
Desi Arnaz, Jr. announced
his intention to marry
Liza Minnelli. The
marriage never took place.

Desi, Jr. and the girl he married, actress Linda
Purl (her blond hair dyed brunette for a role).
The couple is now divorced.

Lucie with Marvin Hamlisch, composer of *They're Playing Our Song*. The vehicle brought Lucie Broadway stardom.

Brother and sister in the late seventies.

Lucie with Laurence
Luckinbill, her second
husband.

With husband Gary Morton and (left) Army
Archerd at the premiere of *Mame*. The film was
a major disappointment, but Lucy's marriage was
a big success.

With Gary, Vivian and her husband, John Dodd.
Vivian didn't want to do any more "Lucy's."

With one of her numerous
awards. "She is
happiest when working,"
observe her friends.

Lucy wired CBS President James Aubrey that "the rigors of a weekly half-hour program combined with the added task as president of Desilu made it impossible to do justice to both jobs," and that she felt she could be of "greater service" to Desilu by concentrating on her duties as president and only doing an occasional one-hour special. Aubrey remained calm, saying he was sorry to lose her weekly show but would "look forward" to her comedy specials.

However, the matter was far from closed.

Palm Springs was Lucy's usual getaway spot. To unwind after her grueling work week, she spent most weekends there with Gary and the kids.

Did the kids see much of Desi? "Their daddy has a house right down the road from ours, so they get to see him often," Lucy said. Did she visit Desi too? "Of course not—I have my own husband to look after," she replied. "I see Desi on business only. He still directs some TV episodes."

Although the children lived with Gary and Lucy, they spent many weekends and a lot of the summer with Desi. Lucy always said, "He'll never have any trouble getting the children any time he wants them."

There was a genuine affection and understanding between Lucy and Gary, but not the romantic spark there had been between Lucy and Desi. "With him, a home isn't just a place to change your clothes," Lucy observed about her new husband. "He loves every room. And I'm contented because someone is doing with me the things he likes to do, and I'm doing with someone what I like to do."

"Lucy can't run a company by herself," Gary later said. "Maybe with me around, when she walks on the set, her mind is at peace. I pop in from time to time, on conferences, rehearsals. I can tell from her if things are going well, if the *laughter* is there. She's a thoroughbred, very honest with me, a friend to whom I can talk about anything. She never leaves me out of her life; that's important for a man."

Morton acted with Lucy's children in amateur theatricals in

their garage theatre, and he played golf with little Desi. "In fact," recalls a friend, "he even played golf with *big* Desi, which everyone considered a fantastic display of unnecessarily civilized behavior."

The children were always referred to as "little Desi and little Lucie."

"It has always been little Lucie and big Lucy, never, God forbid, young Lucie and ....", a friend notes, rolling her eyes upward in mock horror.

How did big Lucy spend her rare free time? She had never been particularly sports-minded, but was mildly interested in golf and riding. "I think I might make a golfer," Lucy once said. "I want to have another go at that. Several years ago I took nine lessons. Then the instructor put me in a foursome with three other girls. On the fourth tee I hit my ball a powerful whack and it disappeared. I went home when I couldn't find it—didn't know you could use another ball. But I have a trophy from the last time I played. I'm a thirty handicap, a happy hacker. I love the game, but never had time for it.

"I'm best at riding. When I lived in the east years ago, I used to go on hunts. They used a little worn-out fox, but I never laid eyes on him. I went along for the steak breakfast.

"There's another sport with horses I'm interested in: I play long shots. Once at Del Mar I put two dollars on the daily double and it paid $1,300. I wasn't even at the track, just sent the money in."

While Lucy might venture a couple of dollars on a long shot at the races, her career was not something she would gamble with. "At the last minute," Lucy finally signed for another season with CBS. Insiders noted that Lucy had been prompt to reevaluate her situation when ABC dropped "The Greatest Show on Earth." Without "The Lucy Show," Desilu would have had no shows on the air at all.

James Aubrey announced, "Lucy has exercised a woman's prerogative and will be back on the CBS Television Network this fall." Her time slot for 1964 would be changed from 8:30 to 9 P.M.

It was felt that the new spot would improve her ratings, which had slipped from the top five to between ten and fifteen.

During the season Lucy reunited with pal Bob Hope for a special, "The Lucille Ball Comedy Hour." Jack Gould noted: "It was the counterpoint of Miss Ball's distinctive wackiness and Mr. Hope's handling of the throwaway lines that provided the needed stage chemistry to keep a viewer looking." He concluded, "There is nothing wrong with corn when it's professionally done."

As if Lucille's schedule wasn't already bulging, in the fall of 1964 the world's foremost tycoon-actress-wife-mother took on still another job. It was a radio interview program on CBS, with husband Gary producing and occasionally joining her on the air.

"CBS didn't have to twist my arm when it was suggested that I might want to take over the radio spot Garry Moore was vacating. I love radio. I did some radio work before television, but it was situation comedy stuff. I've never done this sort of thing before."

"Let's Talk to Lucy" would be a Monday-through-Friday morning talk program. "I'll find people wherever I can and we'll gab."

She would take a portable tape recorder along wherever she went—on the set or wherever she might meet celebrities to interview.

She had already taped interviews with Bing Crosby, Danny Kaye, Jack Benny, Dean Martin and his wife Jeanne, Red Skelton, Bob Hope, Agnes Moorehead and Hedda Hopper.

Describing the show's modus operandi: "It's not difficult, I have people do research. All I have to do is be near a tape recorder. It's just a matter of spending a half-hour with a friend of mine. The show will be heard ten minutes a day. My staff has to cut it down to broadcast time. I have no trouble talking. I'm usually interested in what I'm discussing. It's easy and it's fun."

Lucy enjoyed the show because, like most show people, she is starstruck. When Barbra Streisand was her guest, Lucy asked her how it felt to be only twenty-one, a big recording artist and star of the Broadway hit *Funny Girl.*

"Not much," replied Barbra.

"That cool really flustered Lucille," cousin Cleo remarked. "It violated everything she believes in. For Lucy nothing came easy."

About Streisand, Lucy recalled, "I didn't know one thing about her. She'd just moved into her New York apartment and I was completely in awe of her. I couldn't believe anyone twenty-one could have this feeling for songs or be so good. She came in from the kitchen with this compote with peaches in it, eating. I said, 'All right, honey, sit down. Could you get a little closer to the mike?' She didn't and I didn't dare ask her again. So finally I asked her a question and she nodded, she didn't answer. I cut and said, 'Barbra, this is radio.' She said, 'Okay.' And she moved in and there was the sound of her spooning the peaches."

By now, Oscar Katz, a former CBS program executive, had taken over "the major chores" at Desilu.

"All I have to do now is to attend directors' meetings, policy sessions and approve or disapprove potential programs," said Lucille.

Then the inevitable question: Will Lucy be back for another season with "The Lucy Show?" The inevitable answer: "I don't know. Two or three times, I didn't think I'd be back this season. I lost my long-time writers, the network suggested a one-hour weekly show, with which I'm not about to kill myself. I wanted to do a series of specials, which the network didn't want. So, here I am, back at the old stand. Who can tell about next season? All I know is that I'm not tired of working. I love it."

However, Vivian Vance *was* tired of working and announced that she wanted out. Viv was weary of commuting to the coast and wanted to stay home in Connecticut with her husband. She agreed to appear in some episodes for the third season but that would be the end.

At first Lucy thought she could persuade Vivian to change her mind. She even went to Connecticut to apply a little friendly pressure. But she later abandoned her efforts. "I didn't want to bother her after our initial crying spell—we cried ourselves out."

So Lucy lined up guest stars, including Ann Sothern and Joan Blondell. But she noted there would be no regulars—"Nobody can replace Vivian Vance."

Gale Gordon had already joined the series, and now his role would be beefed up to provide the inevitable straight man-reactor to Lucy's antics.

By now Jim Aubrey had been deposed as chief of CBS. Lucy was having her continuing problems with the networks. As always, she was finding it difficult to sell Desilu's products. One of the new pilots she was excited about was "My Son, the Doctor." Lucy noted, "Naively, I believed that if you had a good series you could sell it. I guess there's more to it than that."

She was still upset over the failure to sell the Donald O'Connor series and Ethel Merman's show. Lucy appreciated Merman's approach to her work, which was similar to her own. "That Merman, she's a trouper—somebody who gets to work with no fuss, no mess. Not somebody who gets temperamental like Jack Palance, and you can quote me."

Somehow Lucy found time to engage in a few civic and educational activities during the year. She was a guest lecturer at the tenth annual Sam Goldwyn Creative Writing Awards at UCLA.

Goldwyn himself was on hand. His relationship with Lucy had remained cordial through the years. Lucy sometimes referred to him as "the man who started the Ball rolling."

Before addressing the students she was checking her notes. A reporter asked, "Dr. Ball, where did you matriculate?"

"I never did that in my life," she said tongue-in-cheek.

"But where did you get your degree?"

"Oh. Well, I graduated from the Goldwyn Girl line."

"Let's see, that was Class of 19...?"

"We won't go into that."

Lucy commented to the audience, "You students are well protected here in this wonderful university where you get the best of instruction and advice. You are surrounded by love. But I know you must be worrying about what will happen to you when you go out in the world and there will be no one to guide you and look after you. I think it will help you if you will remember to recognize the small successes that you will have. Don't let the brightness of that big goal blind you to what happens on the way toward the goal. Meet one wave at a time and enjoy what progress you make. I want you please not to be taken up in the undertow of pessimism. Never lose your interest in people."

In the summer of 1964 Lucy and Gary went to New York. August 31 was declared "Lucy Day" at the World's Fair at Flushing Meadows. Crowds of screaming, camera-clicking fair-goers were on hand to welcome television's most popular star.

"I've never seen anything like this in my life," noted one of the burly police captains, surveying the crowds. "We've had a lot of public figures at the Fair, but Lucy pulled more people than any ten of them put together."

She arrived at 9:45 A.M. with two busloads of newsmen invited by CBS. Gary, her mother and Hedda Hopper accompanied her. Lucy started the day by putting her handprints in concrete at the Hollywood Pavilion. Hedda also put her handprints in, but first had to remove six rings.

The day was billed as an international salute, since Lucy's show was now seen in forty-four countries. None of the foreigners working at pavilions and exhibits seemed to have any trouble recognizing "the redhead."

Fair officials noted that Gary proved to be more than just an added attraction. "He gagged his way through many embarrassing pauses at the stops along the way and he was helpful in winning over other performers by joining in their song and dance routines."

In Los Angeles, Lucy and Margaret Hickey, public affairs editor of the *Ladies' Home Journal,* were honored by the Los Angeles chapter of Theta Sigma Phi. Lucy was given the "Woman in the News" award, and Miss Hickey the "Woman Behind the News" award.

Lucy also found time to give advice to kids who wanted to break into show business. "I get fifty to sixty letters a week from these kids around the country, and a hundred or more show up every week at the Desilu studio gate," Lucy said. "Most of them have no experience, no hobbies. They don't excel in anything, yet they all want to know how to become a star. They never ask, 'What should I learn?'

"None of these kids would be dumb enough to sign up to be house builders or secretaries without first getting some experience. But they come to Hollywood with no agent, and no chance of getting into the Screen Actors Guild, and no idea of what they can really do. I had one tell me that she wanted to belong to the 'Star Guild,' whatever that is.

"After they sit on a stool at Schwab's Drug Store, and some of them grow old there while claiming to be out-of-work actors, then they begin running with a pack in this town. What happens to a lot of them after that I don't even want to talk about.

"If I do get time to talk to any of these kids, I tell them that show business in Buffalo is the same as here, and they should stay put in their schools or workshops or little theaters and learn all they can. I don't think they believe show business is the same in Buffalo, but it's true."

She felt that the increasing number of "fame seekers" in town was due to the quick and freaky success of teen-age stars like The Beatles.

Oddly enough, in a short time, her own son would enjoy a similar "freaky success."

No matter how busy Lucy became, she tried to keep communications open between her children and herself while at the same time keeping close reins on them. "We *touch* in our house," she noted. "I come home dead-tired, and if I feel my kids stiffen, I say, 'Honey, don't stiffen up. Momma needs you tonight. There's so little time. Let's take advantage of the kisses and hugs while we have them.'"

"I'm observing, watching to see how much of my philosophy

of life has rubbed off on them," she remarked on another occasion.

Desi, Jr. was a dynamo and there was no holding him back. His sister has laughingly remarked, "Desi's been thirty-four since we were kids!"

The boy was having problems in Catholic school. He later noted, "I was overweight and confused about the Catholic faith—which even then was difficult for me to accept—and so I made up for all my insecurities by being the class clown. Only the school people didn't think I was very funny. I did things like writing a paper on religion using all the dirty words I could think of and sneaking a snare drum into a concert and tangling repeatedly with the priests and nuns over points of theology that didn't make sense to me."

When he was twelve years old, Desi, Jr., with his pals, Dino Martin, thirteen-year-old son of Dean Martin, and Billy Hinsche, fourteen-year-old son of a business executive, formed a trio: Dino, Desi and Billy. It wasn't difficult to start this ball rolling. The trio gained invaluable experience performing as part of "The Lucy Show's" warm-ups. Billy's father, Otto, handled their business affairs. Dino's father's friend, Frank Sinatra, gave the kids a recording contract and the group was on its way.

Today the musical group is totally forgotten, but at the time the trio enjoyed a more than modest celebrity with the teenyboppers.

Dino (now known as Dean Paul Martin) has recently spoken of those days and the group's brief but incredible success. According to Martin, Desi loved the adulation of the fans and would often endanger the lives of the trio at a concert by announcing the group's departure.

"You have to understand that the big thing in those days was the escape. That was the most important part of a concert, not the music. I'm *serious:* it was scary, especially every damn time Desi made that announcement."

Discussing a sold-out concert in Milwaukee in the mid-sixties, Martin recalled, "Before the show, I said, 'Desi, *don't* do it tonight.' We finished the next-to-last song. I could see him mentally battling with it, and finally he leapt up and yelled, 'Thank you, this is gonna be our last song, we love you!'"

Martin continues, "Just then, I saw the perimeter fence start to fold down. I threw my guitar down and started running from second base to the helicopter. Billy was running, 50,000 people were running behind us, and Desi started hyperventilating. He was only thirteen years old, with a fat little round face, no neck and a fat little snowman body. Plus, for forty minutes, he'd been beating the drums hard. *Plus,* he knew he really screwed up and I was probably gonna beat the shit out of him for it.

"He was running, and all of a sudden I saw his eyes roll back. It was one of the most dramatic moments of my life. Desi fell to his knees and yelled, 'Go ahead without me! I don't deserve to be saved!' We stopped, scooped him up and threw him in the helicopter; he hit his head and blacked out."

Scenes such as this made life for the youngsters a surreal experience. For, as Martin recalls, "We'd do shows like that on Sunday, and then on Monday we'd go back to school and the nuns would say, 'Where's your homework?'"

The trio was, momentarily, in the big time. Lucy later noted, "I wanted to get Dino, Desi and Billy on my show and waited for a good script. By the time it came along, I couldn't afford them. They had four big hits." She could only afford to pay them $400; the boys had made their TV debut on "Hollywood Palace"; they received $4000 for an appearance on Dean Martin's show. They also appeared on Ed Sullivan's show, earning considerably more than the "Lucy" show budget would allow. In addition, the group also made money from its own music publishing company, which was managed by William Howard, son of Dorothy Lamour and Bill Howard.

Desi's quick success concerned Lucille. And with good reason. The boy had started drinking. The freedom that he had while traveling with the band provided an atmosphere where he was not, despite what his mother thought, under close supervision.

The breakup of his parents' marriage had affected him more

deeply than anyone at the time would admit. Desi, Jr. felt that though the outside world thought he had "everything," he knew that those material advantages meant nothing because they hadn't been sufficient to save his parents' marriage.

Of course Lucy was thrilled that the public loved her son as a performer. "No mother could be more concerned with her kids being happy and succeeding in life than Lucy," stated a friend. "But she was annoyed, too, because the kid didn't have to *earn* the rewards. There had been no struggle at all. Just as she had been flabbergasted by Streisand's nonchalance about 'making it,' she didn't want to see the same thing happen to Desi."

Although a trifle pudgy during his early teens, Desi was proving to be the image of his father. In more ways than one, Lucy knew she was in for a few headaches. She said about the musical group, "they got all this adulation—this uncalled-for adulation—with the little girls screaming, and it's very hard when they come back home for us to get them back to normal."

She thought she would be able to do it "by sticking to the rules. Telling him he's not going out during school months, no matter how big a hit he was with his group when he was out on the road." She meant it.

It was obvious that her children would have show business careers. "Nothing can stop Desi, Jr.," Lucy said. "I can't imagine him not making it from the way he acts. He's become a really great drummer. He plays the organ, the piano, the vibes. Lucie is a fine little actress, and she'll have a big career if that's what she wants to do."

As contract time for Lucy rolled around once again, it was no secret that whether or not she would renew would be determined by how well Desilu did in selling five new series pilots.

The studio had come up with several interesting shows. In addition to "My Son, the Doctor," Oscar Katz announced that CBS was considering a comedy, "My Lucky Penny," starring Brenda Vaccaro, Richard Benjamin, Joel Gray and Luana Anders. It was about two wives putting their husbands through dental school.

Desilu had also had ABC interested in "Frank Merriwell," a series based on the famous turn-of-the-century dime novels. The show featured Beau Bridges and Tisha Sterling, daughter of Ann Sothern. Two other Desilu properties were: "The Good Old Days," starring Darryl Hickman, and "Star Trek," starring Jeff Hunter and Peter Duryea, son of Dan Duryea.

None of the series sold. Lucille re-signed with CBS.

One aspect of being president of Desilu which Lucille didn't relish was the annual stockholders meeting. "Lucy didn't like being responsible to other people and having to explain her every business decision," an associate recalls. But since Desilu was a public company, she had no choice, and she no longer had Desi to "handle things" at these meetings.

Many times during business meetings Lucy would turn controls over to Milton A. "Mickey" Rudin, her whip-sharp attorney. Lucy, used to having people depend on her, depended heavily on Rudin for business advice.

One of the problems she faced from many Desilu stockholders was that they had thought of Lucille Ball and Desi Arnaz as a one-unit institution, and those investors who had bought stock in Desilu on the basis of faith in the two stars no longer had that faith to fall back on. They respected Lucille, of course, but the directors of the company were merely businessmen and since Desi's departure stockholders began to take a keener interest in how their money was being spent.

There was quite a furor at the annual Desilu meeting in August, 1965, held at the little theater on the lot. John Gilbert, a man who owned one hundred shares of stock and was described as "a person who makes a profession of attending stockholders' meetings and asking pointed questions," charged that Lucy's income—close to $500,000 a year—was equal to the loss the company sustained. He referred to the fact that the year's net profit of $455,000 was a drop from the almost $800,000 profit of the previous fiscal year. Gilbert and other shareholders were also upset that the stock had dropped from a high of twenty-nine to seven. They also noted that one director of Desilu did not even own any stock. And many protested the firm's no-dividend policy.

Gilbert was vehement, and several times his shouts interrupted the meeting. An attempt was made to rule him out of order, but he continued to toss charges at the company's management. Lucy had been conducting the meeting, but Mickey Rudin took over in her behalf. Rudin, who was also a company director and Desilu's chief counsel, ordered John Reeves, Desilu's chief of security, to toss Gilbert out.

Reeves and Gilbert struggled. Gilbert's glasses were knocked to the floor. The two men fell into the aisle and began wrestling. Lucy began shouting: "Leave him alone. Let him go back to his seat."

Gilbert was released and sat down.

But by now the mêlée involved most of the close to one hundred stockholders present. Lucy's flaming temper rose a number of times as she "stared knives" at Gilbert through most of the meeting. At one point she noted, "I've read about him. He's all that they say."

"Thank you," Gilbert retorted.

In defense of Lucy, Rudin noted that she was paid as both president of the company and as an entertainer, "and she is about two hundred per cent underpaid" in relation to other stars.

The main argument was about the lack of dividends. Lucille read from a written statement: "Use of cash for corporate purposes is needed. Directors have decided it is in the best interests of the company not to pay dividends. Our money is being used to support the company."

At one point the debate became so heated that one stockholder suggested a short recess so that things could "cool off." The recess was declared. Lucy huddled on stage with her aides and Gilbert remained in the audience surrounded by his "supporters." Lucy cracked: "Mr. Gilbert, do you mind if I go to the ladies' room?" He graciously gave his permission and Lucy stormed out.

When the meeting was called to order, the bickering increased. The directors sat staring at the ceiling, becoming more
red faced. Lucy chain-smoked and took some aspirin. "Bufferin
and water on the house," she called.

When one stockholder suggested that company officers take
only a dollar a year with their salaries going for dividends, Lucy
snapped: "How long could I keep these valued advisers at a
dollar a year? This isn't war—it's the TV business."

Gilbert had the last word. He summed up the meeting: "This
has been a real show. Too bad it wasn't on television. It might
have increased our revenues."

Several minority stockholders proceeded to file suit against
Desilu, charging that Lucy's compensation had been excessive
during the last three fiscal years. The suit charged that in 1962,
before Lucy took over the majority of stock, she received
$175,000 a year. Since then she received $375,000 in 1963,
$735,000 in 1964 and $490,000 in 1965. The suit said that from
the moment she bought out her husband, she had "engaged in a
plan and scheme to use her control and dominance over the
corporation to obtain for herself excessive and illegal compensation." The stockholders also maintained that Lucy had only been
rendering part-time service to Desilu.

The company replied that Lucy had been paid $100,000 per
year for services as president, and $390,000 for services as an
actress, with sixty-seven per cent of the latter sum to be deferred
for payment in later years. But Desilu would retain total residual
rights of the new "Lucy" show, and Lucy would not share in any
residuals. Thus, the company explained, her huge salary was not
only justified but a bargain, since they had already secured
substantial minimum guarantees for reruns of the show.

In the fall of 1965 President Lucy authoritatively declared: "I
don't like the way television programming is going. There is too
much sameness, too much repeating of the old formulas. There
is no real exploring of new avenues for entertainment." This from
the woman who was in the thirteenth year of portraying
essentially the same character.

She voiced concern over the networks' scheduling more movies during prime time hours. "It seems to me that the networks are abandoning their duty to create new entertainment for television. They are making of TV little more than a second-run movie house."

For the 1965-66 season the "Lucy" locale was changed from Connecticut to California. Gale Gordon, Lucy's talented second banana who portrayed her cantakerous banker-boss, remained in strong support. Her TV daughter was all but written out of the script, and her TV son would appear in only a few shows.

With the absence of Vivian Vance other guest stars were used, including Milton Berle, Danny Thomas, Mickey Rooney and Art Linkletter. Bill Frawley even made a brief guest appearance on one episode. (Frawley, who was now a regular on the Fred MacMurray series, "My Three Sons," died suddenly in March, 1966. Desi took out a full-page ad in the trade papers as a farewell to his friend.)

That winter, Lucy announced she was quitting. She agreed to do two specials the following year, but wanted to drop the series. "I have things I want to do—specials and pictures." CBS programming chief Mike Dann commented: "CBS is certainly not happy about Miss Ball's decision." Industry gossip said this time Lucille wasn't bluffing. They based this prediction on the fact that she hadn't asked for anything.

But it seemed to others like a different version of the annual renewal ceremony. Lucy could parry like the best politician: "When it comes time for me next season, I'll ask myself again about doing a weekly series. I don't know what my answer will be. How long do I want to be bitten? But I'll tell you this: I'm not retiring. I have no intention of retiring."

Lucy had obviously tired of the annual allegations that she "held up the networks" to take Desilu's products. "No matter what the impressions may have been," she said, "I don't play games about the series. Look, I am a company woman—not just mine. I belong to CBS. I reserve my opinion for what's best for my company and CBS."

The network still needed her and Desilu signed a spectacular $12,000,000 deal with CBS in 1966. The package involved a renewal of "The Lucy Show"; two one-hour Lucille Ball specials; and the purchase by CBS of reruns of "The Lucy Show," to be used as a daytime network strip (one a day) when the show ended its prime-time run.

Each new "Lucy" show was budgeted at $90,000. CBS agreed to put up $600,000 for development of pilots by Desilu Studios. In addition, part of the pact included Desilu supplying summer replacements for "The Lucy Show" in 1966 and 1967. The trade noted that Desilu's unsold pilots were the most likely replacements.

In the spring, Lucy went to London to film a special, "Lucy in London," with guest stars Anthony Newley and the then red-hot Dave Clark Five. Discussing the special, Lucy said, "I've been around for fifteen years. I find getting out to new places is invigorating. My mind seems to work a little easier. I could think of lots of things to do for TV in different places."

The show, broadcast that October, was "not Lucy's finest hour," according to critic Jack Gould, but he noted "that she may have hit upon an engaging innovation." He referred to the use of gifted writers, directors and cameramen of British and European television. "It could lead to television that might be fresh and different," Gould concluded. It didn't.

Lucy was suffering from a slight case of laryngitis and was "saving her voice" so Mickey Rudin chaired Desilu's 1966 annual stockholders' meeting. Although revenues had slipped slightly to $18,897,000, the profit went up from $455,000 to $735,000. The ruckus at the last annual meeting obviously had figured in corporate thinking since the company declared a five per cent stock dividend on its common and class B common stock. It was the first dividend of any kind that Desilu had paid since 1961 and its initial stock dividend.

Lucille Ball and "The Lucy Show" were still the company's principal assets, although it was producing two other shows for the season and renting its facilities to other companies.

Desilu had sold 132 reruns of Lucy shows to CBS for a minimum of $6,600,000. Lucy's salary, though considerably reduced to $75,000 as president and $156,000 as an actress, again drew complaints from the stockholders.

John Gilbert was at the meeting again and proposed a resolution that would limit Lucille's salary to $90,000 in any year in which the company paid no dividends. Naturally, the resolution was defeated. Desilu contended that Lucille was underpaid and that other studios would pay far more for her services and talents.

Desilu had been buying its own stock and had acquired 136,569 shares during the fiscal year. Rudin told stockholders that the company treasury had more than 200,000 shares and Desilu would consider acquisition or merger through a stock swap only. He noted, "I should also explain the possibility that other companies may want to purchase the Desilu stock, but no discussions have been held." He added that Lucille Ball wouldn't sell her shares unless the same offer was made to all shareholders.

Was Lucy planning to sell Desilu, now that it seemed the company was rolling at last? For the new season, in addition to "The Lucy Show," the studio had sold "Mission: Impossible" to CBS. "Star Trek," which had failed to sell the year before, had been reworked and reshot with different stars, William Shatner and Leonard Nimoy, and Desilu sold it to NBC.

Lucy was furious with gossip that CBS had bought "Mission: Impossible" in order to persuade Lucy to sign. She claimed that the series had been purchased by CBS long before any agreement was reached with her. Desilu again stated they never at any time demanded that CBS buy a Desilu series as part of a price for Lucy's renewal.

Interestingly, "Mission: Impossible" did not fare well in the ratings initially. But it was "kept on the air" and later proved to be an enormous success, Desilu's most successful dramatic series since "The Untouchables."

Lucy's pressures at work were increasing. When Desi was running the company Desilu had been hailed as being responsible for more film production than several major motion picture studios combined. Now the stature and prestige of the company had slipped despite the sale of the two new shows.

Early in 1967, Gulf and Western Industries, which had acquired Paramount Pictures the previous year, made Lucy an offer for Desilu that they were hoping she couldn't refuse. The deal was in the neighborhood of $17,000,000 in stock. Lucy's share would be over $10,000,000, since she owned sixty per cent of Desilu stock.

At first, it wasn't easy to convince Lucille to sell, even though Mickey Rudin and others kept warning her that the day of the independent TV producer was drawing to a close. "You can't face the networks and buck the major studios alone," they had advised her.

Hollywood was in transition and although Lucy didn't want her people swallowed up by a conglomerate, "She could see the handwriting on the wall and Lucy was never one to miss the bus."

In February, while the Gulf and Western deal was pending, Lucille "fled" to Miami to try to talk Jackie Gleason into co-starring with her in a film about Lillian Russell and Diamond Jim Brady.

Rudin tried desperately to reach her by phone to get her to make a decision on the sale. The deal was being arranged so that Lucy would receive a substantial capital gain. It would relieve her of the headache of being Madame President. But on the other hand, part of her liked playing that role.

She was afraid of a corporate takeover. Desilu was one of the more pleasant and casual lots in town. She could be outspoken—she didn't think the creative end of the business should be left in the hands of people who sold cheese.

Rudin couldn't reach her by phone so he flew to Florida. Lucy has described ensuing events. "Everybody had heard about the merger. Panic! Still, I couldn't make up my mind. Mickey came down. He had to have an answer, he said. Twenty-four hours or we blow the deal!

"Well, we went over the whole thing again and I started to cry.

'I need an hour,' I told him, 'I've gotta have an hour.' More thinking. I said to him, 'Do you know, Mickey, I haven't even seen this man?'" She was referring to high-powered Gulf and Western boss, Charles Bludhorn.

" 'Now Lucy,' Rudin said, 'I've told you about him. Will you talk to him on the phone?'

" 'No,' I said, 'I like to see a man's eyes, shake his hand.'

"Well, I talked to him anyway and do you know what he said? He said, 'Miss Ball, one of the things I am prepared to like about you is that you care.' I cried again. Then I said yes."

At the time of the takeover, Desilu stock was trading at about fourteen and a half. Bludhorn announced that Desilu Productions would continue as a separate corporate entity and Lucy would remain as president of the subsidiary.

Bludhorn said, "Miss Ball is one of the greatest artists of our time. We are glad to welcome her to the Gulf and Western team. We look forward to a fine association with her."

When the shareholders, who always made Lucy a little uneasy anyway, voted overwhelmingly for the merger, it seemed she had made the right decision.

Observers noted that for Lucy, who was still paying off the almost $3,000,000 she had paid Desi, the $10,000,000 loomed large.

The merger clearly left her free to concentrate on acting activities. Hollywood insiders said part of the deal was a commitment from Paramount to star Lucy in one or two films each year, if she wanted to do them.

Lucy later met Charlie Bludhorn, but not until after the deal had been consummated. One afternoon, when he was at Paramount, the Austrian-born businessman-turned-movie mogul walked over to the Desilu lot.

Lucy got a charge out of the story that Bludhorn and his aides had a tough time getting into Desilu. A skeptical studio cop at first wouldn't let his new boss, whom he didn't know, through the studio gate.

About Bludhorn, Lucy said: "He travels fast, talks fast and acts on impulse. I just hope he stays alive."

With benefit of hindsight, it seems that Lucy sold Desilu at the wrong time. After years of not being able to sell pilots or hit with a successful show other than "Lucy," the year of the takeover Desilu had two hits: "Mission: Impossible" and "Star Trek," with a third subsequent winner, "Mannix," in preparation.

Lucy was committed for one more season of "The Lucy Show." But now she was at least free of her corporate headaches. Her tycoon days were over and she could focus in once again on her career as an actress. To the surprise of many, perhaps even herself, Lucille Ball would soon be the star of a hit movie.

15

"The Beardsley Story" was a script which had been lying around Desilu for years. The Beardsleys are a real-life family from Northern California. Helen North, a widowed Navy nurse with eight children, met and married Navy lieutenant Frank Beardsley, a widower with ten children. The Beardsleys then proceeded to have more children of their own. The family had been written up in *Life* and Lucy, impressed, had bought the film rights.

Now Paramount would make the film, under the title *Yours, Mine and Ours*. Melville Shavelson was signed to direct. He recalls, "At the time I was called to do *Yours, Mine and Ours* no one really wanted to do a picture with Lucy. That's the reason it hadn't been made up to that time." Shavelson was referring to the fact that *Critic's Choice* had been a dud, "and Lucy's box-office in movies was considered zero, even though she was one of the top TV favorites."

It was no secret that Lucille Ball would be difficult to direct in a film, since for the last dozen years she had, in effect, been directing herself and everyone else. Shavelson noted at the time, "On her television show she runs everything and she likes that. And she doesn't want to do it any other way; she doesn't want to play second fiddle to anyone."

There were script problems from the beginning. Shavelson remembers, "When I came into the project Lucy had owned the story for years and they had about five screenplays. *All* of the screenplays were similar to the Lucy television show. They were farcical comedy shows with Lucy and seventeen kids. Well, that's a joke, not reality, and I said, 'Well, somebody really lived this life. Somebody better go talk to these people and find out how it happened.'

"They turned out to be very intelligent people, their reasoning and everything else made sense. And a great deal of material that was in the picture I got from the Beardsleys themselves. None of it had ever appeared in any script at all because nobody was interested in what the reality of the situation was."

Shavelson's main concern was that Lucille Ball had typed herself as the "Lucy" character and didn't feel confident playing any other character, especially after *Critic's Choice*. The public wanted her as "Lucy" and she knew it, "so if you give the public something fresh or different, you run a big, big gamble," notes Shavelson.

When he started on the film, Lucy had him test her own children for parts. "I could've used Desi," notes Shavelson, "he has quality and ability. But I didn't use him because he was making more money with his group than I could afford to pay. Besides, I felt that if one of the kids in the movie was her real child it might subconsciously disturb the audience."

Shavelson didn't want to use little Lucie. "The girl was pudgy and had baby fat. She didn't look too good at the time and didn't make a good test. I told Lucy I was rejecting her. I thought it would be a big struggle, but Lucille said, 'Okay.'"

Henry Fonda was signed to co-star, but not without an

argument. Shavelson recollects, "Fonda was near the bottom of a career and he didn't want to make the movie. I spent a whole day talking him into his role. Fonda has always been one of my favorite actors.

"'Please, nobody's going to believe me as a lieutenant,' Fonda said.

"So we made him a warrant officer," notes Shavelson.

Shavelson licked the problem of writing the Helen North character for Lucy realistically while retaining certain aspects of the comedy the public expected from Lucille Ball.

In the final script, the role was not typically "Lucy." "We knew she had to be a specific person and come alive as that person in order to make this picture work, because the film was about real people," states Shavelson. "Had it been Lucy playing 'Lucy,' the film would have had a certain audience, but it would have been fairly limited."

Shavelson had his hands full with Lucy. On one typical occasion on the set she commanded, *"Cut.* Let's do it again. There's a shadow on Hank's chin. Mel, move that light three inches to the left. Now stay where you are, Hank." ("She's the same girl she was at MGM," beamed co-star Van Johnson, observing her.)

She never hesitated to voice her opinions about how scenes should be shot, where things should go and on numerous other aspects of production, in front of the crew. "This undermines a director's relationship with the crew," remarked a director who has "been through it" with Lucy.

But, Mel Shavelson understood Lucy. According to him, "The biggest scene in the picture is where Lucy had to be drunk and crying and laughing at the same time. I felt it was a key scene in the picture. I had written the scene for Lucy and I knew she was capable of it. She felt she wasn't, and when it came time to do the scene she refused to do it. She wanted to change it to either one way or the other. I insisted that she go through with it and she finally did. It was tough, but she did a great job. I don't know anybody else who could have carried off both of those emotions at the same time. It's that mixture of the tragic and the comic simultaneously. Only a comedienne can do that, because a comedienne can play legitimate. But it's extremely hard for a legitimate actor to play comedy successfully."

The scene, in which Beardsley's children get their prospective stepmother drunk, was the highlight of the film.

During shooting of the movie, Lucy gave innumerable interviews. "You always got the feeling that she regarded the interviews as a chore," recalls an associate. "But as the star and co-producer she knew she owed it to the picture to help publicize it. It really was a chore, too, considering that under that 102-degree heat it was a real problem to preserve her heavy movie make-up."

She was continuing as president of Desilu until April of 1968. Lucy said she turned down offers more lucrative than Bludhorn's and noted, "I'd been assured that Mr. Bludhorn had no intention of razing Paramount."

She also said, "I sold everything to them because they want to propagate the species. Others just wanted the property, I suspect, to bulldoze everything and get into real estate."

Yours, Mine and Ours was an unexpected super-hit. It grossed over $17,000,000, and was the biggest box-office winner that Lucy has ever made. And she was furious about it. Mel Shavelson contends, "Lucy could never forgive me for not warning her in advance that this was going to be such a successful picture." She hadn't provided a tax shelter for her profits. Her share as an actress ran to over $2,000,000, but she didn't keep much of it.

In addition, Desilu's share went to the new Desilu owners, Gulf and Western. The conglomerate made millions they hadn't counted on from *Yours, Mine and Ours*, paying them back a considerable percentage of their total cost for Desilu.

Lucy's exclusive contract with CBS would run until 1970. "The Lucy Show" was under the Paramount TV banner for the 1967-68 season. Gary Morton took over as executive producer, a move that had been expected for years.

"Anyone married to me has an uphill climb," Lucy noted.

"Gary and I coped by anticipating. We knew we shouldn't be separated eight, nine months a year, so he tapered off his act, found other things to do—making investments, building things. He plays the golf circuit, Palm Springs, Pebble Beach. . . .

"He didn't come into the business for six years. I didn't want to put him in a position in which he would be ridiculed. I could tell that he was grasping things—casting, story line. I said, 'You've been a big help to me. You should be paid for it.'"

Cleo became producer of the show. Lucy said, "I have been after Cleo for five years to take this job because she is so good at it." And she added, "Cleo thought a long time before becoming producer, wondering if it wasn't overdoing family. 'Nobody seems to be suffering from it,' I told her."

Lucy liked to keep the program a close family operation. "Unlike a lot of comedy stars, Lucy is not gregarious," an associate explains. "It takes time to become one of Lucy's friends, but when the barrier is crossed you're a friend for life."

Audience warm-ups for the show were a family affair as well. Gary would do comedy bits, introduce Lucille's loyal and durable mother, who had missed only one or two of the "Lucy" shows filmed to date, and he would then introduce Cleo, who by this time had divorced Ken Morgan and married *Los Angeles Times* television critic Cecil Smith. Even Smith appeared on a couple of Lucy shows.

Lucie Arnaz (who had also appeared in a half-dozen episodes) was attending Immaculate Heart High School in Los Angeles. Desi, Jr. was at La Jolla High and later switched to Beverly Hills High. He wasn't a good student. Lucy, at the time, said, "When he brought home two D's, he was grounded a month for each. We pulled all the plugs out of the wall. There's nothing in Desi's room that can't be unplugged, and I go up and unplug. I worked so hard the first time I was exhausted and had to go to bed."

She also noted, "He couldn't have friends in and he couldn't go out. He knew we meant it."

Lucy pointed out that sending the kids to their rooms without unplugging was not punishment, since they had TV, stereo, tape recorder, *et al.* About young Lucie, Lucy remarked that she got B's, and occasionally an A, "which indicates she's a talented girl. But she's just getting along in her studies."

The truth of the matter was that Lucie Arnaz had become infatuated, at fifteen, with a young man several years older than she. Although her mother tried to persuade her to date others, the girl insisted that she would wait for Phil. For public consumption, the story was that at *sixteen,* Lucie had met Phil Vandervort Menegaux on the set of a TV show. She told a friend that when he drove her home and dropped her off, he said, "So long. See you in five years." She knew he meant it, so she called the TV station, got his telephone number and tracked him down. They started dating.

At first her parents were concerned, because Vandervort was much older than Lucie—he was twenty-two. Even though she was dating, Lucie still "stuck close to home." Lucille has told of the time when her family wanted to screen some films at home. "So up went the paintings and on came *Thunderball.* Five adults and a few kids sitting around. Well, the blood is spurting, the bullets are flying, the sharks are biting, and then this 007 guy climbs into bed with this dame and I yelled 'Stop the film! What the hell kind of picture is this?' My daughter, who is sixteen now and in the middle of a big romance, said, 'Oh Mother, my God— we've seen it three times!' So I showed *Blow-Up,* that awful Italian thing. Well, that was worse. I said, 'I have had it, get me a western.' And so help me they're in the fort, see, with the Indians coming through the gate, and I'll be damned if the girl doesn't make the sign of the cross, rip her clothes off and climb on top of this cowboy—Rod Taylor or somebody—and they're crawling all over each other in bed like there's no tomorrow! Ugh! Everybody's taking their clothes off but me. You'll never catch me in the buff, kiddo."

Appearances were all-important to Lucille Ball. She felt she was bringing up her kids the way she had run her life. In a no-nonsense fashion. The children were well-liked in Hollywood circles and they had the reputation for being well-behaved. But underlying problems hadn't yet surfaced.

Though Desi, Sr. was now mostly out of the public eye, he made a few headlines in the late 1960s which seemed to support stories that he was still a hot-headed, temperamental Latin.

There was the time when he was annoyed by beach bums in front of his Del Mar home. He attempted to scare them away by "shooting blanks at them." Desi called the sheriff, but it was he who was arrested, not the beach bums.

Desi later explained that he was in his bathrobe, preparing to eat dinner at about 9 P.M. when nine youths started a ruckus in front of his house. Little Lucie and a girl friend were visiting, and Desi said that he went out to try to talk to the "beach bums" creating the disturbance. "All they did was to holler and cuss at me. I put a .38 revolver in my bathrobe pocket, loaded with blanks. I thought I could scare them by shooting into the sand at my own feet. I fired two shots. The shots didn't even faze them. They just hollered and cussed more, even louder. Then I went into the house and called the sheriff myself. I was sitting on my front porch when the sheriff's car drove up."

According to Desi, when he said "Thank God you're here!" the deputies said: "You're under arrest."

The deputies later reported that Desi had approached a parked car and told the young men in it, "I've got a .38 and I'll shoot your tires and car."

Then he fired one shot past one of the boys and another at his feet. One of the sheriff's deputies said, "Arnaz apparently thought the boys were on his property and wanted to scare them off." He noted, "The car was on public property."

The gun had been a present to Desi from the cast of "The Untouchables," and he commented: "I have never aimed a gun at anybody in my life."

Desi was freed on $1,000 bail and later released.

Another publicized incident concerned a multi-million dollar suit against Desi, pending in the courts for several years, which was finally settled. The suit involved one Jack Young, a former maintenance man at the Thunderbird Club in Palm Springs, and his wife. They sued Desi for the staggering sum or $34,000,000 for "orally and physically assaulting" them back in 1964. The suit was later revised down to $100,000, and famed attorney Melvin Belli represented the Youngs.

Supposedly Desi, his wife Edie, and Jimmy Durante and his wife had gone to the country club to find Desi's mother. The Youngs claimed that Desi became enraged when Young took what Desi thought was too much time to respond to a request for information. They accused Desi of hurling an ashtray at Mrs. Young, hitting Young and verbally attacking both.

At the trial, Young testified that Desi had described working people as "low-down dirt under my feet." A witness for the defendant was comedian Durante and after hearing the evidence the jury deliberated about ninety minutes. Their verdict: Desi was innocent.

Desi also made news when he suffered a freak accident in the summer of 1967 which would affect his health for years. Desi and Edie had taken Lucie and Desi, Jr. on a boat trip to Baja California, Mexico. They were visiting the tiny (about eight hundred people) village of San Juanito and at one point Desi and the family sat on a veranda. A heavy man came along and sat on the same porch. It broke in half and they all fell to the ground. But Desi, unfortunately, fell on a broken tree, which pierced his left side.

A doctor was flown in from the States immediately. Then Arnaz was flown to La Jolla's Scripps Memorial Hospital, outside of Del Mar, and operated on at once to remove several blood clots.

A few weeks later Desi announced plans to build a $250,000 hospital for San Juanito, in gratitude to "the Man away up there."

By this time Desi had reentered show business. He had found a book he wanted to make into a film and had flown to New York to arrange financing. Then, according to an account related by Desi, "I got a call from Bill Paley, the head man at CBS. He says, 'I hear you're going back to work but not in TV.... You have something against TV?' he says. 'How can I have anything against TV,' I say, 'when I borrow fifty thousand and make ten million?'... So anyway, Paley talked me into coming back. Funny thing is that after all that my show ends up on NBC."

Desi's idea for a new TV show was a situation comedy, "The Mothers-in-Law," starring Eve Arden and Kaye Ballard in the title roles, with Herb Rudley and Roger C. Carmel as their husbands.

There had been stories that Desi was not only an ex-tycoon but worse—a Lucy-less ex-tycoon. "What could he do without her?" asked show business pundits.

Eve Arden was not a clown like Lucy. "No," Desi said, "Eve is more a Rosalind Russell, more an *It Happened One Night* comedienne. I don't know anyone who can deliver a line like Eve." Desi had seen Kaye in night clubs and liked her, knowing her broad comedy style would blend well with Eve's.

"The Mothers-in-Law," whose competition was the second half of Ed Sullivan's top-rated show on CBS and "The FBI" on ABC, was not a big hit but it showed promise. Desi used Desi, Jr. in two episodes.

NBC renewed the program for a second season, but the renewal was based on the cast's working for their first season's salary. Roger C. Carmel objected to this, since his contract called for large raise. Desi fired him and hired Richard Deacon. The show was left in its tough Sunday night time slot and never saw a third season.

Desi, as always, survived. Many people voiced the opinion that he had reentered TV because he needed the money. Arnaz, according to one long-time friend, has gone through more money than most bank tellers. Desi discounted the rumors. "I'm not a multi-millionaire the way I should be, but I have enough left so I can do only the things I want to do, not just something everybody else is doing."

Desi and Edie had many residences—a house in Palm Springs, one in Del Mar, a breeding farm in Corona and a resort hotel in La Paz, Mexico.

Lucie Arnaz once explained, "At the end of every season, Mother comes in and says, 'Well, kids, it's the last TV show I'm doing,' with a tear trickling down her cheek. So down to the studio Desi and I have to go. Everybody cries. The band plays

'Auld Lang Syne' and that's it for another year."

Although Lucille Ball's commitment to Paramount was over, she had no intention of retiring. She formed a new company, Lucille Ball Productions, with herself as president and Gary as vice president. Lucy revealed, "When Paramount bought out Desilu they also bought out the format of 'The Lucy Show.' It became theirs completely. So I either had to negotiate with them to use the format or I had to find a new one."

She found a new one— "Here's Lucy"—and also announced that her new company would plan motion pictures, films for TV and television specials.

Since Lucy was finding it more and more difficult to keep her kids under supervision, she decided to take action. Unlike most working mothers, she had a unique solution: take the children to work with her.

Mel Shavelson says that it was after filming *Yours, Mine and Ours* that Lucy made the decision to incorporate her children into her television program. In Shavelson's opinion, she did it because "she was worried about what was happening to Desi, Jr. and also what might happen to Lucie. If she could bring them onto her TV show she could watch them all the time."

For public consumption, Lucy offered another explanation: "Lucie and Desi had been wanting to work with me. The idea fitted in to the scheme that I had long had for them. I feel that too many kids nowadays go right into college without knowing what they want to do. For many of them, the experience is wasted.... I feel that when they do go to college—and I think it's very important to do so in today's world—they will have a much better idea of what they want to do."

Neither of the Arnaz children would opt for college. In fact, in the 1960s, the future of American colleges looked bleak. Youngsters across the country had forsaken higher education. It was a period of revolt against the Establishment. The assassinations of President John F. Kennedy and Martin Luther King had disillusioned the young (and many adults) in America. They began rebelling against social conventions and the political establishment. The flower children had congregated in San Francisco, calling for Peace and Love.

In the twenties, society had labeled convention-defyers as "Bohemians." In the fifties, they were called "Beatniks." Now, in the sixties, those opposed to the Establishment—those who flaunted convention by letting their hair grow long, growing beards, wearing dirty clothes, going shoeless and braless—were called "Hippies."

A drug which heretofore had only been popular among a very small group now found wide acceptance—it was called "pot," "grass," "maryjane." The youngsters took to marijuana and considered it a socially acceptable drug, just as their parents considered liquor socially acceptable. Society protested that pot would lead to stronger substances, and indeed it did. Soon many youngsters were espousing LSD, mescaline and other mind-expanding drugs.

Parents all over the country were having trouble keeping their children "in line," and Lucille Ball was no exception. Even she admitted at the time that she had deliberately taken the kids out of school because "I didn't like that scene. It was the usual— pregnant girls, drugs. A lot of girls who boarded there were unhappy misfits." She noted that all the friends Lucie brought home "were the rejected," something Lucille said she understood—but was not going to allow.

Lucy also contended that her children "were as sick of that weird high school scene as I was. I made them a proposition— told them to think it over for a month. Do you want to be on the show? I told them the salary would be scale, that most would be put in trust." And she admitted, "They wanted to be in show business and I wanted to keep an eye on them."

Desi, Jr. didn't like to rehearse in front of his mother, or anyone else. "He doesn't want to work out the kinks while anyone is watching," stated Lucy. "He's very self-conscious." Observers agreed. They recalled that Desi's self-consciousness was evident at rehearsals for the show. He would become upset when he missed a cue or did something wrong.

"I've been a tough taskmaster with them," Lucy told a friend. "My children have the discipline and desire to work hard and learn." But she added, "It isn't always easy. Especially with Desi."

Lucy gave the kids three-year contracts, subject to annual options, and each would receive $17,600 the first year, $20,400 the second and $25,200 the third. Twenty per cent of the money paid to them was put into government bonds. Forty per cent was set aside for taxes.

In "Here's Lucy," Lucille played a widowed secretary, Lucille Carter; Desi, Jr., her son Craig; Lucie, her daughter Kim. Her brother-in-law was portrayed by Gale Gordon. When the show premiered, some critics were unimpressed with the Arnaz offspring. *Women's Wear Daily* was positively negative, saying not only did the kids have "no talent" but the show was pure "treacle." Even the trade paper, *The Hollywood Reporter*, called it "one giant marshmallow."

Lucy's reaction: "Listen, that a *good* review. I usually get okay personal notices, but the show gets knocked regular."

The New York Times, however, noted: "The youngsters know how to trade lines with the veteran star. And Miss Ball should have a ball trying to bridge the generation gap."

Lucy insisted that bringing the kids on the show brought the family closer together. She told friends, "We each had our own interests before. Now we get home and begin to talk—not only about the work we've been doing all day, but about politics and everything else."

However, Desi, Jr. gave a clearer picture of the *true* situation when he revealed, "These were difficult times with my mother. My sister and I had two quite different relationships with her: parent-child at home and employer-employee at work. It isn't a very good arrangement. She would treat us—rightfully so—as cast members at work, but we would still take things personally that probably weren't intended that way. When most people are hassled at work, they can blow off steam when they get home. But it didn't work that way for us because we just continued the same arguments when we got home. My stepfather was always the peacemaker."

By trying to keep the kids close to her, Lucy had in effect created yet another problem: not only were Lucie and Desi, Jr. the children of stars, but now, because of the TV show, they were recognizable celebrities themselves. And Lucy admitted, despite her precautions, that her children were spoiled. But she noted that the triumph was that they lived through being spoiled. "They had to learn who their real friends are and who are the leaners, the phonies. They've been terribly hurt several times." Lucille described a time when Lucie cried to her, "The only reason she liked me was that you're my mother."

At first, Lucie had been the harder child to raise. Lucy noted, "They go through stages. First it was the girl, then it was the boy. I have a feeling that possibly from now on it will continue to be Desi."

How right she was!

Desi, Jr. was indeed harder to control, since he had had a taste of "freedom" while traveling with his group. In addition, his willfulness and charm and lust for life made it difficult to discipine him.

There had been the traumatic discovery by Lucy that the boy had a drinking problem. When confronted, Desi, Jr. promised to stop but at the time no one realized that he would take up an even more dangerous habit.

There was a problem Lucille Ball admitted she shared with millions of other parents—a lack of communication. Lucy's lament: "You try to keep close. You travel together, laugh together, do everything together. But the kids won't really confide—won't ask you things."

When Lucy brought this to her daughter's attention, Lucie's answer was, "There's nothing I want to know, Mom."

Lucie was a typical teen-ager—lots of clothes, messy room, friends, dating. Desi was more organized. "His room looked like an office," a friend recalls. "It was neat and uncluttered. There was a large desk, and he took the responsibility of running his music publishing company seriously." "I've got all these companies but no money," he moaned as a teen-ager.

Lucy kept him on a strict budget. She tried to make a point of not letting their wealth go to the children's heads. "I told them it won't always be this way," she said. "People in show business don't have real money like people in Boston or Pasadena. I've tried to teach them moderation."

Despite her protests, it was obvious the kids had all the material possessions one would expect. Lucie had a Mercedes sports car. Desi had an Astin-Martin. Both had all the clothes and paraphernalia they could possibly use. And they knew their parents lived as wealthily as anyone in Pasadena. Lucy herself drove a silver Rolls-Royce (which she had bought for $8000 from Hedda Hopper's estate). She drove the car herself, never feeling comfortable in chauffeur-driven autos.

Although the kids had come to accept and appreciate Gary, he never for one moment was considered a father replacement. Both Lucie and Desi, Jr. loved their father and spent a lot of time with him..

In the opinion of a prominent producer, another reason Lucy wanted the kids on her show was to get them involved in *her* life so they would be with her and not Desi.

"They are close to their father," Lucy admitted at the time. But she pointed out, "Their father has an easier life with them because it is usually vacation time and more fun for everyone. In Beverly Hills it's school and homework; early to bed and not so many dates, just on weekends."

Desi, Sr. took over The Candy Store, a popular Hollywood discotheque, for Desi, Jr.'s sixteenth birthday in January 1969. When Desi, Sr. was asked if he was going to buy his son a car for this birthday, he laughed "Are you kidding? That kid made more money last year than I did."

For his sixteenth birthday, Desi wrote his son a touching letter containing a lot of the same advice his father had given him:

Dear Desi,
    Well pardner, you are now sixteen, and in my book that means you are no longer a child; you are a man.
    You will get your driver's license and you will drive your

own car. A note of warning about driving, particularly about driving on the road that lies before you—the one we all have to travel, the road of life.

It is very much like the road from Las Cruces to La Paz. There are stetches that are so smooth and beautiful that they take your breath away, and then there are others that are so ugly and rough that you wish you had never gotten on the damn thing, and you wonder if you will ever get through.

Somewhere during the way, you will get into a particularly bad spot that presents a very difficult problem, and you may not know exactly what to do. When that happens, I'd advise you not to do anything. Examine the situation first. Turn it upside down and sideways as many times as you have to. But then, when you have finally made up your mind, do not let anything or anybody stop you. If there is a mountain in your way, go through it.

Sometimes you will make it; sometimes you will not. But if you are honest and thorough in your decision, you will learn something either way. We should learn as much from our mistakes as we do from our successes.

And when you do come up with a minus, try to convert it into a plus. You will be surprised how many times it will work. Use a setback as a stepping stone to better times ahead.

And don't be afraid to make mistakes; we all do. Nobody bats five hundred. Even if you did, that means you were wrong half of the time. But don't worry about it. Don't be ashamed of it. Because, that is the way it is. That is *the* bag.

Remember, good things do not come easy, and you will have your share of woe—the road is lined with pitfalls. But, you will make it, if when you fall, you try and try again. Persevere. Keep swinging. And don't forget that the Man Upstairs is always there, and all of us need His help. And no matter how unworthy you think yourself of it, don't be afraid to ask Him for it.

Good luck, son.

Love

Dad

It was clear that Desi Arnaz, in his way, tried to instill in his son the same tenets as Lucille tried to instill in the boy—belief in God and in yourself, hard work and perseverance.

At the time, Desi, Jr. noted about his father, "On the way up he lost sight of the things that were really meaningful to him. So there was a bad period when his values were all scrambled. But now he's found them again. Now he can admit his own mistakes and tell me how to avoid them. Now he has a wife geared to those attitudes and a new way of life and a house in Mexico and a boat, and he works as much as he has to. I see a good deal of him, and the only absolute condition of our relationship is that we always tell each other the truth as we see it."

The truth about what was really going on between Lucy, Desi and their son was not made public. Concerning her children Ball gave out statements such as: "I'm strict about their friendships. There are certain homes where they're not allowed to go; the atmosphere is entirely too free, not enough discipline, no parental supervision. There have been times when either one or both of the children were never going to forgive me—like when I separated Lucie from the girl who had been a lifelong friend for no more reason than that they'd been born in neighboring bassinets at Cedars. I had to barge in when it became apparent that Lucie's life and her choice of friends were being determined by the other girl's thinking. Lucie was being ridiculously pushed and pulled, but when I ended it, she was bitterly resentful and I was, for a little while, 'the enemy.'"

According to Lucy, there was "a difference between being concerned and being nosey, but it took me a while to convince Lucie and Desi of *that*. They finally understood and that helped in our little matter of communication, too."

Their little matter of communication had exploded into a huge matter of concern. For years Lucille Ball had had to put up a good front for the outside world concerning her real life with Desi Arnaz. Now Desi, Jr. forced her into a similar situation. Her inner circle knew that she was in agony. For a while, on the set of "Here's Lucy," her son's behavior and appearance seemed normal. But soon everyone would know that he had a heavy drug problem. He was smoking marijuana, using cocaine, experimenting with psychedelic drugs like LSD and Mescaline. He later admitted that at this point he was already using amphetamines, barbiturates and dropping the popular drug of the day, quaaludes. In addition, he had even returned to drinking. By his own admission, at night he would "sneak out of the house" to join his friends to take drugs and drink.

Sometimes his mother and stepfather would catch him. There would be tearful scenes, pleadings and promises. All to no avail.

Throughout this nightmare, the intense work schedule for mother and children continued. Lucy was now taking the show on location around the country and the cost of each episode had spiraled to $110,000. The location shows would cost around $200,000 apiece. Veteran director George Marshall, who had directed movies starring some of cinema's comedy greats— Laurel and Hardy among them—was signed to direct to boost the quality of the show.

More frothy interviews on the future of "Here's Lucy." "We want to bring something a little different to the show," Lucy said. "It will be the kind of thing with which American families can identify—a trip in a camper." She said her kids were deciding whether they wanted to continue their show business careers. "Now they're finally experiencing the tough discipline working on location."

By this time, Lucie wanted to move out and get her own apartment. Lucy, like any mother, was horrified. The universal cry—"What can you do in your own apartment that you can't do here?"

There are two versions of events which occurred at the time of Lucie's moving to her own apartment. Mama Lucille's version was calm and intelligent: "Thank heavens she broke it to us gradually. She kept buying little pieces of furniture here and there and led us into her announcement. Then she cooperated by moving into a neighborhood we wanted and the type of building that is protected well. It had to come and I'm glad she handled it the way she did."

"Young Lucie has her own apartment now," Lucy said in February, 1970. "She's learning to cook her own meals, budget and run her own life. I believe in this. You're obligated to teach a child how to stand on his own feet."

Desi, Jr., however, later told the real story of the anguished scenes when his eighteen-year-old sister moved out. "By the end of the first year of the show, we were on the point of breaking up, and it was clear that we were going to have to make some adjustments at home. So Gary became the mediator, and we managed to work together and live together pretty well until my sister turned eighteen and announced she was cutting out to set up her own apartment. My mother didn't see it that way, and things got pretty tense. There was a big scene when my sister left, but two weeks later everyone had a great revelation and the whole emotional thing seemed rather silly to me."

At the start of the 1970 season, Lucy hired Jerry Paris, noted as one of the best directors in the TV industry. Paris's credentials were impressive. He had won an Emmy and directed the top TV comedies: "The Dick Van Dyke Show," "That Girl," "The Partridge Family," "Love American Style." The opening segment of the Lucy show was going to co-star Elizabeth Taylor, Richard Burton and the sixty-nine-carat Burton diamond.

How did Lucy land the Burtons for her show? She met them at a party in Hollywood. Elizabeth and Richard were great fans of Lucy's, and Burton casually suggested, "Why don't you have Elizabeth and me on your show sometime?"

Lucy was flabbergasted. Never one to miss an opportunity, she said, "Love to have you on the show. When can you do it?"

The Burtons' only available time was immediately, so Lucy flew into action. She had her writers whip together a script centering around the Burtons and Elizabeth's fabulous solitaire.

Lucy was "in awe" of the Burtons, like everyone else. "You can't help being in awe of them," she laughed. During dress rehearsal, Richard had a line that was supposed to get a guffaw, but instead received only a mild twitter from the audience. Lucy, naturally, didn't command the Burtons the way she did the rest of her cast and crew. However, she couldn't stand by and let Burton lose the laugh. She suggested to him that he punch the line across with more force.

Burton stared at her, sort of a "thanks, kid, I'll think about it" expression on his face. However, came the air-show taping, Burton took her advice. The line got the big laugh it should have, and Richard Burton had learned a bit about comedy from the red-headed maestro.

It was the casting coup of the television decade and the Burton-Taylor show was used to launch Lucy's new season. The rating was tremendous and although Lucy's competition, "Laugh-In," was then at its peak as the number-one show, Lucy managed to give them the roughest possible contest.

Jerry Paris, however, was extremely unhappy. He and Lucy quickly parted company, although he was initially signed to direct three more segments. Paris said at the time, "It wasn't Lucy's fault. The other shows were supposed to be filmed in Hawaii. CBS didn't want to spend the money to go there."

He was being diplomatic, but later he was outspoken about Lucy, saying she was her own woman, and man, and director, as well as star. "She runs her own ship," he noted. "Here's my analysis of it in a nutshell: Lucy has been left alone with so few directors after the divorce from Desi that she's had to work back of the camera as well as in front of it.

"That's a pity," he observed. "Lucy is the finest comedienne in the world. But it's very hard for a performer to see herself that way—from the back of the camera. Experienced actresses as well as apprentices need good directors. I think if she'd given it a chance more with me, we'd have swung together. But she's not used to a good director, so she didn't recognize one."

A cameraman who has worked on both Marlo Thomas's "That Girl" as well as "Here's Lucy" notes, "If Marlo Thomas has a velvet glove, Lucy has an iron fist. She's a hard-working burlesque comedienne and on that set she has total authority."

By now Desi, Jr.'s "problem" could no longer be hidden. If Lucy, as she later stated, was unaware of the extent of her son's condition, insulated as she was by other well-meaning family members, it was now brought right on to the sound stage. Young Arnaz has recalled that during this period his moods fluctuated tremendously and he felt ill most of the time. During that third

"Here's Lucy" season he was so high on drugs that he often lacked coordination and on one occasion couldn't perform a drum solo.

This was the first time he had to admit that he was addicted. He asked his parents for help. They took him to a doctor who recommended a detoxification center. It would be the first of what would prove to be many attempts to kick the habit.

It was announced that Desi, Jr. was leaving "Here's Lucy" because he was going to attend the California Institute of Arts to study music and drama.

Lucy, as always, was concerned with public opinion. The young Desi once explained, "The basic concern of my mother and stepfather has been protection of the family name—don't do or say anything that might expose us in a bad light. I never felt it was all that important—and neither did my dad, who hasn't done too well on this score. I guess that's one big reason I feel such a powerful bond of affection with my dad—a bond that has actually grown since my parents divorced. Temperamentally, we're much alike. My father is Latin and terribly sentimental. Simple things like home and family and honesty turn him on. Business doesn't, so when he got totally hung up in things that were fairly low on his scale of importance, he ended up hating himself—and that's when he got in trouble."

If Lucille's major concern was "protection of the family name," she was in for a few jolts in the new decade. Desi, Sr.'s romantic hijinks as a young man were, in the words of a friend, "chopped liver" compared to the approach taken by his offspring.

The detoxification program that young Arnaz was involved with had substituted one drug for another—prescribed medication in place of street drugs. Soon Desi, Jr., as he later recalled, began abusing the medication and again taking cocaine and marijuana. And since the doctors had told him moderate social drinking was all right, he soon found himself back where he had started.

Insiders knew that by this point Desi, Jr.'s parents had no control over him. He had left home and was living with an older woman. He was still underage when he met actress Patty Duke. It was not unlike his parents' first meeting. Desi, Jr.'s description at the time: "Right off, we fell in love."

Patty was six years older than Desi—the same age difference as between Lucille and Desi, Sr. She had been married at eighteen and was recently divorced from Harry Falk, Jr., a young director. She already had won an Academy Award and countless other prizes for her superb performances on the stage and in films.

But her personal life had always been desperately unhappy. Her father, a cabdriver, had deserted the family when Patty was a baby. She was raised by guardians, John and Ethel Ross, who were also her theatrical agents. Early publicity said Patty was an orphan who had been adopted by the Rosses, but in fact her mother was living.

Desi and Patty began steady dating. They were sophisticated children of show business and Desi has recalled that shortly after their affair began she told him she was convinced she was incapable of getting pregnant. "At least the doctors told her that there was a forty to fifty per cent chance of her never having babies because she had previously miscarried," said Desi.

Naturally, like most young people in love, Desi and Patty talked about having children. However, Desi later explained, "I didn't want to get married. I wasn't financially secure.....I couldn't afford marriage and I didn't want to get married in any event. I know it sounds young, illegal, immature and all the rest of it, but maybe if two people love each other and they can live happily together, maybe they don't need that marriage contract."

Desi explained his attraction to Patty. "Patty is a lot like my mother, the same drive, and strong will, a perfectionist.... But I'm never going to get married. Marriage is unrealistic, expecting you to devote a whole life unselfishly to just one person. Do you know people age unbelievably when they marry? From what I've seen, eighty-five per cent of married couples are miserable; fourteen per cent just average; one per cent happy."

With statements like these, Desi was expressing the views of the new generation. But his mother was from the old generation.

Desi accompanied Patty to the Emmy Awards, where she won the Best Actress award for her performance in the motion picture for television, *My Sweet Charlie.* All America watched as Patty, receiving the Emmy, thanked the Academy and then—looking straight at Desi Arnaz, Jr.—said, "And...thank *you.*"

The affair had become inescapably public.

In August, Desi got his first movie role, a starring one in Hal Wallis's production for Universal, *Red Sky at Morning.* It would be filmed on location in New Mexico and before Desi left Hollywood, "Patty told me that she thought she was pregnant. We had had some false pregnancy alarms before, so we weren't quite sure."

He and Patty must have quarreled, since, as he said, he didn't want to get married and even if he did, he was underage. Desi went to New Mexico for the film, and Patty resumed her career.

"We were sort of uptight during this period," Desi remembered. "But we talked all the time and when I got back from New Mexico, she was in Palm Springs and she was five months pregnant."

Patty was emotionally distraught. She suddenly eloped to Las Vegas with a rock music promoter named Mike Tell. She had known him for one day. "A week later," Desi said, "she announced her pregnancy, not by him but by me."

Nineteen days after her elopement Patty announced that she was divorcing Tell. Desi's reaction was one of "mixed emotions." "I was happier than I had ever been before in my life," he said. "Patty was also happy. She was more tranquil, more at peace with herself than I'd ever seen her. People didn't interfere with us during this period, and we were happy. We were looking forward to the birth of our child, a child who was innocent."

Every fan magazine in the country had a field day and was making Lucille Ball out as "the wicked witch of the west" by not allowing her son to marry Patty Duke and legitimize his child.

Desi, Jr. subsequently contended that both his mother and father stood by him and Patty during the trying ordeal. "My mother was great about everything. She had Patty over to the house. She looked after her. She was gentle. Yet all the while the fan magazines made my mother furious. They conjured up such fictions as 'Lucy Throws Patty Out of House...' 'You're Not Good Enough for Desi, Cries Lucy,' 'Keep Away From My Son, Warns Lucille Ball.' It was sickening, infuriating...."

"The truth was that Patty and my mother got along beautifully. And my dad, Desi. Patty and I went down to his place in Baja California, and he was magnificent. 'Be honest with yourself,' he advised. 'Do what you think best. I am behind you a hundred per cent.'"

The furor increased before the birth of the baby. It was almost impossible to pass a newsstand without noticing piles of fan magazines with pictures of Lucille, Patty and Desi, Jr. on the covers. The headlines: "Why Lucille Ball's Son Is So Bitter About His Own Mother"; "Patty Duke Begs Desi, Jr. to Believe Her: You Made Me Pregnant." The implication was that Desi, Jr. wanted to marry Patty; Desi, Sr. would have gone along with it; but Lucille absolutely refused to give her permission.

On January 19, 1971, Desi celebrated his eighteenth birthday with a party at the Luau. Although Gary Morton and Lucie were on hand, Lucille was not. And beaming, pregnant Patty was very much in attendance.

A month later, on February 25, she gave birth to a son.

Desi, Jr. visited his son the day after he was born and described the experience: "It was an incredible sensation. He looks just like me." The baby was born by caesarean and weighed only five pounds. Patty named him Sean Patrick Duke. "That is the name she wants," Desi said, "but he is my son and I love him just as I love his mother."

Lucille was then candid in describing the entire Patty Duke episode. "I worked for years for a quiet personal life and to have it personally impinged upon, with no recourse, is hard. I brought Patty to the house, feeling very maternal about her, saying look at this clever girl, what a big talent she is. Now, I can thank her for useless notoriety. She's living in some fantastic dream world, and we're the victims of it. Desi being the tender age of seventeen when they met, she used him. She hasn't proved or asked for anything. I asked Desi if he wanted to marry her and he said no. My daughter helped outfit the baby, which Patty brought to the house, but did she ever say thank you?"

Some reports quoted Patty as replying, "Lucy never brought me into her house. Sean was two months old before I ever even spoke to Lucy—and then the only reason I was at their house was because Desi had begged me to come. Let me tell you something—Desi may have been seventeen, but he knew the score. She makes it sound like I led him down the garden path and that's not the way it was. Not at all. That other thing is totally untrue, too. Lucie Arnaz did go shopping with me. We went to Saks in Beverly Hills. She helped me pick out clothes, but every penny went on my charge. And I even paid the bill for the lunch we had afterwards, I think. I don't know what Lucy means by 'I never thanked her'—what was I to thank her for, for shopping with me?"

At first Desi, Jr. visited his son two or three times a week—"as frequently as I can." And he also stated, "I am prepared to do what is best for all of us." He noted after the baby's birth that "the relationship between Patty and me has altered. Our passion is not as tempestuous as it once was."

Young Arnaz didn't like to talk publicly about his son, but finally revealed his views on Patty and the baby because he was annoyed with the fan magazine approach to the situation. "The magazines day after day are filled with the most incredible articles," he noted. "The writers, especially in fan magazines, seem to create their own dialogue. I am constantly amazed when I read what I am supposed to have said.

"I would avoid the subject completely if it weren't for the fact that my mother in this whole thing has been turned into a heavy.

"Supposedly, my mother doesn't want me to acknowledge our child. She doesn't want me to see Patty again. I'm supposed to forget that whole unmarried-father bit. Patty isn't good enough for me. Supposedly, Lucille Ball has barred Patty Duke from entering our house, threatening to ruin her, tried to buy her off. All lies! My mother has been the kindest, most gentle, most understanding mother any son could ask for. She and my dad have treated Patty with love and respect and tenderness. They think the world of Patty Duke. However we want to work out our problems, it's okay with them."

Desi, Jr. took Patty and Sean to visit with Desi and Edie in Mexico.

Patty bought a house in Bel-Air and then came another surprise. In Desi's words: "Because she is an honest and decent and forthright girl," Patty told him that she had fallen in love with some other "lucky young man" and planned to marry him. At the time, Desi said, "Naturally, my male vanity is a trifle shattered that she has fallen out of love with me and in love with someone else. But, at the ripe old age of eighteen, I feel sure that I will be able to overcome it."

Patty Duke subsequently married actor John Astin, with whom she had more children. She used the name Patty Duke Astin until recently, when, after many years, she and the actor divorced.

Today, when Desi Arnaz, Jr. appears on call-in interview programs, which he frequently does, and a "fan" might be crass enough to bring up his affair with Patty and the matter of Sean being his child, he refuses to even acknowledge the question.

Patty Duke, still one of the industry's most highly regarded actresses, is also now President of the Screen Actor's Guild. She has recently signed to write her memoirs. One must wait to see what her definitive word will be on the Desi affair and the part Lucille Ball played in it.

16

In the early 1970s, there were rumors that Desi Arnaz, Sr. was seriously ill. He had had several operations and seemed to age a great deal overnight. When there are rumors of a "serious illness" they usually refer to one dread disease.

"Everybody but everybody was sure I had cancer," Desi told a friend. "The reason they thought I had the Big C is because they heard I had surgery four times during the last two years." He could laugh about it, admitting, "I haven't been around much." Nonetheless, friends said that despite his bouts with the knife he looked fit, even though he had gotten a bit paunchy. The hospital stays had been for diverticulitis and a hematoma that developed after he took a nasty spill on his power boat.

"Only high class people like L.B.J. get diverticulitis," joshed Desi. "No really," he added, "it's very common. And neither of the difficulties had anything to do with cancer. Actually, I haven't felt better in fifteen years. I've put on about twenty-five pounds, but that's because I haven't been doing anything but fishing and drinking beer since I sold my interest in Desilu."

Desi expressed hope of someday doing a film with his son. Many people felt this was Desi's prime reason for continuing to perform sporadically.

Desi was called on to perform as father-of-the-bride when, three days after her twentieth birthday, on July 20, 1971, Lucie married twenty-six-year-old Phil Vandervort. It was the Hollywood society wedding of the season. Her new husband was described as a documentary film maker.

The Saturday afternoon wedding and lawn reception took place at the Roxbury Drive estate. Crowds of people gathered outside, straining to catch a glimpse of celebrities. Lucy's neighbors turned on their sprinklers to keep the crowds off their lawns.

More than two hundred guests attended, including columnist Rona Barrett, Beau Bridges, Lloyd Bridges, Carol Burnett, Ken Berry, Dino Martin, Jr., and his wife Olivia Hussey, Ruta Lee, the Ross Martins, Buddy Hackett, Jack Carter, and Virginia Graham.

The bride wore a dress she had designed herself. "We've Only Just Begun" replaced "I Love You Truly" as the wedding theme.

Lucie's maid of honor was Wanda Clark, big Lucy's secretary. The four bridesmaids were Lisa Pharron, Cindy Barnes, Alice Brittingham and Naomi Parry. Cee Cee Durante, Jimmy's daughter was the flower girl and Lucie's cousin Marcus, son of Cleo and Cecil Smith, was ring bearer.

Dick Gautier (Conrad Birdie in the film version of *Bye Bye Birdie* and currently a TV show emcee) was Vandervort's best man. Ushers were Ed Hall, Steven Hitter, Ben Stone and Desi Arnaz, Jr.

One of the highlights of the reception was when Desi, Sr. danced with Lucille. Gary Morton cut in. "That's the second time you've cut in on me," Desi kidded.

The bride was radiant, but brother Desi, without trying, almost stole the show. The baby fat was gone and like the frog who turned into a prince, Junior had become a "hunk." He was incredibly handsome in his tux and those on the scene recall he was a meticulous host, visiting with friends, chatting with business associates. Women at the party were "swooning" over him and everyone gossiped about the eighteen-year-old's current romance, a rumored on-again, off-again affair with the estranged wife of a "major, major" figure in show business. "Shades of *The Graduate*," laughed a family friend.

It was a busy year for the young Arnaz professionally as well. He had filmed an episode of "Night Gallery" and had been on "Mod Squad." He starred in a television movie of the week, "Mr. and Mrs. Bo Jo Jones." It seemed only a matter of time before he would become a major star.

Brother-in-law Vandervort joined Lucille Ball Productions as a production associate soon after the marriage.

While Lucy's television series continued successfully with its usual devoted audience, a major policy change was on the horizon at CBS. A new programming vice president, Fred Silverman, held the reins. Silverman was outspoken, an unusual trait for an executive in his position. He said Rod Taylor's expensive CBS "Bearcat" series, "looks chintzy, even with all the money we're spending." And he called Doris Day "too Pollyannaish, too saccharine."

Perennials like Red Skelton, Ed Sullivan and Jackie Gleason (who wanted to do a variety show but CBS only wanted him to do weekly "Honeymooners" episodes) had top ratings, but, in the eyes of Silverman, they had no long-range future. Their fans were dependable but growing older, and new, youthful fans were not watching.

Lucy knew who made up her TV audience. "Kids watch me during the day. Women and older men at night. Teenagers no. They look at 'Mod Squad.'"

Although Lucy was high in the ratings, talk filtered through that her show was on Silverman's "cancel" list. There were reports that Silverman made off-the-cuff comments about Lucy's show which Gary overheard and a verbal battle ensued.

Gary later said, "Lucy and I read a blind item in a west coast column which said, 'Which top CBS star is trying to get Fred Silverman fired?' Lucy turned to me and said, 'Who's the top CBS star?' She had no idea the item was referring to her."

Morton told friends that Silverman's reputation was riding on three yet-to-debut shows: "Funny Face," with Sandy Duncan; "Cannon," with William Conrad; and Sonny and Cher's summer series.

It was indeed true, as Gary Morton implied, that Silverman's future was on the line with the three series in question. However, they all proved to be hits.

Whatever differences Lucy and Silverman had, the situation was resolved. Lucille Ball remained with CBS.

In the words of Desi, Jr. at the time: "Mom is still hung up on the excitement of what she's doing. Not that it isn't meaningful, she gives a lot of pleasure to millions of people every week. But sometimes, it seems to be making up for a void somewhere. The great entertainers I know—including my mother—have so much of whatever is inside them that it has to come out, and so they work it off in show business. This compulsion drives her to be doing things that right now are really unnecessary, because she doesn't have to work that hard any more."

Desi, Jr. was still hung up on the excitement of what *he* was doing. And his private life had overwhelmingly captured the interest of the press and public.

A close family friend noted in what was undoubtedly an understatement, "Desi, Jr. seems to gravitate towards women who have certain qualities that Lucy has—ambition, drive—but usually lack her other qualities, like stability and discipline."

"It's obvious that a certain 'helpless' quality in a woman is irresistible to him," conjectured another one of his pals. "A gamin quality—little girl lost—these things turn him on."

Desi was turned on instantly by saucer-eyed, twenty-six-year-old Liza Minnelli. It was an immediate attraction for both. Once again he had chosen a girl with a successful career, but with a garbled private life.

Liza was from a show business family. Her parents, Judy

Garland and Vincente Minnelli, were two of Hollywood's brightest luminaries. However, they divorced when Liza was four and although there was lots of love from both parents, the child's formative years were spent in a somewhat less-than-stable atmosphere.

Liza's romance with Desi immediately became front-page news. Reporters eagerly recounted Liza's previous exploits—her stormy marriage to young singer Peter Allen, the man her mother wanted her to marry, which ended in divorce; her affair with Rex Kramer, guitarist in the group from her night club act. (In an extremely candid appraisal of the Liza-Kramer affair, Peter Allen said: "Rex was exactly the opposite from me. He was a country boy who hated the city and loved girls.")

Liza's affair with Rex ended amidst an outburst of bad publicity. His ex-wife sued for $500,000, charging alienation of affections. After the brouhaha subsided, Liza said she realized all along that Rex was not really in love with her but was in fact using her.

Liza's romance with French singing star Charles Aznavour was, according to Aznavour, *"amitié amoureuse."* "I had it with Piaf and I have it with Liza. It's less than love and more than friendship. It's better than romance."

It seemed to be old-fashioned love between Desi and Liza, although they didn't exactly race to the altar. They exchanged wedding bands which symbolized, in Liza's words, their "bond of union and understanding."

Liza further described their relationship. "Desi understands the need for calmness the way I do. He has a steadiness that's very important to me. I hate abrupt changes of emotion, and I can't live in that kind of atmosphere."

Years later, Desi, Jr. revealed that during this time he was still drinking heavily and taking drugs. Liza was no stranger to the scene—her mother's addictions were legend. Both Desi, Jr. and Liza would endure future hospitalization for their drug dependency. But that was years away—at the time they were involved, the public knew of no "dark side" to this glittering young couple.

Early in 1972 Liza spent time with Lucy at Snowmass, "skiing." Lucy and Gary had bought a home in the exclusive ski resort.

"Lucy wanted to make sure that she and Liza understood each other," according to one intimate. "Lucy has accepted the fact that Desi, Jr. is a 'chip off the old block' and she's trying to make the best of it."

Lucy understood Liza's background and realized Liza's need for a family. "I was one of the first to ever see Liza," remembered Lucy. "I was in the hospital with Judy within hours because we were such good friends. Liza spent one summer with us because Judy was on the road. Liza thought I was her mother."

How did Lucille view the relationship between Liza and Desi, Jr.? "They're engaged. But they're not getting married. They're too busy."

As far as young Lucie was concerned, when she told an interviewer, "I love Liza. Listen, he could do a lot worse—and he did!", Lucy interjected: "Okay, cut her off."

On another occasion, Lucy stated that Desi and Liza "are wildly in love and that's all I know."

Lucy was still bitter about Patty Duke. "She made a career of magazines for a year." Lucy told writer Kay Gardella. "She went every way—up, down and around—and then suddenly it all stopped and she revamped her stories. They changed every day and it was really something for a while. It was a real barrage and it had very little to to with us." (By the summer of '72 Patty had signed to star in "Love Child," an episode of Universal's "Owen Marshall" TV series in which she'd play a girl whose out-of-wedlock baby becomes the subject of child custody litigation.)

Desi Arnaz, Jr. and Sr. accompanied Liza to the world premiere of *Cabaret* in New York in the spring of 1972. Desi, Jr. then flew to Puerto Rico to be with her while she tried out her new night club act. They were also together at the Oscar ceremonies in April. Then young Desi flew to Tokyo for his second film, *Marco Polo*. Liza joined him later on.

"Desi will never marry her," said one Hollywood wag. "Why

should he?" But others noted that Desi was capable of impulsive and romantic actions.

In any case, Lucille was "thankful that Liza's not giving out interviews at Desi's expense."

Lucie Arnaz's marriage was in trouble. Lucille Balls' coverup statements— "It's very tough the first year...," describing the split as "an amiable separation for a while...a little spat...everything is very amiable...," didn't make it any easier for her to accept her daughter's situation.

Much to Lucy's displeasure, young Lucie became more outspoken after separating from her husband. She was tired of the "little Lucie" tag. When a friend telephoned Lucy and Lucie answered the phone, the caller asked, "Is this little Lucie?"

"No," answered the girl. "This is *young* Lucie. Do you want to talk to my mother?" Lucille picked up the phone. "This is *old* Lucy speaking," she snarled.

Lucie's complaint was that "To most people I'm still *little* Lucie. Almost everybody I meet starts out by asking me about my mother.... People even ask me why I don't have red hair. Well, I don't because my mother's hair color comes in a little bottle. Mine is a combination of the auburn hair my mother used to have and my father's one-time black hair."

Lucie had also "had it" concerning her reputation for being shy. "Me? *Shy?* Only when I do something professionally, and that's because my brother always outdid me. When we went to mother's taping and were introduced to the audience, it was Desi who stood up and bowed and bowed and bowed. I just grinned sheepishly. Oh, how Desi loved all the attention!"

After the split and subsequent quick divorce from Vandervort, Lucie Arnaz was being squired around town by female impressionist Jim Bailey, who, ironically, had rocketed to stardom via his extraordinary impersonation of Liza Minnelli's late mother, Judy Garland.

Lucie's role in her mother's TV show had been considerably expanded since her brother's departure. Through these years she had gained invaluable experience working with such pros as Jack Benny, Dinah Shore, Ginger Rogers, Carol Burnett and even Patty Andrews. A memorable "Here's Lucy" episode presented Lucille, Patty and Lucie spoofing The Andrew Sisters, the most famous singing trio of the 1940s.

By the fourth season, it seemed time for Lucie to move on. Mama had her writers fashion a script, "Kim Moves Out." The teleplay paralleled what Lucy and Gary would like people to believe was the real life situation when Lucie had moved into her own apartment. Lucille Ball Productions tried to spin-off this episode into a series, "The Lucie Arnaz Show."

CBS didn't buy, but ironically an accident soon occurred which made it necessary for Lucie to stay with her mother's series anyway.

Lucille Ball's form of relaxation during these days was skiing. She loved her home at Snowmass. But she observed, "Honey, I have to be careful. If I break a leg five hundred people are out of work."

Lucy did break her leg skiing. It was, in fact, a serious break, known as a butterfly shatter, requiring months in a brace and four silver screws in her leg. "The doctor tells me that I will never be able to ski again, and I love the sport!"

Lucy's sense of humor supposedly didn't desert her when, with Gary on the sidelines, she described her ordeal in the hospital to a group of friends. "It was like a scene from 'M.A.S.H.'"

Gary interjected, "That place was really very nice. Next year we'll go back so Lucy can break the other leg."

Lucy forced a smile.

The doctors and nurses at the hospital won't ever forget Lucille Ball—reports were that she was "difficult as hell," giving one and all the third degree regarding every single move made to minister to her—"*What* are you doing?" "*Why* are you doing it that way?" "*How* do you know that's the *proper* thing to do?"-type comments ad infinitum, driving one and all to distraction. On the one hand, her attitude was totally understandable. On the other, it appeared she was running things as if on the set of "Here's Lucy."

It was not an easy time for anyone involved. She was *determined* the "Here's Lucy" show would go on, and it did. Undaunted, Lucy had writers whip together scripts with the "Lucy" character laid up with a broken leg.

Lucille Ball and work. They were synonymous. Desi, Jr. even came back to "Here's Lucy" for one episode, which guest-starred Joe Namath.

A top writer observed, "The Lucy character is really an ingenue, and Lucille is getting away with it—she's playing an ingenue. As you know it is completely acting. The Lucy that she plays in 'The Lucy Show' has nothing to do with Lucille Ball. In most cases television is an X-ray and you can't exist very long unless you're playing yourself. She's playing somebody else."

In one episode of the program, "Lucy Meets Lucille Ball," the writers even underscored the fact that the Lucy character and the *real* Lucille Ball were not one and the same.

Regarding her "Lucy" scripts, Lucille Ball noted, "I need a strong father or husband figure as a catalyst. I have to be an inadequate somebody, because I don't want the authority for Lucy. Every damned movie script sent me seems to cast me as a lady with authority, like Eve Arden or Roz Russell, but that's not me."

Apparently Lucy was soon convinced that she *could* be an "authority figure" in a film. *Mame* was to be a lavish, multi-million-dollar star vehicle requiring the title character to be on screen virtually the entire running time. The property had originally been a smash Broadway play (in 1956) and then a blockbuster film (in 1959), both starring Rosalind Russell. *Auntie Mame* then metamorphosed into a tour-de-force musical for Angela Lansbury (1966), who scored a smashing success as the singing-dancing *Mame*. Now, when the time had come to film the new *Mame*, Lansbury was not remotely considered box-office by the motion picture industry. Barbra Streisand was too young for the role (and had flopped in *Hello, Dolly!*); Elizabeth Taylor was strictly a dramatic actress. Doris Day had retired from films. "Lucy as *Mame*" was a package that certainly could excite the motion picture exhibitors.

But Ball wasn't "campaigning" for the role. After all the years, she hadn't yet wearied of the "Lucy" character! "No, I'm a rooter, I look for ruts. My Cousin Cleo is always prodding me to move. She once said Lucy was my security blanket. Maybe. I'm not erudite in any way like Cleo. But why should I change? Lucy deals in fundamental, everyday things exaggerated, with a happy ending. She has a basic childishness that hopefully most of us never lose. That's why she cries a lot like a kid—the WAAH act—instead of getting drunk."

The character of "Mame," however, was one which Lucy surely could relate to on a crucial level. It dealt with the intimate relationship between a woman and a child whom she rears with love and devotion—only to have him, as a young adult, come perilously close to adopting a value system and lifestyle totally alien to everything she has taught him.

The film would be quite an undertaking; the glamour of the venture aside, it would be grueling work for the leading lady. But the prospect was too exciting to pass up, and with Cleo and others urging her on in the background, Lucy agreed to do the film. She was adamant that her rendition of "Mame" would *not* be a version of the "Lucy" character. Nor, she said, would "Mame" be an ultra-sophisticate as portrayed by Rosalind Russell. Lucy's would be a "Mame" for the entire family—and hopes were high as contracts were signed and it was announced that Lucille Ball would make her triumphant return to the screen in her most glamorous and challenging role ever. ("I think Cher should play it," declared Rosalind Russell. Twenty-seven-year-old Cher was at the peak of her glamour girl popularity, and Miss Russell noted that "she could bring something fresh to it.")

The dancing the role required would not have been a major problem for Lucy, but her broken leg had changed all that. Now it would be a problem—but also a challenge. A far more serious obstacle was the singing. Lucy was the first to admit she was no singer. Sure, she could carry a tune, but she definitely was not *a singer.* Lansbury was a terrific singer—she had belted out the Jerry Herman *Mame* score to perfection. How Lucille would manage that facet of the performance remained to be seen.

It was understood there would be no dubbing by any other actress's voice—Lucy would sing all the songs. Whatever she lacked in voice, she'd make up for in presence; at least that is what the moviemakers were banking on.

A top supporting cast was assembled. The role of "Mame's" Tallulah Bankhead-like sidekick, "Vera Charles" would be played by Beatrice Arthur. Arthur had played the role on Broadway with Lansbury and was currently riding the crest as TV's "Maude."

Robert Preston would be Lucy's leading man. And the director of the film was to be Gene Saks, who had directed the smash-hit on Broadway. In the late 1960s Saks had directed the hit film versions of several of Neil Simon's plays. His wife of twenty-three years happened to be Bea Arthur, which generated the kind of gossip Hollywood thrives on: Would there be dissension because Saks would favor his wife over Lucy? Would there be rivalry and hostility between Lucy and Bea Arthur, who was no slouch in the taking-charge department? Lucy was quick to deny all innuendoes. She was vocal in her admiration of Bea Arthur and said she wouldn't have signed for the picture if the studio had wanted to sign anyone else for the "Vera Charles" role. And Ball sang Saks's praises to the skies.

Choreographer Onna White had the job of directing the dancing Lucy—and it was to prove a formidable assignment.

The start of production was delayed almost a year to enable Lucy to be in the best possible shape. As the cameras rolled, in January 1973, Lucille Ball also announced that she would return for a sixth season of "Here's Lucy."

Lucy shrewdly analyzed herself and what she had become by this stage of the game. "I don't think I'm too versatile, but that's sort of beside the point," she noted. Regarding another season of "Here's Lucy": "If millions like this, it would be pretty silly of me to go astray. I've learned a lot about my trade over the years...I do what I do with all my strength and heart."

Lucy poo-poohed any deep psychological analysis of why she was a comedienne. "Listen, honey, have you heard me say anything funny? I tell you I don't *think* funny. That's the difference between a wit and a comedian. My daugher Lucie thinks funny. So does Steve Allen, Buddy Hackett...Dean Martin...Oh, I can tell a funny story about something that happened to me. But I'm more of a hard-working hack with an instinct for timing, who knows the mechanics of comedy."

Mame was in production for six months. Lucille Ball, at sixty-two, had taken on a mind-boggling schedule for herself. She had no social life whatever during this period and the self-discipline she displayed was awesome. One is reminded of Gloria Swanson's analysis of what makes a star: "Energy."

Filmmaking lacked an ingredient Lucy had grown used to. A friend noted, "Making a film is tedious work and lacks the spontaneity of a live audience, which Lucy thrives on."

As production on *Mame* progressed, it was obvious that two men really had their tasks cut out for them. Makeup wizard Hal King had the job of seeing that Lucy presented the illusion of being ageless and glamorous under the merciless scrutiny of the wide-screen Technicolor camera. Director of photography Phil Lathrop, whose expertise with lighting and camera angles was well known, was also challenged on this film.

On Lucy's television show, there were virtually no close-ups of Lucille Ball. Lucy looked about as she had looked for years. She was careful not to disenchant people. A friend of Gary's related a revealing anecdote: "Once, my parents were coming to Los Angeles and were dying to meet Lucy. Gary's a doll. He's always ready to please and he said he'd see what he could do."

However, when the elderly couple went backstage to meet Lucy they were only allowed to see her from a distance. "She waved to them from across the set," said Gary's friend. "He later told me she wouldn't let them get any closer because she doesn't like her friends to see her close up and be disillusioned."

A famous actress who worked with Lucy claimed, in the early 1970s, that "Lucy had her face lifted, but everybody should look that good after a face lift. I've seen a lot of those women who've had their faces lifted, but their bodies look like they have to be carried to get in and out of a car. Lucy's got a good body. She works so hard her body is always tuned up. I've never seen her get sloppy fat. She's always kept herself in good shape.

"She's still glamorous in her way. I mean, my God, I don't know of anybody that's had a span of years like that woman has had. Let's face it. How long has she been on the screen? At least forty years."

It was more than forty years. And for their work on *Mame*, Hal King and Phil Lathrop deserved much praise because, all things considered, they made Lucy look good.

It wasn't easy. There were strained relationships during production. One of the most unflattering reports concerned a confrontation between Lucille and Hal King. He told her he was ill and wanted to retire, and she allegedly was so furious that she slapped him in the face.

Makeup and lighting were not the least of the problems. Lucy's gravelly baritone voice was simply not equipped to do justice to the score. The big ballad, "If He Walked Into My Life," had been a highlight of the play and became a hit song. It required a belting, musical voice—but Lucy ended up talking-singing it, a la Rex Harrison's style in *My Fair Lady*.

When the picture was finally completed, however, hopes were high. The public, as always, would have the final say—and there was a strong "want-to-see" factor built-in.

As the picture was being edited, scored and prepared for release—and being hailed as "Lucille Ball's greatest achievement"—Lucy returned to the small screen for the sixth, and final, season of "Here's Lucy." The series had grown tired, and although she could have signed for another five years, she didn't.

When *Mame* was ready for release, Lucy was ready to publicize it. The picture had its world premiere in New York in February, 1974, and the media coverage was extensive. New York's diminutive mayor, Abe Beame, came to the Lincoln Center gala preview, and Lucy and Bea Arthur tried not to tower over him. Lucy was frankly self-conscious about it, but the trio still resembled, to quote a wag of the day, "Two showgirls posing with a midget."

Mame opened at Radio City Music Hall and initial grosses were big. But reviews were bad and word-of-mouth was not good. *Mame* was not remotely the hit it could have been and should have been, considering the talents involved. Lucy had made a big-screen comeback in a picture which didn't perform so well on the big screen. However, ironically, today *Mame* plays very well on Lucy's home turf, television.

Most people who knew her said that Lucille would never stop working—and her own answer to the question, "Will you ever retire?" was usually: "Yes. When I drop in my tracks!" However, the mid-1970s finally saw Lucille Ball cutting back drastically on her work schedule.

There would be no more weekly TV series. The last month of shooting "Here's Lucy" had been tearful and sentimental. Ball knew that she was giving up her "wonderful arena," and though she might continue to work occasionally she would miss "that wonderful treadmill."

During the 1974-5 season Lucy appeared in only two specials, "Happy Anniversary and Goodbye," with Art Carney, and "Lucy Gets Lucky," with Dean Martin.

The next season she starred again with Carney, and with Jackie Gleason, in "3 for 2." TV fans expected new heights of hilarity when "Lucy" paired with "Ralph Kramden." But the vehicle was not "Lucy" and "Kramden" and not a comedy—both veteran stars wanted to present other facets of their talent, and as drama the show missed its mark.

Unfortunately for Lucille Ball and her family, there was still a great deal of drama in her son's personal life. His relationship with Liza Minelli had ended when she began an affair with Peter Sellers.

Desi, Jr. was still fighting his drug and alcohol problems. He again asked his family's help, and so began another long period of anguish for Lucy, Desi, Sr., Lucie and Gary. Desi, Jr. went in and out of detoxification centers.

Between periods of hospitalization, Desi, Jr. was still making the young-Hollywood social scene and was always in the center of things. But his once-promising career now consisted of TV movies-of-the-week and guest shots on series such as "Streets of San Francisco," "The Love Boat" and "Fantasy Island."

Lucille, too, continued sporadically appearing on television. There was a two-hour special to celebrate Lucy's long affiliation with her network: "CBS Salutes Lucy: The First 25 Years." The audience, of course, tuned in. And the next year, there was a "Lucy" Reunion Special—again the fans were there by the millions, but this was Ball's last major "Lucy" production for CBS-TV to date.

In 1978, the year Ball guest-hosted a now-forgettable one-shot country-western variety hour for CBS, her daughter finally scored a *major* success. Lucie played the lead in the Broadway-bound musical, *They're Playing Our Song*, with Robert Klein. It was a Neil Simon script, a Marvin Hamlisch-Carol Bayer Sager score. Critics praised the twenty-seven-year-old Lucie for all the right reasons—she was no longer merely "the daughter of Lucille Ball and Desi Arnaz" but finally a star in her own right.

She had been working steadily. After her mother's series went off the air, Lucie had done a couple of movies-of-the-week and guest shots on TV series. And she spent a great deal of time gaining experience doing musicals in summer stock.

It was after her hit on Broadway that Lucie Arnaz revealed she had had a serious romance with Burt Reynolds. Lucille Ball had wisely kept mum regarding her daughter's involvement with Reynolds. One can speculate on Mama's feelings—she was certainly privy to all the gossip regarding Reynolds' numerous and varied ladies. Dinah Shore, a woman almost as old as Lucille Ball, had been one of the actor's most widely publicized relationships. Others in Reynolds' love life were almost young enough to be his daughters.

When Lucie Arnaz, basking in the glow of her notices for *They're Playing Our Song,* decided to discuss her affair with Reynolds, she related how their relationship had been a special one, and now that it was over, they were friends. Lucie said she was genuinely happy for Sally Field, Burt's then highly-publicized girlfriend.

Lucie, living and working in New York, now met a man who, in her words to her mother, was "another Gary." He was someone she felt she could spend the rest of her life with. (Lucille Ball later said, "That was the ultimate compliment to my husband.")

Laurence Luckinbill was seventeen years Lucie's senior. On the plus side, he was a successful stage, film and television actor and a published writer. At the time he and Lucie met, he was starring in Neil Simon's Broadway hit, "Chapter Two." But there was another fact that certainly couldn't be ignored. He was in the midst of a divorce from his first wife, soap opera star Robin Strasser, the mother of his two sons.

According to Lucie's account, at first it was she who pursued Luckinbill. After knowing each other as friends for some time, Lucie frankly told him she wanted more than that. So, apparently, did he. Their romance began. Her career, too, was on the upswing. She signed to co-star with Neil Diamond and Laurence Olivier in *The Jazz Singer.*

Her brother, Desi, had also made a few theatrical films (most notably he played the young bridegroom in Robert Altman's 1977 *A Wedding*). But Arnaz's career seemed anchored in movies-for-television. In two of these, "Having Babies" and "Black Market Baby," Desi starred with a pretty and accomplished young actress, Linda Purl. The youngsters fell in love and in late 1979 decided to marry.

Purl, a blonde with a turned-up nose, was from a non-show-business background. Desi later said that Linda never touched drugs, but drank socially. At the time of their marriage, in January 1980, Desi vowed to Linda that he was off drugs.

The couple wanted a traditional wedding—but wanted to

write their own ceremony. This presented problems at the various churches they consulted in the Los Angeles area. So the wedding eventually took place at the Wise Temple, although neither bride nor groom was Jewish. It was a large wedding. There were over 125 guests. The bride wore a traditional gown and veil and carried white roses. A huge reception followed at the then-fashionable Bistro in Beverly Hills. Afterwards the couple left for a honeymoon in Mexico and Spain.

Lucy was happy that her son had settled down. And happy that his problems seemed under control and he wasn't making news. Then, suddenly, it was sensible and reliable Lucie who was making the columns! She and Luckinbill had signed to star in the Broadway hit *Whose Life Is It Anyway?* They would alternate playing the lead part. It was during this tour that it became evident that the unwed Miss Arnaz was pregnant.

Lucie waited until the baby was almost due before deciding to marry. Then in June, in an apple orchard near Kingston, New York, Lucie and Luckinbill were wed. Though informal, it was still a gala affair. Lucy and Gary, Desi and Edie, Desi, Jr. and Linda, were all there. A few of the Luckinbills' New York friends, including Tommy Tune and Swoozie Kurtz, were also in attendance. At his daughter's request, Desi, Sr. sang "Forever Darling."

Some months later Lucie gave birth to a son, whom the Luckinbills named Simon after their pal, Neil Simon. Almost immediately Lucille Ball began reveling in her new role— grandmother, and for a short while it appeared that the entire "Lucy-Desi" family had achieved stability and happiness.

Then Desi, Jr.'s marriage fell apart. The young man was still battling his addiction to alcohol and, no doubt because of the lifestyle he was leading, peer pressure had been strong for him to return to using marijuana, and ultimately, cocaine. When Linda discovered that her husband was again hooked on drugs, she called the marriage quits.

After his wife left him, young Arnaz spiraled back into the abyss. Eventually his physical health was in jeopardy, and he was convinced to check himself into the Scripps Hospital Dependency Center in La Jolla. There he was detoxified and underwent in-depth psychological treatment. Programs of this type concentrate not only on the individual's problem but on how the family caused and supported the problem. The psychiatric sessions at Scripps included not only Desi, Jr. but his mother and father, his sister and stepfather. No one could deny that in crisis the family pulled together.

For a while Lucille Ball concentrated on family and downplayed any professional interests. She concentrated most of her energies, for the first time, on charitable interests. She worked for the Motion Picture and Television Hospital and also for the Los Angeles Childrens' Hospital. For years the star sponsored the annual Lucille Ball Backgammon Tournament with proceeds donated to the Children's Hospital.

Lucy spent more time with her family and friends. She also spent considerable time and money decorating her New York apartment. The Mortons wanted a suitable place in Gotham so that Lucy could be near Lucie and the grandchildren (the Luckinbills had a second son, Joseph).

Lucy's Manhattan "pad" was indeed a showplace. It rated a special layout in *Architectural Digest*. A fitting palace for the queen of television.

In 1983 Lucille Ball was inducted into the Television Hall of Fame. To those who asked how a workaholic could be happy away from "the business," Lucy replied that she was happy to be "retired" from the ratrace. She occasionally lectured to college students. Her TV appearances were limited to talk shows, awards presentations and tributes. Often the shows were in her honor and standing ovations for the legendary redhead were the order of the day.

It's interesting to note that while Lucy does not mind appearing on TV, she will *not* pose for still photographs. "I hate to have my picture taken. People don't stare at a TV the way they stare at photographs. When you stare at a picture, you start to see every wrinkle, every tiny line. People see me one way—as

'Lucy'—and they shouldn't have to think about that character's getting old. People should think things stay the same, even though they don't."

But the lure of the soundstage was apparently still strong. Lucy was quietly on the lookout for a suitable vehicle. There was an announcement that Lucy would star with Lucie in a television movie, "I Never Loved My Daughter," which was about a dying entertainer. Miss Arnaz quickly declared, "My mother and I would die before doing that story." And Gary Morton quickly announced that he had only agreed to read the script, and had not committed Lucy to the project.

Lucie Arnaz did, however, admit that she and her mother were looking for scripts to star both of them. Although the mother of two, Lucie continued her career. She traveled a good deal, but the Luckinbills' home base was a fabulous apartment on New York's Central Park West. Lucie and Larry had seemingly found a way to make their marriage work. There were several ground rules: one, they had set up their lives in New York and not California. For another thing, they worked at maintaining their separate identities and careers, although they would occasionally work together. (They made a movie-for-TV, "The Mating Season.") They tried not to spend too much time apart, and when they were separated, they made sure they did not date, see or spend time with other people no matter how innocent it might appear. They knew the temptations.

When CBS wanted Lucie for a series, she agreed, providing the show would be shot in New York. The network met her condition. But although well produced, the series flopped. Brother Desi, too, tried a new TV series. "Automan," despite a big publicity campaign from ABC, failed to catch on.

Recently Arnaz, Jr. has become a spokesman in the War against Drugs. He has become a follower of Vernon Howard, author of dozens of books on self-improvement and applied psychology. Some people contend that Howard has a cult following. In any event, Arnaz, Jr. has toured the country espousing the work of Howard.

Today, when Desi, Jr. makes personal appearances, he's intelligent and articulate on his past and present. But he visibly bristles when pressed to comment on his parents—he makes it crystal clear that he is his own man, not "that kid born on television." (Ironically, Richard Keith, the "Little Ricky" from "I Love Lucy," had faced problems similar to Desi, Jr.'s—drugs and alcohol.)

Arnaz, Jr. often states that he doesn't want to talk about his parents or the mistaken image people have of them—or him. He says, in effect, that the overwhelming interest and curiosity the public has displayed in him, and the unending pressures it entailed, almost did him in, and he won't fall prey to the syndrome any more.

Lucie Arnaz says more or less the same thing. She tells interviewers that *now* is *now,* and she doesn't want to talk about *then* or her mother and her father—she is her *own* person with her *own* career, her *own* family and she's happy to talk about *that.* In 1985, the Luckinbills had a third child, a daughter, Kate Desiree.

Meantime Grandma Lucy was not ready for total retirement. The constant search for good material finally produced an excellent and challenging script. Lucille Ball tackled it with her usual tenacity and exhuberance.

No one can accuse Miss Ball of taking the easy way out. The project she decided on was unconventional, to say the least. It was a story with social significance as well. Lucy had played a wide range of roles during her long career, but never had she undertaken such a gruesome character part.

"Stone Pillow" would present her in the role of a bag lady, and Lucy had decided on playing the controversial role not only because she "has to grow up sometime," but because she was desperate "to work with a great director." George Schaefer was a TV veteran, the man largely responsible for the highly acclaimed "Hallmark Hall of Fame" dramas.

Together, Lucy and Schaefer, working with Rose Goldemberg's script (she had written "The Burning Bed"), fashioned a memorable portrait of a feisty, pathetic, homeless woman adrift on the treacherous streets of New York City.

Lucy pulled out all the stops. She was going for broke in her attempt to break new ground as an actress. It was an incredibly demanding physical ordeal—Lucy, dressed in layers of heavy woollens, filmed the drama on location on the streets of Manhattan, in April and May (the story was set in wintertime). It was an unusually warm and humid spring, with temperatures in the nineties. Lucy became ill, but that wasn't the worst of it. While filming a fight scene, she was injured—and, since she was seventy-four, recovery was to be a very slow and painful process.

Lucy sometimes had second thoughts on how she was required to look in the film. Of course she was playing the role without makeup—at least without the famous Lucy eye-and-lip makeup, her trademarks. And the equally famous Lucy hairdo was changed for this venture into a matted mess tucked under a wool cap.

The distance between "Flora Belle," the "Stone Pillow" character (named by Lucy for her grandmother), and the way anyone had ever seen Lucille Ball look before in public, was virtually unmeasurable. By design the cameraman's job was now to *exaggerate* the years. (Simone Signoret once observed that it's easy to play an old woman when you're thirty, or even thirty-five; but when you're over forty-five, it can be traumatic.)

Lucy was certainly cognizant that she was taking a big chance with this project. "Flora Belle" would be doing things on screen that no character that image-conscious Lucy had played before had *ever* done. In one scene "Flora Belle" had to take a roll of toilet paper from her piled-up-with-junk shopping cart, and waddle into a back alley to use it as a comfort station. Another scene had her scrounging around garbage cans for her supper.

Interestingly, however, the character offered Ball some legitimate opportunities to inject fleeting glimpses of what seemed the old "Lucy" character. But it was "Lucy" over-the-edge and in old-age; the moments of zaniness, however, were somehow appropriate to "Flora Belle."

After production on "Stone Pillow" was wrapped, the press carried numerous and alarming stories on Ball's rapidly failing health. One report went so far as to claim she suffered a stroke. But there had been a lifetime of mishaps, accidents, injuries. Lucille subsequently popped up on various talk shows, seeming healthy and reasonably happy. When Joan Rivers interviewed her on "The Tonight Show," and wished Lucy "twenty-five more years in the business," Lucy retorted, adamantly, "Please, I hope not! Do you know how old I'll be in twenty-five years?"

"Stone Pillow" was not screened far in advance for TV critics—never a good sign, since that indicated the network was nervous about the response (as was Lucy). Lucy was outspoken about how she feared the telefilm would be received—not because of the quality of the venture, but she had dire misgivings about how she looked in the production. A tight lid was initially clamped over releasing still photographs of her "in costume." She feared people wouldn't understand that she was "in character makeup"—they would think that was how Lucille Ball really looked!

Lucy needn't have worried. When the picture aired, late in 1985, her appearance *was* a shock, but Lucy could still make you laugh and cry at the same time, a feat few performers are capable of. She was recognized as being television's "Great Actress" as well as its "Great Comedienne."

Equally important, the film garnered very high ratings. The public still tuned in to watch Lucy no matter what kind of role she played.

In recent years it is fascinating to observe that it is not when she is discussing Desi or the children that the Ball composure goes to pieces. Lucy usually becomes highly emotional when the subject of her late best friend and co-worker, Vivian Vance, comes up. (Vance died in 1979.) On more than one occasion an interview-in-progress has stopped dead while Lucy, in tears, talking about Vivian, struggles to recover herself.

On Merv Griffin's TV show, publicizing "Stone Pillow," Lucy seemed more mellow than usual—but then came a revealing tableau. The "old" behind-the-scenes Lucy emerged when husband Gary Morton (they have now been married longer than

Lucy was married to Desi) joined his wife on camera. Griffin
had asked Morton to come on stage. Morton did and was very
funny and appealing but, as far as Lucy was concerned, he
wasn't dressed properly and she said so. She felt he should be
wearing a shirt and tie instead of the informal attire he sported
(although he hadn't planned on being on the show). If Lucy had
made a similar on-the-air comment to her first husband, the
fireworks would have been seen in Fresno. Gary Morton,
however, didn't make any kind of scene—he dutifully buttoned
his shirt.

It was apparent that Lucy-the-producer, Lucy-the-image-
conscious star, couldn't relax quite enough, even at this very late
stage of the game, to allow Gary to just be himself.

In the Spring of 1986, there was a surprise announcement.
Lucille Ball would return to the small screen on a weekly basis.
The vehicle, on the ABC network, would be a comedy series
titled, as this book goes to press, "Life with Lucy." Gary will co-
produce with Aaron Spelling, whose company created "Dy-
nasty" and "The Love Boat," among other popular series.

Not everyone was pleased by the news. "We still love you,
Lucy. But we'd love you even more if you left 'Lucy' alone,"
wrote New York *Daily News* columnist George Maksian. He didn't
want her to retire and pointed out there were "lots of other roles
Miss Ball could play." He thought she would have been terrific as
one of "The Golden Girls," NBC's hit sitcom featuring three ladies
who are no longer ingenues. Maksian concluded, "My complaint is
that Lucy should leave 'Lucy' be."

Only time will tell if Lucille Ball can make a triumphant
return in a weekly series. Lucie and Desi, Jr. will make
appearances on the show. Gary will be there to provide his wife
with the close family behind-the-scenes support she requires.

Lucy is peacock-proud that her marriage to Morton has
endured. "I didn't make the same mistake twice!" is the oft-
repeated anthem for her private life.

Desi Arnaz, too, until recently had a long and happy second

marriage (sadly, his wife Edie died in 1985).

But no matter to the public that Lucy and Desi were married longer to other people than to each other. Theirs is the once-in-a-lifetime relationship immortalized on film.

No matter that the Ricardo family or the "Here's Lucy" Carter family bore no resemblance to the real-life Arnaz family.

No matter that Lucille Ball's private life held tragedy and sorrows. That she has detractors. And that off-camera she is not a funny person.

No matter that she is seventy-five and a grandmother. No matter whether the upcoming sitcom survives or not.

Endless syndication of "I Love Lucy," "The Lucy Show" and "Here's Lucy" reinforces in the public mind that Lucille Ball is forever young; forever married to Desi; forever the "zany" mother; forever funny; forever loved—forever LUCY.

INDEX

Ackerman, Harry, 95, 115
Anderson-Milton Dramatic
    School, 24, 25
Andes, Keith, 169
Arden, Eve, 47, 104
Arnaz, Desiderio II (Desi's
    father), 33, 35
Arnaz, Desi (Desiderio Alberto
    Arnaz y de Acha III):
  act with Lucille, 62-63, 85-86
  affair with Lucille, 56-58
  arrest of, 219
  Broadway stardom of, 53, 54
  business sense of, 61, 104
  as Desilu president, 141
  development of "Ricky"
      character, 96
  as director, 152-154
  divorce proceedings of, 69-70
  drinking problem of, 14, 148
  enters Army, 67
  escape from Cuban revolution,
      34-35
  extramarital affairs of, 68-69
  first band of, 54-55
  first meeting with Lucille,
      54-55
  forms Desilu Productions, 85
  illness of, 239-40
  "I Love Lucy" premieres, 100
  marriage to Lucille, 58-59
  in Miami, 35-37
  movie career of, 61, 66-67
  as pioneer of TV production,
      98

  relations with Desi, Jr.,
      226-28
  remarriage of, 190
  resignation as director of
      Desilu, 186
  selling of stock in Desilu,
      184-85, 187
  singing start of, 38
  youth of, 33-35
Arnaz, Desi, Jr., 107, 138, 139,
    141, 147, 157, 159, 194, 202,
    221, 224, 230, 242, 254,
    257-58
  affair with Liza Minnelli, 16,
      242-43
  affair with Patty Duke, 235-37
  drinking problem of, 16, 225,
      243, 252, 255
  drug problem of, 231-232,
      243, 252-53
  on his birth, 108
  on his father, 228
  marriage to Linda Purl
  as rock star, 200-201
  school years of, 191-, 217
  self-consciousness of, 223
Arnaz, Dolores (Desi's mother),
    33
Arnaz, Lucie Desiree, 99, 138,
    141, 157, 191, 194, 215, 217,
    218, 221, 222, 224, 225,
    229, 245, 257, 258, 261
  marriage to Laurence
      Luckinbill, 254-55

marriage to Phil Vandervort, 240-41
moves to own apartment, 229-30
romance with Burt Reynolds, 253
Asher, William, 105
Astaire, Fred, 65
Aubrey, James Jr., 183, 193, 197

"Babalu," 38
Baker, Phil, 47, 48
Ball, Fred (Lucille's brother), 20, 25, 45, 68, 121
Ball, Henry (Lucille's father), 19
Ball, Lucille:
accused of Cummunist Party membership, 110
act with Desi, 62-63, 85-86
affair with Alexander Hall, 51
affair with Desi, 54-55
arrival in Hollywood, 39
birth of daughter Lucie, 99
birth of son Desi, Jr., 107-108
breakup with Desi, 157
buys out shares of Desilu stock, 184-85, 187
childhood of, 20-26
Columbia Pictures, move to, 41
development of "Lucy" character, 96
divorce of, 13-14, 69-70, 158-59, 160-61
dyes hair red, 65
early films of, 40
family problems of, 16-17, 149, 154, 155
first meeting with Desi, 54-55
forms Desilu Productions, 85
forms Lucille Ball Productions, 222
as Goldwyn Girl, 40
Gone With the Wind, audition for, 49-51
illness of, 239

image of, 15
Jamestown, N.Y., return to, 30
lifestyle of, 17
last show with Desi, 156
marriage to Desi, 58-59
marriage to Gary Morton
merges Desilu with Gulf and Western, 210-11
MGM, move to, 64-65
miscarriage of, 86
as model, 29-30, 31
moves to New York, 24-25
named Best TV Comedienne of 1952, 108
pregnancy, as TV event, 104-106
premieres in "I Love Lucy," 17, 100
problems with her children, 222, 225
produces pilot film for TV series, 94-95
public relations biographies of, 48
RKO, move to, 42, 43
shooting incident, 25-26
second marriage of, 15, 176-79
stars in "Here's Lucy," 222, 224
stars in "Lucy Show
"Stone Pillow," (TV play), appears in, 258-59
as show girl, 27-30, 31
social life in Hollywood, 49
testifies before HUAC, 111, 117-21
tours in Dream Girl, 77-78
voted Queen of Comedy (1946), 76
Wildcat, opens in, 172
Beardsley, Frank, 213
Benadaret, Bea, 79, 99
Bergen, Edgar, 63, 64
Berkeley, Busby, 39, 174
Berle, Milton, 94, 103, 152
Berns, Larry, 109

Big Street, The, 63, 64, 73
Biow, Milton H., 95, 96, 97
Bludhorn, Charles, 210
Bowman, Lee, 79
Bracken, Eddie, 56
Brier, Royce, 127
Burton, Richard, 230-31

Cantor, Eddie, 40, 48
Carnegie, Hattie, 29, 30, 31
Carroll, Bob Jr., 79, 95, 100
Carroll, Earl, 26, 27
Carter, Jack, 177, 179
Chesley, Harry, 109
Cohn, Harry, 42, 81, 83, 87, 88,
    90, 136
Coleman, Cy, 168
Colt, Alvin, 170
Crawford, Broderick, 49
Critic's Choice, 183, 213, 214
Cuban Pete, 74
Cuban revolution (1939), 33, 34
Cugat, Xavier, 53
Cuneo, Larry, 100

Dagmar, 93
Daniels, Marc, 95, 99, 105
Daugherty, Fred, 149
Delvalle, Jaime, 109
De Mille, Cecil B., 87, 88, 89,
    90, 91, 191
Denning, Richard, 79
Desilu (ranch), 61
Desilu Productions, 85, 136,
    140, 141, 149, 150, 151, 161,
    163, 182, 184, 185, 189, 196,
    216
    purchases RKO Studios,
        142-43
    sale of, 208-11
    stockholders' meeting (1965),
        203-205
Desilu Workshop, 145
Dodds, John, 182
Donahue, Jack, 72
Donleavy, Brian, 49
Drake, Bernard, 23

Dream Girl (Rice), 77, 78, 79,
    168
DuBarry Was a Lady, 65
Duke, Patty, 16, 233-37, 244

Eltinge, Julian, 23

Facts of Life, 162, 163, 164, 167
Falk, Harry Jr., 233
Fancy Pants, 82
Fitzgerald, F. Scott, 57
Fonda, Henry, 43, 63, 179, 180,
    181, 214-15
Forever Darling, 136, 138, 140
Frank, Mel, 163
Frawley, William, 99, 133, 144,
    156, 206
Freund, Karl, 65, 98, 99

Gardella, Kay, 184, 244
General Artists Corporation, 94
Gilbert, John, 203-205, 208
Gleason, Jackie, 209
Goldwyn, Sam, 31, 39, 40, 41
Goldwyn Girls, 39
Gordon, Gale, 79, 99, 206, 224
Gould, Jack, 183-84, 195
Grable, Betty, 57, 63
Graham, Sheila, 57, 84
Green, Dick, 42
Greatest Show on Earth, 87,
    90-91
Guilaroff, Sidney, 65
Gulf and Western, 210, 216

Haley, Jack, 48
Hall, Alexander, 51, 136
Harris, Joseph, 107
Healy, Ted, 41
Hepburn, Katherine, 43, 44, 47
"Here's Lucy," 224, 232, 249,
    262
Hirsch, Clement, 190
Hirsch, Edith Mack, 190, 220,
    221, 262
Holden, William, 81
Hollow, Sylvia, 31

Holly, Edwin E., 185
Hollywood Ten, The, 112
Hoover, J. Edgar, 114, 115
Hope, Bob, 66, 79, 80, 82, 152,
    162, 163, 183, 195
Hopper, Hedda, 113, 114, 143,
    144, 154
Horton, Edward Everett, 77
House Un-American Activities
    Committee (HUAC), 111,
    112, 113
Hughes, Gordon, 79
Hughes, Howard, 142-43
Hunt, Cleo (Lucille's cousin),
    21, 23, 45, 68, 75, 160, 164,
    217
Hunt, Desiree (DeDe) (Lucille's
    mother), 19, 20, 22, 24, 25,
    41, 68, 107, 121, 179
Hunt, Fred C., ("Grandpa"), 20,
    21, 22, 25-26, 45, 67-68,
    117, 118, 121
Hunt, Lola (Lucille's aunt), 21,
    26

"I Love Lucy," 17, 95, 97, 98,
    99, 101, 103, 104, 109, 113,
    132, 136, 137, 140, 262
    last epidsode of, 14
    premiere of, 100

Jackson, Donald L., 115, 122
Jacobson, David, 109
Jell-O, 136
John Murray Anderson-Robert
    Milton Dramatic School,
    24, 25
Johns, Glynis, 189, 192

Katz, Oscar, 196, 202
Katzman, Sam, 90
Keaton, Buster, 72
Keith, Richard, 138, 139, 191
Kidd, Michael, 168, 169, 170,
    171
King, Hal, 100

Koerner, Charlie
Kratzert, Gert, 30

La Conga (nightclub), 54
Laughton, Charles, 63
Leigh, Carolyn, 168
Lester, Jerry, 93
"Levin, Hymie," 88
Levy, Ralph, 95
"Little Ricky," 137
Lloyd, Harold, 57
Lombard, Carole, 62, 77
Long, Long Trailer, The, 109,
    111, 134, 135, 140
Lucille Ball Productions, 222,
    241
Luckinbill, Laurence, 16, 254,
    255
"Lucy Show, The," 182, 183,
    184, 196, 207, 211, 216, 262
Lyons, Alfred, 95, 104, 114

McCall, David O., 151
McCarthy, Senator Joseph, 112,
    113
MacMurray, Fred, 51, 206
Maksian, George, 261
Mame, 247, 248, 249, 250, 251,
    252
Martin, Dino, 200-201
Marx Brothers, The, 48
Mayer, Louis B., 65, 111, 113
Menotti, Carlo, 169
Miller, Ann, 46, 47, 55
Milton, Robert, 25
Minnelli, Liza, 16, 242-43
Miss Grant Takes Richmond, 81
Morgan, Ken, 68, 75, 112, 164
Morrison, Charley, 133
Morton, Gary, 177-79, 180, 181,
    184, 193-94, 216, 235, 241,
    242, 246, 260, 261
Motion Picture Center, 136, 152,
    143
Mulvey, Jim, 31
Murchison, Clint, 1515
Murphy, George, 57

"My Favorite Husband" (radio show), 79, 85, 136

Nash, Richard, 168
Nelson, W. Argyle, 185
Niccolette, Nick, 53
Nolan, Lloyd, 51, 67, 75, 77, 174
North, Helen, 213

Ober, Philip, 182
O'Brien, John P., 58
Oppenheimer, Jess, 79, 95, 99, 104, 107
Orcutt, Flora Belle (Lucille's grandmother), 21

Paley, William S., 95, 97, 144, 220
Paris, Jerry, 231
Parsons, Louella, 86, 90, 105
Peale, Dr. Norman Vincent, 173, 179
Pegler, Westbrook, 126-27
Penner, Joe, 47
Pepper, Barbara, 40
Peterson, Ed (Lucille's stepfather), 22-23, 41
Philip Morris, 95, 96, 97, 104, 114, 116, 127, 135
Piazza, Ben, 49
Price, Will, 49
Pugh, Madelyn, 95, 100
Purl, Linda, 259

Raft, George, 41
Reed, Rex, 188
Reeves, John, 204
Reynolds, Burt, 16, 253
Rice, Elmer, 77
Robinson, Hubbell, 95
Rogers, Ginger, 42, 47, 57, 145
Rogers, Lela, 42
Rudin, Mickey, 160, 204, 207, 209
Runyon, Damon, 62, 64

Saks, Gene, 249
Selznick, David O., 49-51
Sharpe, Don, 95
Shavelson, Melville, 79, 98, 213, 214, 215
Silverman, Fred, 242
Skelton, Red, 65, 83, 103
Sorrowful Jones, 79, 82
Sothern, Ann (Harriet Lake), 42, 66, 143, 144
Stage Door, 46-47
Stewart, James, 43
Stewart, Paula, 177, 179
"Stone Pillow" (TV play), 259-60
Streisand, Barbra, 195-96, 247
Strickling, Howard, 112, 113
Sullivan, Ed, 93, 126

Taylor, Elizabeth, 230, 231
Taylor, Yvette, 80
Tearle, Conway, 45, 46
They're Playing Our Song, 253
Thibodeau, Keith. See Keith, Richard
Thompson, Maury, 145
Thorpe, Jerry, 185
Three Stooges, The, 41

Vance, Vivian, 99, 100, 101, 108, 133, 144, 156, 182, 183, 196-97, 261
Vandervort, Phil, 218, 240, 241

Welles, Orson, 49, 52
Wheeler, William, 117-21
White, Oona, 249
Wildcat, 168, 170, 171, 172, 173, 174, 175, 176, 177, 179, 188
Wilson, Earle, 74, 179
Winchell, Walter, 110, 111, 112, 113, 128, 150

Young, Jack, 219
Yours, Mine and Ours, 213, 216, 222

Zaura Productions, 136